*Life, Liberty
and the Pursuit
of Happiness*

PEGGY NOONAN

Life, Liberty
and the Pursuit
of Happiness

ADAMS PUBLISHING
Holbrook, Massachusetts

Published by Adams Media Corporation
260 Center Street, Holbrook, MA 02343
by arrangement with Random House, Inc.

ISBN 1-55850-509-1

Printed in the United States of America.

J I H G F E D C B A

Library of Congress Cataloging-in-Publication Data
Noonan, Peggy.
    Life, liberty, and the pursuit of happiness / Peggy Noonan.
       p.   cm.
    Originally published : New York : Random House, ©1994.
    ISBN: 1-55850-509-1
    1. Noonan, Peggy. 2. New York (N.Y.)—Biography. 3. United States—
Politics and government—1989– 4. Speechwriters—United States—
Biography. I. Title.
    [F128.55.N497   1995]
    974.7'1043'0922—dc20   94–46829
                                                                CIP

This book is available at quantity discounts for bulk purchases.
For information, call 1-800-872-5627.

To some members of my troupe—

L.S., F.R., J.C., J.P.,

M.G., W.S., A.H.,

S.W., S.G., M.M., W.M.

The search is what anyone would undertake if he were not sunk in the everydayness of his own life. . . . To become aware of the possibility of the search is to be onto something. Not to be onto something is to be in despair.

The movies are onto the search but they screw it up. The search always ends in despair. They like to show a fellow coming to himself in a strange place—but what does he do? He takes up with the local librarian, sets about proving to the local children what a nice fellow he is, and settles down with a vengeance. In two weeks he is so sunk in everydayness that he might just as well be dead.

What do you seek—God? you ask with a smile.

I hesitate to answer, since all other Americans have settled the matter for themselves, and to give such an answer would amount to setting myself a goal which everyone else has reached—and therefore raising a question in which no one has the slightest interest. Who wants to be dead last among 180 million Americans? For, as everyone knows the polls report that 98% of Americans believe in God and the remaining two percent are atheists and agnostics—which leaves not a single percentage point for a seeker.

WALKER PERCY
The Moviegoer

Contents

PART I

Life

*W*hen last we met, George Bush had just been inaugurated president, Ronald Reagan was waving good-bye to Washington in a helicopter flyby, and I had just come back to New York, where I finished a book about being a speechwriter for both. Ultimately my son and I ensconced ourselves in the top of a house in one of Manhattan's old brownstone neighborhoods, where I set up shop as a writer.

When I had been back in town a year a friend from Washington called me and asked, "Who do you see, what ring are you in?" I laughed at the usage. Which ring of the tree, of Saturn, of thieves.

I told her that I didn't think I had a ring. Because of the particular facts of my life—a Republican in a Democratic town, a conservative in a liberal town, a person associated with politics in a neighborhood dominated by commerce and the arts, a single person in a couple society, a mother of a young child whose friends are often people whose children are grown or not yet born, a writer who works at home and so lacks the society of the office, a person whose life is pedestrian and yet privileged—I am not naturally part of any group. But also because of the facts of my life I know and have dealings with many people, and am invited to visit their circles, their rings. It is a various world.

This is in part about that world. It is not a book about big events, but about the day-to-day of thinking and living in a particular era. It is not so much about politics as about life viewed from an inescapably political perspective. And if there is any revolution in it, it is one that is happening within me.

I'll tell you when its ideas began to emerge: one day in 1992, when I was sitting in a good and overpriced East Side salon, and experienced a certain bubbling up of thoughts that were really themes.

It was the kind of salon where the women look beautiful and perfect even before they get the haircut. They glide in, their soft leather heels going click on the faux marble floor, and they ease into the chair— good suit, short skirt, StairMastered legs—and say *Yes, thank you* to the stout Guatemalan lady who asks if they'd like some water, some cappuccino. Then Oscar comes and stands behind them and he looks at the client, and himself, in the mirror. He is young, blond, high-cheekboned, full-lipped. His black shirt is buttoned at the neck, his black pants gathered at the waist and feet. He is like a beautiful young statue, like Michelangelo's *David* if it had a Conair 2000 in its hand. He leans to kiss his client twice. *Ooooh, you look so well,* he says. She smiles in the mirror, shakes her head and says, *Do I need a trim!* But she doesn't, she is perfect, and when she leaves she'll be even more perfect. We are high above the avenues of Manhattan, in midtown, the heart of the gold souk, and I am sockless in my sneakers feeling strange.

I am new here, do not know these people, it is a self-conscious place, a busy buzzing self-conscious place ringed with mirrors ringed with lights. In such circumstances there is really only one option: *Do not avoid, dive.* Immerse yourself in the sensory reality, emerge where you emerge.

Lie back, breathe in, nestle your head in the porcelain groove. Fold your hands on the front of your black cotton kimono, notice the soft-white tiled ceiling. The spray sound somehow surprises. The woman who wets my hair is good-natured and brisk.

Too cool? Is too cool or hot?

Your scalp constricts and then eases, soothes. She massages your head and then, sensing tightness, your neck; her fingers are broad and blunt. Soft water. Sweet chemical smell. The sound of the traffic as it filters up to these high floors is muffled and gentle. Zoom and zoom.

Unclench your mind. Daydream. About . . . cars. On pedestals, turning. The cars in commercials look so handsome now, their shine is so warm, like chocolate. That brown truck in Dallas, with the bumper sticker. I was in a taxi on the way to the airport and an old gray pickup was behind us bearing down, and as it veered off onto a toll road I saw it: POLITICIANS PREFER UNARMED PEASANTS. A few weeks ago I went to Mass in the church I went to as a child, on Long Island. In the parking lot of Saint Rose of Lima there was a Ford wagon with a bumper sticker that said, MY BOSS IS A JEWISH CARPENTER. And Susan, my best friend when we were twelve, laughed and said, "I like that."

We had been driving all around Massapequa, showing my son the beige brick grade school we'd attended, the houses we'd lived in. At a little Cape Cod I told him, "I used to live there when I was your age," and he looked in a kind of surprised, surveying way and said, "You did?" The whole weekend I thought of old black-and-white films of the workers in the early fifties who put up the split-levels and ranch houses that sheltered so many of my generation. Now, out there, it's Buttafuoco-land—prosperous, satisfied, dumb—but then it was GI Bill land, and full of yearning.

Parenthood, motherhood, then.

Recently I asked Joe, my brother-in-law, at his fortieth birthday party, "What was the best thing about your mother when you were growing up?" And immediately he said, "That she was there."

"There for you," I said.

"No," he said, "actually there. In the kitchen. For twenty years she stood in the kitchen stirring the gravy. Every day I came home from school, she was there. When I came home with a broken arm or blood coming out of my lip, she was at the door. That's the big change. Kids have no one home now. I don't mean one-parent families, I mean two parents and both are out. And we'll never go back to the old way again, ever."

Thirty, forty years ago, when we were a poorer country. I keep thinking about then. Mothers didn't drive, that's why they were home. They didn't drive or there was just the one car and the father had it, so they were home and did the housework and made dinner. Another world. Some people say the women's movement changed it all but, you know, Henry Ford did as much as anyone. Prosperity and mobility: these have changed our time, changed our country and our lives so completely and dramatically, and the funny thing is we all know it, but I don't think we've ever fully absorbed it. It's like what Václav Havel said, as day by day Communism fell and his true nation emerged: "We haven't had time to be astonished." But there is Old America and New America and, you know, I miss the hungry years.

Okay, now, we're all done.

I sit up, the hair warm and heavy on my neck. She squeezes it like a rope, wraps it in a small white towel, pats me, tells me, *There you go.* And directs me to a swivelly chair that faces a silver wall-long mirror.

I thumb through *Cosmopolitan, Elle, Vogue.* Like the part Adolphe Menjou played in *Stage Door: Young lady, I'm Cosmo el Voge and this play will be cast as I wish!* It is strange to live in a country where what we read smells better than we do. The perfume ads, the Calvin clads. An article on the new immigrants catches my eye, and as I turn to it subscription cards fly to the floor. The Asian broom boy sweeps them away. My grandmother was the lady in the chair on the edge of a dance hall in a big place in Brooklyn in the fifties. She was so big and mild. She cleaned up too, she was an immigrant too. She never yelled at anyone, never spoke harshly, and it was all so long ago and I wish I'd really known her. She died one night of a cerebral hemorrhage as she leaned against the wall on the top step of the stairs just outside her apartment. She had just returned from a meeting of Holy Name. Her husband, my grandfather, had died a few months before. "She wanted to be with him," said my mother, and I thought and think that was true.

—

I keep wondering about who we are these days, all of us. I keep wondering if we're way ahead of our parents—more learned, more tolerant and engaged in the world—or way behind them. They touch my soul, that generation. They are an impenetrable inspiration. They got through the Depression and the war—they got drafted for five years and said Okay, Uncle Sam! and left, and wrote home. They expected so little, their assumptions were so modest. A lot of them, anyway. The women shared the common trauma of a childhood in hard times and the men had the common integrator of the barracks, and I feel that they understood each other. They knew what they shared. When Communism fell we should have had a parade for them, for it meant their war was finally over. We should have one for them anyway, before they leave.

They weren't farmers, or the ones I knew weren't farmers, but they were somehow—closer to the soil, closer to the ground. The ones in Brooklyn, Rochester, wherever, they were closer to the ground.

Affluence detaches. It removes you from the old and eternal, it gets you out of the rain. Affluence and technology detach absolutely. Among other things, they get you playing with thin plastic things like Super Nintendo and not solid things like—I don't know—wood, and water. Anyway, the guy who said "Plastics" to Benjamin twenty-five years ago in *The Graduate* was speaking more truth than we knew.

Also, our parents were ethnic in a way I understood. Back in that old world the Irish knew they were better than the Italians and the Italians knew they were better than the Irish and we all knew we were better than the Jews and they knew they were better than us. Everyone knew they were superior, so everyone got along. I think the prevailing feeling was, everyone's human. Actually, that used to be a saying in America: *Everyone's human.*

They all knew they were Americans and they all knew they weren't, and their kids knew it too, and understood it was their job to become the Americans. Which we certainly have. A while ago a reporter told me how an old Boston pol summed up Mario Cuomo. The pol said, "He's not a real ethnic. He's never been ashamed of his father." The reporter—forty-five, New York, Jewish—laughed with a delighted grunt. The ordeal of ethnicity. *I Remember Papa.*

There were ethnic, religious and racial resentments, but you didn't hear about them all the time. It was a more reticent country. Imagine chatty America being reticent. But it was.

I often want to say to them, to my parents and the parents of my friends, Share your wisdom, tell me what you've learned, tell me what we're doing wrong and right. But, you know, they're still reticent. Loose lips sink ships. Also they tend not to have big abstract things to say about life because they were actually busy living it, and forgot to take notes. They didn't have time, or take time, to reflect. They were not so inclined.

They're like an old guy I met a few years ago when I was looking for a house in Washington. He had gray hair and was stooped in a crouched, still-muscular way and he had just one good eye, the other was scarred and blind. He had an old brick house off George Washington Parkway and I walked through it; it was perfect but too near the highway for a woman with a two-year-old. When I was in the basement I saw his World War II memorabilia—he still had framed citations on the wall, and I could see he'd seen action island-hopping in the South Pacific. And one of the old framed papers said Guadalcanal, and this was exciting, so I said to him, for the most interesting things you hear in life come by accident, "Did you know Richard Tregaskis?" And his good eye kind of squinted. I thought he might not recognize the reference, so I said, "He was the one who wrote, *Guadalcanal Diary.*" And the squint gets deeper and he says, "Yeah, well, I was a grunt. We'd already done the work and left by the time the writers came." I sort of smiled and asked if I could use the bathroom, where I plucked a piece of shrapnel from my heart.

Now they're all retired, and most of the ones I know are in pretty good shape. Susan's parents go to Atlantic City and catch a few shows, play the slots. They own their house. My father—army infantry, Italy under Blood 'n' Guts—has a small apartment in Santo Domingo and swims and says he can feel the sun to his bones. My mother lives here in town and flies off when one of her children is having a baby, to be a continuity, to say by her presence, We did this too, years ago, so don't worry. Lisa's parents just got back from Europe. George's father, who for twenty-five years worked in the Newark welfare office, married a woman with a farm in Pennsylvania. Now he walks in the mud in big rubber boots, holding a piece of corn. He's happy. There was more divorce than I think we've noted in our parents' generation, and a lot of them did it in a funny way, not after a year or ten years but after twenty-five, thirty-five years. After a life. There are always serious and individual reasons for such things, but I would include the seventies, the decade when America went crazy, the decade when, as John Updike said, the sixties had finally percolated down to everybody. Bill Clinton talks about change, but change was yesterday. The real revolution hit twenty years ago. He should know, it formed him. It made him.

—

Are you done with that? The magazine?

I am startled, smile and nod. Another lady in a black cotton robe. We all look so undefended with our hair wet and the towels around our necks.

Sorry. I wanted to catch my horoscope, while I'm here.

"Page 267," I say. "A good month for Scorpios."

I read my horoscope too, can't help it. I told the women in my Bible-study group and they said, "Try not to." But one later took me aside and said, "I know, I sometimes go to a psychic." And we laughed. Everyone wants to know what's going to happen. Actually that's not completely it. Chesterton or somebody said, When people stop believing in God they don't start believing in nothing, they start believing in anything.

My generation, we believe in work.

A few years ago people were saying we'd become a service society, a nation of burger pushers. But so many of us—research assistants, insurance salesmen, secretaries, doctors, editors of newsletters, teachers, bureaucrats, lawyers, travel agents, assistants of all kinds and stripe, welfare caseworkers—push words! We are paper people, and sometimes it feels thin as a piece of No. 10 bond. Not because it isn't wood and soil and babies birthed in the night but because it's such silly stuff—depositions and advertising schedules and the subject for the seminar. (As if you have to schedule Americans to speak. As if you have to assign them topics.) Anyway, the paper thing was happening in our parents' time too. With us it's just more so.

An odd thing is that prosperity plus mobility have not resulted in less effort. Everyone works so hard! Or at least everyone's always working. The other night during a shampoo commercial it occurred to me I was looking at one of our last forms of national communal worship. In the morning, across this broad land, we stand and worship the shower nozzle, looking upward with hope and faith. *Make me come awake, be alive.* On Friday nights when we go to the cocktail party we eye the hors d'oeuvres tray hungrily, but not for the stuffed mushrooms, for the toothpicks. We could use them to prop open our eyes at dinner. Here's a question: Are we all tired because we're tired, or are we tired because we want exhaustion to be the problem, because if that's the problem you can fix it. A few days off, a weekend hibernating . . .

Maybe what motivates us is simpler than that. The other day I met with a Chinese dissident who has served time in jail, and whose husband is in jail in Beijing. I asked her if the longing for democratic principles that has swept the generation of Tiananmen Square has been accompanied by a rise in religious feeling—a new interest in Buddhism, Taoism, Christianity. She thought for a moment, and looked at me. "Among the young, I would say our religion is money," she said. I nodded, and said, "Oh, that's our religion too." And she smiled as if to say yes, I've heard.

———

Also, there is the issue of how we talk.

Yesterday at 4:00 P.M. I was in the cocktail lounge of a hotel with Betty, breezy businesswoman, native New Yorker and GOP mover. She is one of the few remaining white persons of the professional class who smoke, and when she smokes a funny thing happens—she cocks her head and blows out the smoke and her right eye for a second goes askew and you realize she is watching you, listening to her head, and checking the room. All in half a second. She's got a summer cold, is sipping a hot toddy, is in a hot-pink suit and wearing thick gold earrings. She was saying, "So a former Bush cabinet member, a person well known to you, Peggy, calls me this morning and he's hemming and hawing and how are you and how's Bob and yatta yatta and I'm waiting and talking and finally he says, 'How's your women's group?' And I finally realize, like a duh, what he's calling about. He wants an award."

"How could you tell?"

"Because he could give a shit about my group. He knows we give yearly awards."

"Oh."

"But you can get so fucking exhausted having to constantly smoke out everyone's agenda, ya know? For you too?"

She was clicking her nails. I was eating the assorted nuts.

"I don't know," I said. "I think I forget to think about it. But lately when people call and I don't know why, sometimes I just pause. If they call out of the blue and they start chatting I answer for a while and then finally I say nothing. I used to not do this and chat because I was afraid they'd take my silence wrong or be embarrassed. But now I think I'm doing them a favor by not talking, because they fill the silence with the point of the call. So I'm sort of saving them time."

She nodded thoughtfully. "Silence. That's good. I'll try that. Waiter!" She paid with a company card.

—

But that's not what I fear—modern life, the culture, our style as a people. I think I have, actually, the end-of-the-century jits. It's a big thing when a century ends, a time of fate and foreshadowing. The 1790s gave us a revolution in political thought in France—and the Terror, Napoleon, and war. The 1890s were a pleasant time, a beautiful epoque, and a prelude to the most killing century in the history of man. Start out on a bicycle built for two, wind up at Verdun.

Start out at Sarajevo, wind up at Sarajevo.

And this is the end of a millennium, which, as a political operative would put it, adds resonance.

Here we are now, immersed in good news, saturated with good

fortune—democratic principles sweeping the world, tyrants undone, bouncing Czechs, falling walls, a billion people in China poised to break free, freedom coming inch by inch, prosperity promising to follow on little cat feet—and I'll tell you, it's starting to make me nervous. Makes me want to poke my head out of the sink here and say to all the nice people, "We're letting our emotional guard down, you know. We're starting to believe in good luck. We're starting to think it will continue. I want you all to go home and get a little nervous."

History isn't a straight line, it's loops and curves, and I feel a curve coming. For instance: it's a normal, nice, crisp-as-apples October day and I'm late for lunch, running down the stairs and—the terrible click, the terrible light. A city in siege, the cars clogging the tunnels, the power out, and no newspaper the next day to tell you about the nuteye boy from the nutboy state who carried the suitcase that carried the bomb . . . I know this is morbid, but—we have been protected, I think. And why, knowing history as you do, would you think that that protection would continue?

Are you getting a styling?

She is dark-haired, competent, clipped. I breathe in as if I've been under water.

Are you here for a styling?

She thinks I'm in a trance. All my daydreams wind up daymares. And I wind up sockless in my sneakers being strange.

Uh, just a haircut. I think from Oscar.

Who came and stood behind me and smiled in the mirror. And you know, I shook my hair and said, *Do I need a trim.*

I'll end this part with the fact that once, a few years ago, I saw a woman in a salon like this one have a real daymare.

I was in a chair just like this, and in the long mirror I saw a blond woman with a pale face. Her long hair was all standing up with big pieces of aluminum foil holding up hunks of hair lathered with puffs of white chemicals. She was flipping through a magazine nervously, *flip flip.* Perhaps the words swam before her and the air grew close, I don't know, but all of a sudden she looked up, snapped the magazine shut and almost threw it on the shelf with the combs, as if it had grown hot.

She sort of heaved.

Our eyes met in the mirror.

Then she bolted from the chair and said, to no one, to everyone, "I'm sorry." And she ran through the salon and down the stairs and emerged on Fifty-seventh and ran down the street, her black kimono flapping in the wind, the aluminum foils poking in the air. She looked like a Martian in a panic.

I never found out who she was, or what it was. But it occurred to me that not all the madness on our streets comes from people huddled in doorways. It also comes from salons high in the sky. And I know this is morbid, but sometimes I think she's a kind of emblem for modern life. I mean postmodern life. In the new America.

———

So here I am in the city of New York, a spectacular place and one of extremes. There are the extremes of wealth and poverty, of course, right there on the street for all to see, and extremes of virtue and vice. There is in this place more sin than hell could hold, and enough goodness to light up the world. For every Trade Center bomber there's a teacher with glow-in-the-dark rosary beads, for every Long Island Railroad gunman there are four guys who'll wrestle him to the ground and get the pistol. There be angels here and devils, which keeps things interesting, keeps them as dramatic and Dickensian as any city has ever been.

I lived in Manhattan from 1977 to 1984, and then since 1989. These twelve years are the longest I've ever lived in one place, so I think of New York as home. But like most Manhattanites I don't

answer "New York" when asked where I'm from because my forma-
tive years were spent elsewhere. In a way I always feel that I'm
visiting, that the city really belongs to someone else. Which may be
one of the things that mark the real New Yorker.

I know the city pretty well and watch it closely, taking in the data
peripherally, as people these days do—not full on, where one's
defenses can stop the information from entering, but peripherally,
from the side, where we unconsciously absorb, and find we· have
observed something only when we mention it to a friend.

When I returned in '89, after five years in Washington, people
asked me: What's different, what's changed? Knowing that in this
most fact-fluid of places things would have changed in only five
years. I said I'd seen three changes. The first was in the number of
homeless, and the way people now accept the idea that people can
live in the streets. The second change was the deterioration of the
physical plant—the steam pipes exploding near Gramercy Park, caus-
ing hundreds of apartment dwellers to find another place to live, the
city workers hanging out huge white asbestos-resistant sheeting over
high buildings, the asbestos scandal in the schools, the burst water
pipes, the electrical failure in the subway. It amazed me: the primary
purpose of city government used to be to keep the city standing up.

The third change was in the number of immigrants who, by the
late eighties, had changed the face and facts of the city. I saw it my
first day back, as my brother and I emerged from the Lincoln Tunnel
in a jeep, heading east. We turned onto Forty-second Street and came
upon what looked like a broad avenue in a Third World city in flux.
The theaters, restaurants and sex shops were boarded up in what the
city called revitalization, and filling the streets selling wares, on
squeegie patrol, pushing carts and yelling "Watchyerback!" were
people of all dresses, ages, colors, accents. It was all so vivid, and
vital. In the next few months I would see how Brighton Beach in
Brooklyn has become Little Odessa, full of people speaking Russian

and going to Russian restaurants; and I would go to the small Brooklyn church in which I was christened, which had then been the heart of an Irish-Italian ghetto and was still the heart of a ghetto, although now it is Mexican and Nicaraguan.

There are those who say New York is finished, but I don't think so. There are many reasons, and the biggest is simple and well known: you cannot pick up the Metropolitan Museum and put it in Flagstaff, Arizona. You can't quite pick up Broadway and put it in Evanston, Illinois. You can't quite pick up Wall Street and put it in Atlanta. You cannot pick up the city and disperse it throughout the country; it will not be broken up that way.

The hungry mind of man needs centers to which to gravitate. A few years ago young professionals were saying you didn't need New York anymore because of the fax: You can write a piece anywhere and fax it to *Harper's,* you can make the deal anywhere and fax in the contract and the signatures. Technology was making obsolete not only generations of machines but the idea of the city itself. But seven years into the fax age, the mass dispersal to the hinterlands has not happened. (I put the beginning of the fax age at 1987, the year it had become so commonplace in certain circles that a Bush campaign aide was shocked I did not have one. I had only a vague sense of what a fax was, and thought it was for emergencies. Now half the people I know have them at home, and everyone uses them at work. I keep mine in the closet, and when people call to ask my fax number I say, "Is it possible for you to drop it in the mail?" And they say "Sure!" with an air of discovery. My feeling is very few things in life are so important you have to get them right away.)

The fact is, to gather information, insight and ideas, to hear things that make you connect them with other things, to witness and be part of life at its most booming, modern and dramatic, at its most exposed, you will want to be in something like a city. Perhaps in the city of cities, the city at its citiest: New York. You will want to be near the buzz, of the buzz, in the buzz.

These two things, the buildings and the buzz, the physical plant and the physical presence, will keep New York alive. If the head of the Metropolitan Opera has to be here, then his doctor, tailor and accountant have to be here; if they have to be here, their support system, including the shoeshine guy on Lex and the newspaper stand on Madison, have to be here. And so on. Busy bees, buzzing busily.

If the city will not die, then it will live. But how? The way it always has, by changing. And it is changing, inch by inch and almost in spite of itself.

Here's a sign, a political one.

Near the end of the 1993 mayoral campaign I went to a rally for David Dinkins, our liberal Democrat last-fruit-of-an-old-machine mayor. I wanted to hear the speeches, enjoy the nonsense and the roar. It would be a good rally because it was to be held in the precise heart of New York liberalism—in its left ventricle, in fact, on the Upper West Side of Manhattan, Seventy-third and Broadway, next to an old pushers' haven called Needle Park.

I walked over, and there on the outdoor stage stood the most stellar stars of the Democratic establishment—Dinkins, Mario Cuomo, movie stars, Spike Lee, Danny Glover, famous feminists. And there were more people on the stage than in the audience. On a Sunday afternoon, with one day to go before the election. A hundred, two hundred people showed up, and you could see by their buttons and hats that they were city workers and union people, plus your basic neighborhood weirdos and a few people who saw a crowd and thought there was an accident.

I was astonished. The papers were saying it was a close race, and most put Dinkins in the lead.

I'd planned to stand in the back but there was no back, so I stood up front, twenty feet from the stage. Gloria Steinem spoke and said, "Look behind you—behind you is a revolutionary brother," and even these people looked around and laughed: Hey lady, behind me is probably a pickpocket. At the end, Peter of Peter, Paul and Mary sang "If I Had a Hammer," as clumps of people drifted away.

It was like having a front-row seat on the end of the liberal era.

It's not the end, of course, but the old way is losing steam. Keep trying an idea for thirty years and seeing it fail and even your most politicized citizens, the ones most attached to theories and systems, will begin to drift away.

The immigrants too will change things; they are voting, and this, by and large, is who they are: people for whom family is everything and for whom there are two great torments in their new homeland, crime and taxes, in that order. If it weren't for these they would be immigrants in heaven.

Immigrants, as we all know and as is the tradition, often work odd hours in jobs no one wants—deli counterperson, cabdriver, pizza-parlor guy, cleaning lady, security guard, Chinese-food delivery man. This keeps them kind of close to the ground! It will be hard to convince them that crime is caused by poverty and poverty is eased by income redistribution—i.e., higher taxes on you, Mr. Bangladesh limo driver.

They survive, like everyone else, with stratagems. The other day I was in a cab with a woman cabdriver, a young Jamaican, and I asked her about her job. She said the toughest thing if you're a woman cabdriver is that there's no place to go to the bathroom. Guys just stop the car somewhere and go or, she informed me, carry a bottle and throw it away. But women cabdrivers have to cruise around looking for a friendly gas station or diner or a McDonald's, and it's not always easy. You double-park for three minutes and find a fifty-dollar ticket on your window. The second problem, she said, is violence. I asked if she handles that by working in the day. She said no, she handles it by being sexist: "I don't pick up men." I was having one of those days where the synapses don't quite fire off, so I said, "Why?" And she looked at me in the mirror as if I were really stupid. "Because women don't beat you up," she explained. "Women don't shoot you." I laughed and she said, "Don't get me wrong, honey, I love men, but if there weren't no men in this city there wouldn't be no crime!"

Which, when you think about it, is pretty much true.

Anyway, thirty-nine cabdrivers have been shot and killed so far this year in New York and, as they say, the year isn't over.

Crime, of course, is the city's great leveler, the thing that is always with us, and that gives another meaning to the cry "Watchyerback!"

It is like this throughout the country now, of course. When that little girl, Polly Klass, was abducted from her suburban California home during a slumber party one night in 1993, it was a seminal moment in the recent history of American crime, because it made everyone realize: *There is no safety now.* There is no safe place. The Central Park jogger was running in the park, the boy from Utah who was stabbed to death when he and his family were here for the U.S. Open was in the subway. These are dangerous places. But Polly Klass was in her bedroom; her mother slept a few feet away; the kidnapper who abducted and murdered her was out on parole after an adulthood devoted to violence. The suburbs are frightened, and should be, and the cities are more frightened still.

Here is a very small and typical scene a neighborhood mother told me about when I was newly back in town. I remember it so sharply because I imagined the boy being my own. She was walking along an East Side street in the upper eighties one afternoon when a little boy about ten years old ran up to her wide-eyed and breathless and said, "Lady, can I walk with you like I belong to you?"

Startled, she said yes, and looked in the direction from which he'd run. There, standing on the corner, were three young teenagers, watching. Their eyes said, We'll see you later. "They beat you up and rob you," he said. She walked the boy home, and what struck her at the end was the calm he affected.

I feel about street criminals, any street criminals, anywhere, all of them, the way I felt when I was a girl about the Nazis. As a child I was deeply affected by the book and movie *The Diary of Anne Frank.* It struck me so hard that for years, and I mean well into adulthood, I judged friends by whether or not they would hide me from the SS. This one would hide me in the attic and bring me food forever. This one would even move in with me. This one would say, loudly, to the Nazi detail, "There is no one here!" and then point up and silently mouth, "They're upstairs, behind the bookcase."

I still think regularly about this drama, only partly because some city sirens now make the same sound as the sirens on the Nazi arrest wagons. I think of New York's street criminals as, simply, fascists. They band together for strength and force, they use violence as a tool to intimidate the population, they believe they have a right to take what they want, and they prey on the weak. Their ideology is simple and evil: *I got the power.* They even have snappy uniforms. You can see them on rap videos. Do you find those videos at least vaguely menacing? You're supposed to. They are meant to be menacing.

Anyway, crime has become my big women's issue.

Which is not totally fair. The other night, coming back from the McDonald's near Eighty-fifth Street with my son and one of his friends, we decided to get a cab. It was early but dark, and we were all tired. Naturally I got talking with the cabdriver, naturally it was about crime, and I asked him if, as has been reported in the papers, he has, like many of his co-workers, taken to carrying a gun. He eyeballed me—woman with kids, perfect Taxi and Limousine Commission plant—and said no. But we chatted and he went through the usual list of precautions, and then he got mad. "I won't pick up those kids! Won't pick up the men!" And then he got angrier still and said, "It is not racist, it is not racist!"

I probably need not tell you that he was a black man, age about thirty, with a Caribbean accent and a French-sounding name. It was a real New York moment: a cabdriver in dreadlocks speeding uptown, railing at the wheel, defending himself against unmade charges of racism in a Bob Marley accent.

He isn't racist. I would go so far as to say most people in New York, black and white, are not racist. They are just nervous Bayesians.

Thomas Bayes was the father of probability theory; he was a pioneer in the area of statistical probability. An economist named Walter Williams, who is one tough and brilliant black man, said ten years ago, Look: if you are walking down the street by yourself in the dark and a black lady comes toward you and you cross the street because blacks are violent, then you are a racist and a fool. If you are walking down the street and a middle-aged black man comes toward you and you cross the street, then you are a racist and a fool. But if you are walking down the street by yourself in the dark and a group of black male teenagers comes toward you and you cross the street, then you are not a racist and a fool, you are a Bayesian. You have reason to be afraid. Get over the labels, he said, and deal with the problem.

Here's the saddest thing about Bayesianism.

One of its victims may be Benny. Benny is my son's best friend. They met in the park on Sixty-seventh Street four years ago, when they were two. They chased pigeons together. My son still remembers Benny's first words to him: "You want to climb this?" About a jungle gym neither of them could navigate. Benny is gentle, smart and mischievous, and he and Will hit it off immediately. He and his parents lived across the street from us. In time we got in the habit of going to the park together. In time his mother became a close friend; she is a therapist at a New York hospital and has a very practical sense of people and their subtleties, their bizarreness, their needs; she also sees America clearly, in an unillusioned way, and notices things others and I born here often miss. Benny is black. His mother, from Jamaica, is also black. His father, from England, is so white he is pink. When Benny and Will walk down the street with Tommy Ng, another playmate, they stop traffic. People just stare. I know what they are thinking: This is a beautiful living Benetton ad, these boys have jumped from a magazine to amble down the street for my delight.

Which is exactly what they look like. Their unselfconscious friendship is the nicest part of new America.

Among the delightful things about Benny is that he goes to a Greek Orthodox school, and so has been exposed to yet another culture. When Benny stays over and has dinner with us, my son says grace and makes the sign of the cross and Benny makes a Greek cross and says a prayer that sounds like "Uh yess a fuh fuh, a yess uh fuh fuh." It sounds so pretty and unexpected. Once we were in a shoe store and for some reason the salesman, who was some kind of immigrant, looked at Ben and said, "I bet you speak another language besides English." We weren't sure what that meant. The salesman said, "He speaks Spanish, right?" I said no, and Benny said, "Nice shoes," in Greek, which kind of slamdunked Mr. Interlocutor.

Benny is a happy boy, but as he grows older he will know stresses my son will not know, for it is he who will be whipsawed by our current dramas. It is Benny who, a dozen years from now, will be heading up to Columbia and flailing his arms in the dark as the empty cabs go by. He will by then perhaps be accustomed to being treated differently. The parents of some of his white friends may treat him more self-consciously because he's black. Some of his black peers may treat him differently because he is studious, i.e., acts white. He'll be unable to fortify himself with any nice racial resentment because who is he going to hate? The father he adores is white. The mother he adores is black. The friends he loves are white, black, yellow and beige. It will be hard.

(An irrelevant memory. Children don't notice race. They barely notice color. It's touching and interesting. Once when the boys were five they were sitting in our TV room watching *The Little Mermaid* and eating ice cream. They were right next to each other on the couch, and they both held their bowls in their laps with their hands on them, and Will looked at Ben's bowl, and his arm, and his own bowl and arm. And he looked at me and said, "Mommy, Benny is chocolate and I'm vanilla." And Benny looked at Will's bowl and arm and his own bowl and arm and laughed. I got to say, "And you are both sweet and delicious." When I told Ben's parents they said "Oh how cute," and when they told the story they got it mixed up and called the boys Mr. Salt and Mr. Pepper.)

A final story, which has a point that I think is important. About fifteen years ago my brother, my burly brother Jim who is six three and big, was out late in a subway station after an evening of beer with the boys. It was one of those big stations where you have to walk through long dirty-tiled tunnels to get to your train. My brother was alone, the tunnel was empty. And then he heard a sound, and a woman's voice, and he ran toward it, turning into a tunnel that revealed three teenagers sexually molesting a middle-aged woman. Now my brother is big, as I said, and he had a cast on his forearm, which some weeks before he had broken. He stood and watched for a moment and then was shocked to hear his shocked voice ring out, "What are you *doing?*" He moved toward them and when one of them moved for him, he stopped, planted his feet and swung the arm with the cast and hit the bad guy with a blow to the face that knocked him down stunned and bleeding. (I'm enjoying this, I know, but there is a point.) The other two quickly calculated their chances—two against one, but this guy is crazy—figured forget it, and ran. My brother let the guy he'd hit run away too. Then he helped the woman get herself together and they both went in different directions.

It turned out she went to the police, and the story of the guy in the cast got to a reporter in town who's still on local news and whom I will not name. He found my brother in New Jersey and called him and asked him for an interview. My brother said, "Thanks, but— nah." The reporter said, "But this is a great story, a white guy with a broken arm saves a woman and beats up three black guys! You're a brave guy, you're a hero!"

My brother said, "I wasn't brave, I was half tanked."

The reporter said, "Talk to us." My brother said no.

What upset my brother was the reporter's cynical interest in the racial angle. It made him feel embarrassed, and ashamed. Jimmy didn't think he was slugging a black guy, he thought he was slugging a bad guy.

He called and told me the whole story—after he spoke to the reporter, and then he started to muse on the issue of what was then, fifteen years ago, the unnamed phenomenon of wolf packs. He knew them from being in the city at night and he said they all had two things in common. One is that they're all cowards, and the other is that they all have rage.

I wondered if my brother, in his early twenties himself and not a stranger to anger, had insights I lacked on the reasons behind the rage. He paused, and verbally shrugged. "It's rage at society for not accepting them, or whatever."

We talked a long time about the difficult lives of these kids in this culture. But fifteen years later I think theirs is not rage at society due to racism, or rage at society due to limited job opportunities.

It is not rage at society, it is only rage directed at society. It is the rage of the loveless, and it is directed at society because it is easier, more possible, to aim their anger at an abstract thing—at a society that, as they are constantly told, wants to discriminate against them, will always discriminate against them—than at the individuals, the parents, the young, herself-unloved mother, the absent father, who left their hearts quite dead.

That is why their eyes are dead, those teenagers, because their hearts are dead. They killed their hearts so they could be tough and hard, to show the world they are unfrightened and alive, because inside, they know, they are wounded and dead. I, you, in their circumstances, might do the same.

It has been noted again and again in the press that the thing that tends to trigger a shooting in a school or on a playground is some kind of disrespect, some humiliation. A thirteen-year-old said something to a twelve-year-old, and a gun got pulled. And it makes emotional sense. They *would* be sensitive to humiliation; their whole lives have been the humiliation of being unloved. They have been humiliated by the fact that they are here and no one who is supposed to care cares. Truly, crack and heroin have done something new in human history: They have broken the bond between mother and child. They have made mothers not love their children.

From what I have seen, if you have a parent's love you may or may not turn out okay. But if you have never had a parent's love you will go through life with a parent-shaped hole inside you, and it will most likely, unless you have a very strong soul or very good luck or another power intervenes, leave you thwarted, and disturbed, and possibly dangerous.

But these young men and boys have a kind of power beyond the obvious one: the power of persuasion. The kids who killed the boy from Utah in the subway—some of them were from close, two-parent families. One wonders if it isn't a kind of virus of nihilism that they've caught, that can penetrate even the parent-protected.

These children are not only the biggest single problem in New York's—in the country's—present, they are the biggest single problem in New York's future.

And still it will be eased, in time. There are many reasons to think this. Soon now society will focus on the problem and, in Walter Williams's phrase, start to deal with it. But the main one, for me, is purely intuitive: Young black men will save our country. I'm not sure completely what I mean by this but—they're tough and smart and know how to survive. Think of the ones who go into the service. They go into the armed forces and they are tough and good and have a heart. No one is American the way they are Americans—and against the odds. Did you ever go to a meeting of serious Christians, of whatever stripe or sect? They are there, and leading. I don't mean a photo-op church in Manhattan with a community-leader preacher who's only another politician meeting with the editorial board of *The New York Times*, I mean down back there in the country, in the far reaches, in the suburbs, even, where Christianity is still a religion, and a pretty personal and communal thing. Anyway, something just tells me they're going to save our country.

—

Just as the immigrants will save this city. I feel personally grateful to them because they have done something that has helped keep me, and my son, and my neighborhood safe. My neighborhood is nice, it's pretty, but the thing that keeps it safe late at night, in the dark, is our beacon, our brightly lit twenty-four-hour beacon of busyness, humanity and hope—the Korean deli at the end of the block. As we sleep they are being alive and human and unpacking things and keeping the lights on and keeping the security camera on and keeping a watchman on and making bread, milk and baby Tylenol available to stressed-out parents at 2:00 A.M. They give us a feeling of life and human presence. Also the people who work there are close enough to the old country—to the ground!—to not be totally in the thrall of theories and systems. They don't think everything is politics. They still think a lot is human.

—

When I first came to live in the city, in the seventies, I saw it as straight, cornered and comprehensible. This way is uptown, where the numbers of the streets go up, and this way is downtown, where the numbers of the streets go down. The East Side is over on the east, and the West Side is on the west. They are separated by a park in the center. We call this, "Central Park."

But now, to older eyes, New York seems more layered and circular, and Washington, that city of rings around monuments and ellipses and beltways, seems perhaps not as curved and arched as I'd thought.

For instance: Washington is one town, Politicstown, divided by a train track. On one side are the Bloods, those who live the political life—senators, bureaucrats, staffers, aides. On the other, the Crips—journalists, the media establishment.

New York on the other hand is composed of many towns with many gangs—Moneytown, Advertisingville, Politicstown, Societyville, etc. These might more accurately be seen as feudal kingdoms, and their leaders as feudal lords. Prince Mort of Mediatown, for instance, Princess Donna of Fashionville.

In Washington if you fail, if you fall from power, you are pronounced dead; the Crips rap your obit in the *Post.* You get to hear it in the living room with your kids, on *Capitol Gang.* You're not really dead but you think you are because you've been officially labeled dead, and when you put out the garbage tomorrow the neighbors will be startled, because they heard you're dead too.

This is the reason our politicians have such an exaggerated fear of the normal setbacks of political life, of a lost election or bad press. It's a reason why, when they seriously disagree with policy, they never resign. They hunker down, wait for the weather to change. They call this pragmatism. "It's self-indulgent to go over the cliff, flags flying."

As if the person were acting on principle when he cares only for self.

In New York, failure comes with an escape hatch and is surrounded by a knowing question: Where will he show up next? Blow it in Mediatown and you can still find a place in Publishingville, fail to make it in Societytown and you can repair to Museumville to ponder your next move.

I don't have a circle, which is both good and bad. It is good to belong but perhaps it is better to visit. Still, all outsiders experience more than the usual amount of cognitive dissonance. For instance: there are the thoughts you get when you visit a New York dinner party.

Sometimes the people at these parties, sipping the soup and looking to see if their spouse has landed well, are the most powerful people in the most powerful city in the most powerful nation on earth—meaning that here as everywhere there is iniquity but these, my tablemates, are significant sinners: greenmailers, liars on TV, owners of media organs that pursue their owners' ambitions and grievances.

This man here, this jolly round fellow passing the cream and chatting. He has an innocent eagerness as he listens, an ingenuous engagement in the facts of the story he's telling. He is a man of rough business practice, hugely wealthy, who in the eighties played with companies and broke them up and sold the pieces. He has devoted his life to the accrual of wealth and the buying of beauty, and a good many people have been hurt as he pursued his hard wants.

But what to make of the split facts of his life? He isn't bad: his eyes shine as he talks about his children. He isn't good: he hurts people's lives for money. He gives to charities, the right charities but charities nonetheless. He warms the room when he walks in. His opinions on political questions are well grounded. The host adores him and knows that he came, in spite of a flu he hasn't quite shaken, out of loyalty. If he died tonight he'd go to hell.

It is confusing to dine with such people. No, it is confusing to like them!—to see the human qualities, feel the warmth, hear the human rationales. Ought one to shun this world? Do you comfort yourself that you're only an observer, maintaining a feeling of separateness, even superiority? But in what way are you superior to this man of whom you disapprove and who you hope will like you? Do you philosophize that at the neighborhood barbecue in the ranch houses of Westwood, New Jersey, there is probably an equal amount of venality and calculation, and it's not as dramatic only because they lack the wherewithal to operate on his scale?

These are not social questions but moral questions, questions about How to Live.

And oh—we're back to the rich man—the distance between the vividness of his transgressions and the banality of his persona. He is a jovial little man passing chocolate truffles! No one looks like what they are. I do not mean that you can't tell a book by its cover. As I grow older I think, oddly enough, that you can tell a lot of books by their covers. People give you so many clues about who they are as they walk down the street that it's almost generous of them. (Children are on to this. When a child says, "That man gives me the creeps," listen: he's seeing something you're too smart to see.) Business executives who look clipped, coiffed and arrogant are often—arrogant. Unblinking intellectuals who look at you coldly as you try to answer their questions are often—cold. The smiling, open-faced baby-sitters I see waiting for kids at my son's school are usually easygoing and honest.

What I mean by "People never look like what they are" is: if my businessman actually looked like the part he plays in life, he'd be sitting there at the dinner party with a dagger in his teeth and a hook for a hand.

It would be easier for all of us around him. We could say, "Would you pass the cream, the pirate wants it." It would all be clearer.

—

I have been at home the past few years with a child, and so in some ways have been on Pause. People I know who are married with kids can work outside the house, divide their duties, go on business trips. The family's a going concern, things are settled. But if you're a single parent and you are lucky enough to be able to stay home with a child, you should. To do otherwise would be like inviting friends to a party and then not showing up yourself. It would be rude. Now, however, my son is in first grade, and comes home two days a week from after-school programs at 5:00 P.M., so I no longer have to be in the house during the day. I am fantasizing about working in an office; I am thinking of gray high heels and soft gray suits. Now I wear jeans and a T-shirt and work at a PC surrounded by empty Diet Coke cans. I look like Grace Metalious in the author's picture on the back of *Peyton Place*. I am thinking of leaving the house in the morning and going to my office in A Busy Place.

But I sense that many people roughly my age and in different circumstances are also on Pause. I know the Clintons are running America, I know they're boomers, but that's all—kind of a joke. I know that our perceptions are affected by our biases, that what we see is affected by what we feel, but I see the Clintons and think: This is not authentic, this is not real history, it is manufactured history. He isn't running things, he's running from things; the boomers, ever slow, are still evolving. Someday we will rule; this presidency is just a small burp from history's digestive system.

Anyway, a lot of the rest of us are, on some psychic level, slowing and surveying the terrain. There's no name for this condition, it's not the midlife crisis, it's not a crisis at all. It is more like a kind of equipoise. You're bringing up the kids in a Pennsylvania suburb, grousing with the spouse, considering where you are and thinking about some unnamed but still revelatory future. Or you're fifteen, twenty years into a career and thinking, Is this a vocation or the first answer I could think of? You're dealing with the daily, with you you are in the day-to-day. You're not in a panic, not in a storm, but you're at some post- or pre-evolutionary stage. So for a while you regather and regroup.

And, of course, watch TV. And daydream as you watch TV.

—

I sit at night on the couch in the family room, my spine curled against the pillows, surfing from channel to channel, from 2 to 4 to 7, through Fox and the independents, past PBS, C-Span and Disney. I end in a swell on AMC and wait for a wave. Katharine Hepburn comes on and says, "The calla lillies are in bloom again." I ride it past Pay-per-view and C-Span 2 and wind up, becalmed, on channel 2. The great thing about the stations late at night is that it's like watching TV in the seventies, the same poor fare. The banality is comforting. It's like a glimmer of eternity.

Once I caught a perfect Roddy McDowall wave. He was a child on 5 in *How Green Was My Valley*, then a man in a *Hart to Hart* rerun on 11, and then he was a gray-haired butler on a rerun of *Murder, She Wrote*, on, I think, USA. He aged before my eyes. That was a great night. It was like when Flannery O'Connor saw the chicken walk backward from one side of the backyard to the other. After that, she said, everything was anticlimax.

The best thing I've seen on TV lately was at the end of a *Northern Exposure*, in which everyone was voting, and as people walked to the polls the producers played only music, with no dialogue. It was tender about democracy. And democracy has its tender moments. Today I passed a polling place on Eighty-second Street, and as we drove slowly by on Madison Avenue in heavy traffic there were all these people handing out election literature on the corner. In their midst, a boy and a girl were kissing in a we-just-ducked-eighth-period way and, best of all, a big old lady in a big gray bouffant walked up to a guy and said, "Hi, this is about my son Mahk Snyduh, who's running fuh judge, please take a look and vote for him, thanks." It was so busy and colorful and bustling, and you hoped Mark Snyder would win, and his mother would be happy at the victory party.

Click click. The news, the French anchorman, *My Three Sons.* ("Well, Robby, I'm not sure we'd all agree a basketball game is more important than a geometry final.")

Click, and a swell. Question Time in the British Parliament. John Major stutters slightly this evening. Neil Kinnock bores in with strained flair.

I can ride this wave.

Once, about three years ago, I went to see Margaret Thatcher make a speech in Washington. She had just left Downing Street and this was her first speech in America since her departure. Assembled before her in the ballroom of the Four Seasons Hotel were hundreds of staunch admirers, Republican senators and congressmen and journalists. Thatcher began to speak and it was a good speech, but a funny thing happened. Every time she hit an applause line there would be a second or so of silence before people realized they were supposed to clap. They weren't used to her rhythm, her delivery; they didn't know if she wanted applause. Maybe she would consider it an interruption. Anyway, she'd get to the applause line and there would be a second of silence, and then, from the middle of the room would come the sound of Hear, hear, followed by that growly ruh ruh ruh sound they make in the House of Commons. She'd hit a line, he'd go, "Hear, hear, ruh ruh ruh." I looked over. It was an elderly man sitting at a center table. He was smoking and drinking and as he looked at Thatcher he glistened with admiration.

"Who's that?" I asked the man to my right.

"That's Dennis Thatcher," he said.

At the end of the speech I asked an aide about it, and he laughed and said, "Well, this is the thing. Years ago when Mrs. Thatcher was just starting out, she'd go to big halls like this and no one would be there. A dozen or so people would show up, and she'd make a speech and it would be awkward, she wasn't polished. And when she got to the end of a strong line there would be silence. Dennis would be standing in the back, and he'd sort of go, 'Hear, hear!' to get the crowd going, and they'd applaud. I often went with him. We'd often go 'Hear, hear' together."

"And now she is a great personage of the world, the great British prime minister of the second half of the twentieth century, and Dennis Thatcher—"

"Is still in the back, warding off silence."

"That's wonderful."

"Yes, it is," he said, and made a note.

Anyway, Dennis Thatcher is my idea of the perfect First Lady.

A few months ago, in the summer of '93, I saw her again, but this time in a small group. She was just back from revolutionary Russia, and was bursting with news. It was said of Lenin that he could exhaust you by listening, but she can exhaust you by making you listen; she doesn't waste words, each has a purpose, and she doesn't pause much, so an encounter with her is dense with data.

She told us of the energy and success she'd seen in the provinces. In one, the governor showed her the visible signs of the taking hold of the free-market spirit—the wares and foods on sale in the square, the backyard gardens yielding vegetables and fruit to be sold at a profit. But, she said, she went to Moscow and met with the intellectuals and government people and it was gloomy, gloomy, "We can't make it work, it will never work, the country will collapse." There is such pessimism among the elites, she said. She went to a dinner in Moscow and leaders of the government were there, and former dissidents and writers and bureaucrats. She said she tried to cheer them up.

What did you tell them? I asked.

The hooded eyes blinked, the head tilted forward.

"I told them, 'Now listen, this won't do, *snap out of it!*' "

Hear, hear, ruh ruh ruh.

This is a woman who has never been on Pause. I could have asked her, but she would have said, "Pause. I'm not sure I fully understand your meaning. Life is fast-forward, you see."

———

Click, and a wavelet: from Blair Brown's face to Florence Henderson's to Sally Fields flying over the sand-colored roofs of southern California. Sister Bertrille. You like me, you really like me.

The thing about surfing—you know one of the reasons people channel-surf? Because it's the last immediate power they have. Jay Leno isn't amusing us this evening? Zap, you're gone, Jay. AMC dug a little too low in the old movie bin? Zap, take that, Cornel Wilde. Ted Koppel a bit smug tonight? Zap, try again tomorrow, Ted. You have power, autonomy, you are the king of zappers. You can cut Dick Gephardt off mid-sentence, zap. It's where we insult our rulers now, at home on the couch with a cup of tea.

This is why people are fantasizing about having zappers for their lives. Someone turns to you and says something you don't want to hear, you pick up the mental zapper. A scene in your life begins, the firing scene, the whining scene: Zap.

I love my TV. It's the first thing I put on in the morning, right after I kiss my son, and the last thing I turn off at night, after the lights. I keep it on in the day as I work. When it's off I feel unplugged.

———

But New York, and its circles. There is so much going on in New York in a business sense, in a social sense, in a business-social sense, and so many kinds of relationships. Business friendships, business friendship that turned into actual friendship, and those that are stuck in colleagueship. Small dinner parties among friends, among friends and colleagues, and larger ones among friends, colleagues and people who hate each other.

And there are the big parties at places like the Metropolitan Museum or the Four Seasons or the Public Library. These are interesting because, I feel, they are not so much parties as enactments. Everyone enacts—whatever. A common mission, official approval of the person being honored, the celebration of something new—a book, a fashion line. I don't go to a lot of these but I go to some, and what surprises me is that I always see the same people. They're all successful, big in their field. They are boldface names. It's nice to see them, but I always wonder, Are they always here? Is it a seamless soirée that continues from night to night, that each evening changes its venue but not its cast? And are they having fun?

A friend of mine who has the kind of job that makes him part of the enactment life sat down and told me about what he calls the social stations of the cross: the Literary Lions dinner, the Committee to Protect Journalists dinner, the PEN dinner, the lavish book party for a well-known author. He said, "What you have to know about going to these parties is it's a substitute for life. You never have to be alone, you never have to have real experiences. The people who go to them wind up substituting the illusion of pleasure for pleasure. They derive a sense of themselves from what they're invited to. They want to be in Liz Smith or Suzy in the list of those who attended. They want to be in a list read by plumbers, which is funny since they look down on plumbers. But also, in fairness, there is a business component. It's important to have a certain degree of visibility. It's important to be present and let people know you're there."

He told me one of the many things he admires about his wife is that she usually doesn't accompany him. "She just won't enact, she just won't show!" He usually goes alone, and leaves early.

Tell me about the marriages, I said. Are those couples at the enactments—are they in love, I mean do they love each other? He said, "A lot of these marriages are deals. The marriage is a deal and you both do your part, whatever it is. But one of the good things about the big parties is you can get away from your wife or husband by going with your wife or husband to the party."

—

I keep hearing people use the word "deal" when they talk about other people's marriages. A few weeks ago I had lunch at the neighborhood lunch place, Jackson Hole, with a friend who works in a think tank. His daughter goes to one of the neighborhood private schools, one of the toniest, and he told me that he and his wife are fascinated by the rich parents at the parents' meetings. He said the mother is forty, blond, black hairband, the husband is fifty-eight, trim, in good shape, and they have two children, in kindergarten and second grade. It's her first marriage, his second. They look good together, they love their children, and their marriage is about acquiring and appearing.

Do they love each other?

No. The action for them isn't the love part, it's the having part. Having a pink-cheeked baby in the best stroller in a hundred-dollar dress. Having an attractive wife or a handsome husband with graying hair. She's not interested in him anymore, and he doesn't really much like her. But they have a beautiful apartment on Park in the Eighties. They are a social and economic unit. It's a deal.

Do they sleep together?

Yeah, it's part of the deal.

Mmmmmm.

People can always look clearly at other people's marriages. They don't have illusions about other people's alliances.

Right after this I had breakfast with a friend in from Washington, and looking for inspiration, I asked him what it was like to have a good marriage of twenty-seven years. He said, "Well, we'll always be together." I said, "Oh good, tell me why." And he said, "A deal's a deal."

It occurs to me this usage may not be only cool and clinical. Maybe in an age in which the old societal restraints and sanctions have largely disappeared, people cast about, after a time, for a reason to explain why they are together. And since in our world people tend to respect the contractual agreements to which they have signed their names, they inevitably seize on a metaphor of the business society to explain their private choices: A deal's a deal.

—

But some relationships are easy, some deals easily maintained. There are your friends, people who are in your life from a mix of history, accident and affection, who have no utility for you, nor you for them, save this: They hold your hand. And you theirs. And you meet and talk about the circles in the daily round.

Here is a Thursday-night dinner in a restaurant with Jake and Esther. She is a free-lance writer, funny and gossipy. He is a reporter, book reviewer and essayist. When I think of them I think of a conversation we had once about a businessman we all know in town, a fellow who is very bright and ambitious and a snob, a "This is like the Candy Kitchen" kind of guy. (He just follows. If Coney Island were suddenly in style he'd discover its virtues and give lectures at dinner parties on its down-to-the-bone humanity, its eschewal of the uppity, the Hampton-y.) I don't know why he annoys me. We all forgive jerky things in each other all the time. But it bothers me that he's nice to you if he thinks you're smart, and isn't if he doesn't. He thinks intelligence is a virtue when of course it's not, virtue is a virtue, intelligence is a gift, you ought to just sit down, have a nice glass of water and enjoy your luck.

Anyway, Jake and Esther were laughing and telling stories about him and then Jake said, "But you know, he's my friend, and that's that."

"Why," I said, "what is it?"

"Peggy, we all go through life with a circus troupe walking behind us. You meet who you meet and if you can you become friends, and as the years pass you look back now and then and see Alice swallowing fire, and Johnny juggling names that he drops. It's your circus troupe. And you gotta be good to your troupe."

"And know you're in the circus too."

"Oh yes."

"That's so nice. I think next I'd like to get shot out of the cannon."

"Well, if you get hurt we'll be your clowns, and distract the crowd."

On this evening, this Thursday night at dinner, we were in an Italian restaurant on the East Side. We had met late, ten o'clock, because they were both meeting deadlines. This is the night we discussed being on Pause.

One way you know you're on Pause, we decided, is that all of a sudden you have to make a decision at work, a big decision. You have been offered the job of being, say, *Newsday*'s guy on Clinton for the campaign. This is a significant journalistic position, and not without promise. But instead of jumping up and down, you ponder your reservations and make a list, considering how the new assignment will impact your life—such a job is like a trial separation from a spouse, what if Clinton loses. And then there is another job at a magazine that you've been thinking about, but that is to be bestowed by an owner of known caprice. You are not in control of your fate, and all options look equally insufficient. You are forty-four now, and lack the idiotic excitement of thirty. When you were thirty you were on your way to something. Now you're there. (Oh no!) You cannot make the decision. That is because the decision is only a thin veil covering the real question, which is, What do I want my life to mean? What do I want the obit to say, what do I want for the lead?

When you are thirty and don't know what you want to be, you pick an area and rise; you can't wait to see what you'll become. When you're forty you've become it. (Oh no!) The lead is going to be: Bob Jones, longtime political observer in the days of New York's tabloids and 1993 New York City Rotisserie Baseball champ, died yesterday. . . .

Your thirties are about ambition, your forties fruition. Sometimes the fruit is like the artificial apples and pears people kept in a bowl on the table when we were kids, shiny and succulent-looking but dry, and made of wood.

—

I live on a block full of brownstones in a neighborhood full of children, Carnegie Hill, in the eighties and nineties, near Central Park. The track around the reservoir is a few blocks from my apartment and runners in bright shorts and shirts jog by on the way to it. The other day in the afternoon at the entrance, where runners jog off the cobblestone side of Fifth and run up broad old marble steps to the runners' dirt track, there was an insane man, shouting at people and threatening them in obscene language. Everyone ignored him, and just jogged by.

I stood around inspecting my shoes, wondering if anyone would, the second or third time around the track, ask the guy to stop talking like that. But no one did, including me. We just ignored him, and with seeming ease. People in New York are expert now at not seeming to see what is right in front of their faces.

I always wonder exactly what goes through people's minds when they pass real street crazies who bellow and bark and shout obsceni-ties. It is the modern way to assume they are unmedicated schizophrenics, and I suppose they are, but the level of their pathology is sometimes so biblical, with the growling and shaking of arms, that I have wondered at times if perhaps some of them are not possessed. In which case they would need not medicine but a miracle, a savior to cast out their demons.

But some of them aren't crazy, and work the street life as a job. In front of the Korean deli there are, relieving each other at the end of a shift, two street persons, both male, young, healthy-seeming and polite. They each carry a paper cup, the kind take-out coffee comes in, with change in it. As you leave the deli with change in your hand, they shake the cup at you and say Please. I used to give them my change. Then I saw a sign on the deli cash register: PLEASE DO NOT ENCOURAGE THE MEN OUTSIDE BY GIVING THEM MONEY, THEY USE IT FOR DRUGS. It was signed by a neighborhood association. So I stopped giving money, and they stopped shaking the cup at me, but they also stopped smiling, and saying How you doin' today? I'm no longer a good customer.

The worst thing about what is called the homeless situation is that people are living in the cold and damp of the street. The second worst thing is how it corrupts the people who walk by, making believe they don't see, making believe they don't hear what is being said to them, playing the heavy in the movie of their mind as they shake their head no.

The city of New York in 1987 very famously tried to get a homeless woman who called herself Billie Boggs taken off the streets. Billie, who lived on a good street on the East Side, yelled at people and defecated on the sidewalk. So the city, reasonably enough, put her in a psychiatric hospital. She called the ACLU from a pay phone in the hospital, they took her case, and in court they defended Billie's right to live on the streets. ACLU won. Significant case. Left the city saying, What can we do? Billie returned to her haunts and, after a round of talk shows, television interviews and an appearance at

Harvard Law School, started defecating on the sidewalk again. She was arrested in 1988 for panhandling and screaming obscenities.

I often think of this when I pass someone cleaning up with a pooper scooper after his or her dog. This is where thirty years of urban liberalism have gotten us: in New York dogs can't shit on the sidewalk, but people can.

Still, I love my neighborhood. When you walk south on Fifth on the cobblestones, with the trees arching above, you pass the great museums of the city—the Jewish Museum in the old Warburg mansion; the Cooper-Hewitt, a grand and handsome old mansion with a spacious lawn and arches and an old-fashioned black iron fence; the Guggenheim, huge white and rounded, looking like a big modern cruise ship sailing down the avenue—you expect to see Kathie Lee Gifford dance out onto the big round part on top and belt out the Carnival Cruise Line song. Going south still there are smaller museums in smaller town houses, and Marymount, and the Metropolitan Museum, huge columned stolid and gray, with huge banners that snap in the wind like sails. To the side, the Temple of Dendur, which you can see at night as you go through the park in a cab. You can turn your head and think: There's Egypt.

I take this walk almost every Saturday with my son. He thinks we take this route because it is the only one to F.A.O. Schwarz, where we look at all the wonderful things, the singing bears and dancing ostriches, and buy a toy for under ten dollars, which is the rule. But we take this route because I love it, and want him to see and have imprinted on his brain the glory of New York.

Also this walk is like visiting Europe. The sun-dappled cobblestones, the stately architecture, the brightness and festive atmosphere. Half the people are carrying cameras. I tell my son, one of the things to do with New York is sometimes make believe you're visiting it, like Europe. Then you see it with fresh eyes and find everything interesting, like a discovery. He reminds me he likes the huburbs. That's what he calls them, the huburbs, the hub of towns around the city, like the one in New Jersey where his cousins live, where you can see bugs in the bark and there are pools in back and everyone has cars. He has a point. Then again people tend to want what they don't have or, rather, see the benefit in the thing they don't see when they look out the window in the morning.

His cousin Meaghan, his age, lives in New Jersey and visits us often on weekends. Meaghan tells us as we return one Sunday from a weekend at the Jersey Shore that as soon as she sees the Lincoln Tunnel she says, "Hooray, New York!" She sees it as I do: she thinks she's visiting an exotic capital. She loves it because we do interesting things, not only like go to F.A.O. Schwarz but, on the way there, stop at Harry Cipriani's restaurant to visit the license plate on the wall. There is a license plate framed on the wall at Harry Cipriani's because one morning a cab careened off Fifty-ninth Street, smashed through the front of the restaurant, sped past the bar, crashed through the dining room and came to rest against the back wall. The restaurant was empty, nobody was hurt, and the license plate was put up as a jaunty memorial. When we go in, the maître d' and waiters bow and walk us to the plaque with great formality. Once one of them said, "And from this we learn to be very safe, and always look both ways, and obey your mama."

But the cobblestones. We all like cobblestones, their patterns and nice roughness, the sense they give that here beneath our feet is something that has seen some history. These stones, laid long ago with care and precision, came with the masons' knowledge that after they were gone their work would remain and be of use. Perhaps they put a hand upon each stone and gave it a final push thinking, My hand remains, unseen, forever.

My son practices riding his bike on the cobblestones, leaving our apartment and wobbling between the passersby, with me walking quickly behind him. We go down to the Metropolitan and back. One day we were near the museum when I saw Louis Auchincloss, the novelist. He was sitting on a sunny park bench in a plaid shirt and khaki slacks, yawning over a library book. I had met him six months before, at a book party. He is tall with straight posture and has hooded eyes, and when we stood chatting I had the impression of being closely observed by an eagle. This day I said hello and introduced my son. I wanted my son to meet him so in the year 2007, when he is in college and taking a course on great American novels and reads *The Rector of Justin*, he can remember: I met Auchincloss once. He was in a short-sleeved shirt sitting on a bench. It was in the early 1990s, in New York. My mother said hello and said, "Willy, this is Mr. Auchincloss, who is a writer." And he complimented me on my bike.

It is good to meet people of artistic excellence and achievement. They dress up life, and when you meet them by surprise on a street it's like coming on a peacock in the forest. You see them strut.

Auchincloss said, "Where are you off to?"

I said, "Going home," and gestured north.

"I'm going the same way," he said, "I'll walk you."

We talked about writing, about old New York. "This part of the city has barely changed since I was a boy," he said. "In fact, it's one of the most unchanged areas in Manhattan. I lived on this block when I was seven. Right here in this house."

"This house?"

"Yes."

"The gray house?"

"Yes."

"That's our house."

"No."

"Yes."

"We lived there about a year and a half," he said. "Rented the house when, I think, my parents' apartment was being fixed up. Do you have the whole place?"

"No, we have the third and fourth floors. A woman who writes works on the basement level. Then on the first floor is the office of her husband, who's a psychoanalyst. Then they live on the second floor and we're on three and four."

We parted, Louis walked on to Park Avenue, and we took the bike upstairs, passing a somber-looking patient on the stoop.

Recently I took a friend out onto our little terrace in the back and he stood looking at the view—the backs of the town houses on the next street—and pointed toward a window and said, "That's my analyst's office. That whole street is full of psychiatrists." Right after that a friend of mine who is a psychologist came over and pointed and said, "That's my office."

A few months ago I filled the terrace with flowers, and planted some, and now I'm back there all the time watering and picking off leaves and weeds and sneaking in the Miracle-Gro. I used to have a black thumb: if I bought a tree or a plant it would sit in the corner, look at me prettily and die. But these now thrive. At first now and then when I was out there with my watering can I would hear in the quiet a yelp or a sharp sound and I'd look around to see if someone needed attention or was in trouble. I never saw anything. Now I figure it's just somebody having a breakthrough.

A few weeks ago I told the Auchincloss story to a writer and director who showed a surprising interest in exactly where my house is on the block. I told him and he nodded, with the look on his face highly literate people get when they're trying to remember something boring like a number. He asked if I know a local couple. Yes, I said, they're my landlords, they live downstairs. "I sold them that house," he said.

"Holy mackerel, you lived there too?"

"No, I bought it years ago when I thought I was going to marry someone. But we didn't get married and I decided to sell it, to the people you rent from. Is the big sweeping staircase still there?"

"I don't know. Not in my apartment."

It occurs to me there's a third part to the house saga I've forgotten to mention. I had seen the ad for this apartment in the *Times*, called the agent, she took me over, we rang the bell and who should live here but a reporter I'd known on *The Wall Street Journal*, who was now writing a book.

It is strange and delightful that so many writers have lived here. It makes me happy, as if this is a good place for a writer to be.

—

There is another circle in my life, and it involves motherhood, and the company of mothers.

Once, in Washington, about a month after the birth of my son, I walked into a backyard barbecue full of political people living the political life. It was the first time I'd gone to a party since the baby was born, and as I walked across the lawn toward people I'd worked with at the White House I saw, peripherally, a small group of women standing on the side, near the house. I didn't know any of them, and after sort of seeing them I walked on. But one of them waved in a way that said Come over, come this way. And I did.

They surrounded me and said hello, congratulations, you have a new baby. We moved into a family room in the basement and sat on couches, and we talked about things like whooping cough and DPT shots and the amazingly high fevers babies can get, 105 and 107, fevers that would kill an adult. I started to tell them things I was nervous about, things I hadn't told anyone, and they'd say, I worried about that too, here's what you do. They were generous and encouraging and I liked them, and what struck me was realizing: they've always been at the party. But I never really noticed them and they never really noticed me, and now they have because I am a mother. I have been let into the mother group.

It was like being accepted into a sorority I didn't know existed. And I liked the unspoken rule: Outside the boys talk about Gorbachev but here we talk about important things, like life. Outside we *all* talk about Gorbachev, and that is fine, as Gorbachev is part of life, but here we talk about life at its most compelling and essential. There was a merry superiority to it. Boys will be boys but this be serious.

What I think parents get from children is a very special thing: the experience of unambivalent love. Most of the loves we feel are shaded and complex; they have static. But the love you feel for a child is 50,000-watt, clear channel. And all times in their lives are good, but infancy is, I think, for a new mother, the best. Already I miss my son's lolling babyhood, when he was defenseless before my love and let me kiss and coo. I miss the soft boneless hugging, the rocking in the chair. As they grow older they wiggle away. When I pick up my son from school, when he first sees me, his eyes dance. And then he remembers: the guys. They'll see. He ambles toward me like a guy and says Hi in an offhand manner. I'd like to tell you I give him a wink and a secret tug, but I often go, Hello baby, and put my arms around him. Sometimes he gets embarrassed, sometimes happily so, sometimes comically. He rolls his eyes and makes the guys laugh.

—

When I moved back to New York in '89, knowing a lot of people but not a lot of new mothers, I scoped the neighborhood and figured: the park.

Which is where I met my first New York mother friends, including Benny's mother.

This is what it was like, when my son was a toddler, in the park on Sixty-eighth and First, as the children played. The sound around this moment was a city wind, a wind off the river that is broken by buildings and makes a soft whistle as it goes by your ears.

It is a soft sunny Saturday in spring. The mothers watch and stare in their mother attitudes—sitting on a bench with an arm flung over the back, slouching against the cement turtles. They stand and rock from side to side, unconsciously, as if they were still holding infants. Only mothers and tennis players make this movement.

Trees grow out of soft tar here. The children chase pigeons. The mothers murmur softly in the wind: Aaron's just over the chicken pox, he still has the marks but he's not infectious. Ben, we've discovered, can read. We were going down Park in a cab and he said, "That's the Pan Am building," and I said, "Yes, how do you know?" And he pointed and said, "The word on top, Pan Am."

The first years of motherhood confuse the brain by sending conflicting signals; it both encourages long thoughts and fractures concentration. A kind of impressionism takes hold. One sees small things. The pigeons, for instance. Everything in nature gets something, even the lowly pigeon has scarlet-colored feet. It picks by, and you follow its path with your eyes.

I bring along the *Post*. The mothers read the headlines over my shoulder. Mothers of little children develop a taste for tabloids, in part because the brisk, quick style is suited to the minding of toddlers. Quick bursts of information for those *(Elliot, I told you not on the bars, off!)* who have for years not known the luxury *(Mommy, I have to go pee)* of a consecutive thought. In time these mothers find themselves almost incapable of concentration because, like so many things, concentration is a habit *(What bit you there, was it a tick? Did you see it? Where?)* and by the time a child is two a mother has lost the habit. *(Robbie? Robbie!!!)* At gatherings on the weekend the dads hold forth, but even the mothers most attentive to outside reality rarely speak in paragraphs. (Perhaps part of the empty-nest syndrome is that a woman who hasn't had a consecutive thought in years now has time to have one. This is disconcerting. They walk in trench coats through the university and wonder: What do people think about?)

Of the tabloid headlines the ones that get our quickest attention deal with exotic or child-related crimes, and sex. These are popular because they are primal, have pictures (first-grade photo of pigtailed child who was raped and thrown from a roof; scandal blonde in bikini posing in Georgia State tourism ad) and because to greater and lesser degrees we have personal reference points. We read gossip columns and the people page, staring at pictures of people we do not know and are not, in fact, interested in. But we like the drama that can be discerned, decoded, through the items. For instance: It is interesting to see celebrities deal awkwardly or gracefully with early fame, and then grow incompetent and irrascible with it. We discuss how we would handle the paparazzi. We like the failures and triumphs, the drug use and career slumps, because they show us, no one's happy, or not for long, or not seamlessly. . . . This is quite a comfort to some of the mothers in the park. And I wonder sometimes if, years from now, they will remember this time when their children were young and they read the *Post* and enjoyed the company of women, and know these days were some of the best of their lives. . . .

—

After my first book came out I led something of a double life, as a mommy in the park and a knower of the people in the columns. Some of the other mothers treated me with a new respect, but also at a certain distance.

Once, at this time, I spoke at a fund-raiser at the preschool my son attended, warm and wonderful little St. Thomas More Playgroup. I talked about current politics and about how lucky you are if you get a chance to take part in history, and then, because the crowd was receptive and encouraging and also because I was starting to enjoy the sound of my voice, I gave a too-long answer to a question about what advice I would give to a daughter who thinks she wants to be a writer. Rather than say something short and helpful like "Some Shiite Muslims lock their daughters in cellars rather than let them act out unwholesome desires," I launched into a little disquisition on how if you're a writer you write, that's all, and it's a good life and a lucky thing to be. I talked about how exciting it is when you're writing to try to locate something that is true and real, and then, because I am a fool, I said that at the same time there is a paradox in the job: as you look for what is true you are not yourself being "true." Joan Didion said—correctly, I think—that writers are always betraying somebody: writers are always taking notes.

The evening ended. A few days later at a birthday party for four-year-old Ann, a beautiful girl with big brown eyes like a baby brown colt's, one of the mothers approached me. We were out on the patio of Ann's parents' apartment. I was happy she approached me because when we used to wait for the kids at the end of school she never said Hi. And I thought, Good, this will be the beginning of friendship. She said, "Gee, when you quoted that writer the other night I really understood. My husband always asks me what kind of person you are and I always say, 'I don't know, she's always friendly to me but I never talk to her'—because I don't want you to quote me! So let me just say, everything I say to you is off the record!"

She was perky, as idiots often are. I was taken aback, and sort of nodded and thought, Why do you think anyone would quote you? Did anyone ever tell you you're interesting? But I said nothing. My son might go to grade school with her son, and we'd be in each other's lives for years.

Saying nothing is part of a parent's job. Get along, go along, ease the way. In the private schools of New York this is not always easy. I met a woman recently who is a well-known fashion designer, and we got talking about kids, and schools, and it turned out her son went

to my son's school and she loved it, found it gentle and easygoing
and artistic. But her daughter went to another school, an East Side
girls' school, and she said, "I *hated* the *mahthers*. Dey all wore my
dresses but I *hated* them." I started to laugh. She shook her head.
"Snahhhbby silly," she said, "snahhhbbby silly."

Which some are. But what strikes me more often is how conscien-
tious they are, how involved in their children's lives, whether they
work outside the house or not. They're there dropping off the kids
in the morning, walking away in a camel's-hair coat and heels (account executive in an advertising firm) or leather jackets and Reeboks
(at home with infant). They know which day is gym and which is
music.

I'm more haphazard, like a fifties mother, and am always rushing
in the field-trip-permission slip at the last minute. I feel daunted by
the other mothers' competence.

But I think they're all daunted by each other's competence. I get
the impression everyone's trying to keep up with everyone else, not
in an I-have-a-BMW way but in an I'm-a-good-parent way. A mother
said to me recently, "I think I've noticed something." She is actually
a veteran mother; she has a teenager. She said, "We're all afraid of our
children. It's weird. It's like we all want our kids to approve of us and
like us." And, you know, there's some truth in that.

Maybe we're all insecure—we're raising our kids in a different
way, in the you-can-always-get-me-by-beeper way, and maybe it's
our doubts about it that make us anxious: *I'm doing okay and you're
okay, right? Please be okay! My job pays your tuition!* But maybe it's
boomer narcissism: *I'm pretty wonderful, the fine full flower of my
generation, and I do everything pretty much right and I'm doing this right
too, right? RIGHT?* Which is a bad game to play, as narcissistic parents
tend to produce narcissistic children.

I'll tell you another thing that makes our children a little scary to
us. We, their parents, are connected if only by memory to certain ties

that no longer quite pertain. I know I am Irish, for instance, but my son has no sense of Irishness, and finds my interest in such things exotic. His sense of ethnicity is different from mine: he is an American, pure and simple. I find this all surprising, when it shouldn't be, and disconcerting.

I want sometimes to say to him: You are blood of my blood, flesh of my flesh, and we are of the bogs, you know. But what does he know of the bogs, and what, for that matter, do I? But—I am afraid of losing them! If I were a Jew I'd be afraid of my children losing the shtetl, when I myself never lived there, but had grandparents who did.

You find your kids don't have the old ancestral bitternesses anymore, and you can't school them in that bitterness, as that's not really what we're here for, is it. But part of me wants to say: We don't like the English because in 1846 they took a blight and made it a famine and let the Irish die. And I want my son to get a tough little Jimmy Cagney face, and say, "Yeah, those Brits are dirty rats." But when would I say this, while reading *People* and enjoying a story about the royal family, or the *Journal* and admiring Thatcher's speech? I have thought of taking him to Ireland, but even Ireland seems less Irish than it was. The last time I was there it was Ireland of the microwaves, the Ireland of MTV and skinheads. I think maybe what my son would learn in Ireland now is how to say "fook," which, frankly, he can learn at home.

There is another thing that our children have, and that is, simply, a new mentality about the world. An example:

My son came home from school the other day and ran up the stairs with his backpack in his hand and announced with grave concern, like a perfect little Soviet child, that the air is so dirty now that it makes buildings fall down. It erodes them, he told me, and makes them crumble.

"Who told you this?" I asked, by which I meant who told you this today. Half the cartoons are crammed with environmental warnings, all the good guys have names like Captain Planet. When I was a child I was afraid of Dracula. My son is afraid of capitalist polluters who are making the air unsafe to breathe and making buildings fall down. He has told me, at night, that the sharks are dying in the ocean. He saw this in a book.

Anyway, who told you this, I asked. And he said, "We had a movie in science class, a Green movie."

I tell him, "Sit down."

We sit on the stairs to our apartment.

I tell him, "This is the way it is: the building we live in is a hundred years old, and it's still strong and it can take the air. It will probably be here in a hundred years. And there are always people who will be sloppy and thoughtless and burn things and make the air dirty or put their garbage in the wrong place like a river. But we are doing a pretty good job of controlling this and stopping it, and actually we have a pretty clean country and the air I think is cleaner than when I was a child, and we're not all going to die from pollution."

"We will if we don't stop it," he says somberly.

We forget, we adults, what we do to children's imaginations when we go through one of our national seizures on an issue. Ten years ago Hollywood fell in love with the environmental issue and put enviro messages in all their shows, the messages made their way into the funnies and the magazines, and parents, nice parents, went with concern to school officials and said, "We'd like our children to be better educated on environmental concerns," and the schools came through in their usual clunky way, which is to say with a vengeance, and now I have a little son who thinks he's going to die when our house falls down. It is the duck and cover of our children's lives.

When we go into one of these seizures of fashion we turn a good thing, protecting the environment, into a bad thing, environmental paranoia. We do not educate our children, we traumatize them. We are not giving them a vision of a better world, we are giving them nightmares. And, as they sit in science class watching a Green film, daymares.

Also—this is a rant—I have come to wonder about the worldview or life-view of those who so avidly promote the environmental movement. I get the impression nature is, consciously or unconsciously, their God. Their substitute God. And, like happy little moralists secure in the knowledge that theirs is the one true faith, they are not only instructing our children but manipulating them. Like the strictest old priests in the strictest old country in the strictest year of the nineteenth century, they're scaring them into submission. Obey or you'll burn in hell, whose fumes are not the sulfur of sin but the by-product of nuclear waste.

Also—short rant—when you think about what's being drilled into our children's imagination about the environment, and add it to what is being drummed into their imagination in sex education, you just get the impression that in the year 2010 they're all going to be running around like a bunch of nuts putting condoms on trees.

I'm done now.

Actually, one more thing, but it's not a rant. It's a scene from a great and not sufficiently lauded movie, *Dr. Zhivago*. With Robert Bolt's beautiful, elegant script.

Zhivago is at Lara's small apartment, and her daughter, age about ten, runs in from school and empties her bookbag.

Zhivago sees a picture she'd drawn of a comically evil-looking man with a pointy beard and a hat with a cross on top.

"Who is this?" he says.

"That's the czar. The czar is an enemy of the people."

Zhivago is taken aback. "Well, he didn't know he was an enemy of the people," he says.

"Well, he should know, shouldn't he."

"Well, yes, he should," he says, realizing he's hearing the authentic sound not only of the present, but of the future.

Children don't really believe their parents' explanation of context, their consoling words. They believe society's instruction. They see wisdom in their parents' words only after they've grown older, and been rattled. I feel we should remember this more sharply, and remember that with their nighttime fears we're making them pay a bill they didn't incur.

—

My friend Susan called the other night, and the subject was her daughters, who are beautiful, smart and good but who have just become teenagers and are experimenting with a drug called rebellion. Susan sighs. She can do nothing right, everything is an argument. I tell her of my continuing inadequacy as a mother to cheer her up.

We all worry so much. I remember the effortfulness of the middle-class mothers of Massapequa when I was a child, though I didn't see it at the time. They had so many kids, so many lunch boxes to pack, so many things to wash.

Susan once told me, "My mother's decorating motif was shirts on hangers. I'd come home from school and she'd be at the ironing board with her sprinkling can, slamming down the shirts, with a cigarette dangling from her mouth and her hair in pink rollers. And there'd be shirts hanging all over, on the doors, the bed, the shower rod."

In some ways they worked harder than we do. They did household tasks not only with no help but with no clothes dryer, no microwave. They were always walking around with gray wooden clothespins in their mouths, pushing back an unruly hank of hair, standing in the backyard on thick sturdy legs, like peasants in a Brueghel painting.

The dialogue:

"Okay. Okay now. Susan, it's getting late, your father will be home, you

set the table. No, it's your turn, Bobby was last night with the dishes. Oh.
Well, you set because he's late, he'll clear. Well he can clear before practice.
Because I said so, and you better hope I don't tell your father."

They worked so hard in the house. And I think their children
unconsciously absorbed some connection between Mother waxes the
table, her hand going back and forth back and forth along the brown
wood with the Lemon Pledge, and the old soft cloth that smelled like
chemicals. They connected it to: *My mother cares for the house, my
mother cleans and cares for the house, for the family, for me.* Kids like to
see their parents do house things, they like to see Dad come around
with his toolbox and fix the cabinet when it won't close. They think:
Someone is caring for this house, this family, me. We are a whole and
functioning unit.

Lately I have taken to polishing the furniture when my son is
around. Sometimes I say, "I'm gonna polish this table with furniture
polish, buff it up." He looks at me and wonders why this is interesting
enough to say. "I like this smell," I add.

"Me too," he says. "Mommy, I have something to tell you. Um.
Mommy, on Ace McCloud last night the Cyborgs were all lined up
in front of him. They're just in the Cyborgs, but they turned up on
The Centurions! I was so surprised. And Ace McCloud said, 'There's
a whole lot of troublesome toys here!' Isn't that funny?"

"Yes, that is funny." Pat pat goes the cloth.

Once when he was an infant, when he was about six months old,
there was a nature film on PBS. It was about gorillas and orangutans,
and it showed a mother orangutan cradling her baby and making soft
sounds as she picked leaves off him. My son focused on it, and so did
I. If he had been able to speak and understand, I would have said,
"Isn't that nice?" But he couldn't, so I picked him up and made, softly,
the monkey sound. And he cooed. And it became a habit that when
we hugged I made the monkey sound, and he started making it back,
and in time we gave it inflections. One was sweet, one comic. By the

time he was two and speaking we still used the sounds, and we still do, and I am so much in the habit that when I hug my friends I make the sound and now and then they look at me—"That's interesting, no one's ever made that sound while hugging me before."

It's easier to clearly show love to the preverbal. Words, oddly enough, can get in the way. My friends and I discuss this kind of thing. Our parents didn't, often couldn't, have these discussions. But I think there was something in those first-generation American women, the women of my parents' generation, that equated flamboyant affection with words like "actress" and "sissy."

They didn't get it from their parents. But we luxuriate in giving it, at least when the children are young. Rosemary, the woman who lived in the house in back when I was a little girl, recently said of her daughter, my contemporary: "She's such a good mother. She plays with him all day and hugs him and bites his belly! She's so in love, and patient." Rosemary was astonished. She was never that way. But then she had five of them, and clothespins in her mouth.

—

A talk with Carey, mother of Will's friend Jack and wife of Dan, a wealthy Democrat and party contributor who has just been given a job in the Clinton administration.

She is a woman whose life is changing. She has been at home for six years with two children, which has been no burden, she's been having fun, and her rolling apartment—one room rolls into another, which rolls into another—has just been sold to a show-business couple. She is smart and thoughtful and the only regular problem in her life, she has told me, is Embarrassment At The Dinner Party when somebody says, "What do you do?" and she says, "I'm being a mother."

Not that they don't make nice clucking noises, they do, but—other women at the party are bankers and college presidents, and the men own agencies and are full partners. In the new America she is subtly made to feel she's not contributing. It is one of the strangest things about modern life that women feel defensive about doing something that was, until roughly a quarter century ago, in the whole course of human history, natural.

My sister Kathy deals with the dinner party this way: She says, when asked, in a serious tone, "I'm in human development." She tells me that she's noticing a new tension among her friends. The ones who work, who sell real estate or do some kind of office work, are jealous of the ones who stay home. There's a certain amount of sniping. "Well, yeah, I could do that too if I didn't have a job."

That is the reverse of New York, I tell Kathy.

"Well, in Jersey," she says, "a lot of the women just don't want to go out and work. Their husbands do. They do the kids, the house, they do PTO, they're happy. The ones who work outside need the money, and they resent us guys as lazy and do-nothings."

You mean out there the dream life is . . . like on Long Island when we were kids? Mom at home and dad comes home from work?

"Yeah. Only nobody drinks."

I talked to Carey in a neighborhood lunch place. She was twenty minutes late, and she had that frazzled look of someone thinking, What will I still have time to do after I get this lunch over?

She tells me she's been offered a White House job. She says, "The kids and I will stay in the Hamptons this summer and then we'll join Dan in Washington just before Labor Day and get the kids settled and then they'll start school. And then I think I'll start out working maybe three days a week at the White House."

"White House jobs so absorb you," I say, "you'll be lucky to keep it at three days, it'll expand. When will you get the house all settled in after the move?"

"I don't know, really. I think along the way."

She tells me she is actually a little . . . ambivalent about the White House job, and asks what I think.

I say, "On the one hand it's nice not to have to get up at 5:30 A.M. to do yourself before you do the kids, and it's nice not to go to an office. People who work in offices have a heightened affect, they move their faces all day to register reactions and responses. Smiles, frowns, laughter, the furrowed brow. Your face gets tired and you age quicker.

"On the other hand, it's something, really something, to be immersed in history and part of something like a new administration. It heightens life, and for most people it only happens once, and you'll get to look back and tell your grandchildren about the time you worked for a president and helped him do his job."

She nods, and fusses with the menu.

"You're tired of 'on the one hand, on the other,' aren't you?"

"I really am."

"You want to know what I really think?"

Our faces are warm, our conversation careful, but building within me is that strainer of friendships, that impresser of dunderheads, the didactic impulse. What the heck. Let fly.

"I think," I said, "that of all the ways you can spend your time between now and death, work is just . . . overrated. There are only two reasons to work. One is to support yourself or your family, which is the reason most people work and not to be argued with. The other is if you have a need to share something with other people who are alive. Artists and painters and great thinkers and makers of beautiful cabinets, people who make the best shoes ever, people who have a divine compulsion—they have to work. If Mother Teresa were married to a rich man, she'd still work, because she has to make the world better. Doctors, teachers, lawyers—some of them must work. People who have a compulsion to give. Priests, rabbis, people who just have to play the piano.

"These to me are the only two reasons that make sense. To work just for status is stupid. Who are you impressing? People so dumb they're impressed by a high-sounding job. To work for money when you don't need it is boring, and speaks of a lack of imagination.

"But if you don't need money and you don't have a compulsion you are lucky. You can stay home and be a good mother who is actually there, you can have time for Dan when he comes home with terrible problems, and he will because Washington is full of terrible problems. You can be part of the kids' schools, and you can give the best, most fun, most relaxing dinner parties in town. You can take a book out back into the garden and read it and listen to the birds. You can think about God. You can develop your soul. You can have time for your friends when they call and need you because one's waiting for the biopsy and the other just had this terrible affair. This to me is a very nice life. You'll be the only calm woman in Washington."

We were both startled, and laughed.

She asked why I work. I told her, to support myself and my son and because of compulsion: I want to be immersed in life and name what I see.

A week later she sent me a note. She's thinking she'll put off working for a while, see how it goes. The next time I saw her I told her I'd been embarrassed, later, by my giving in to dat ol' didactic impulse. She laughed and said Never you mind.

A lot of my friends are less lucky than Carey. They have responsible high-level jobs in the professions, families, a husband and children, a mortgage, a life. And they're trying to do everything well and they can't. I think of Donna. She and I started out together at CBS when we were in our late twenties. She worked so hard and was so focused, so versed in the rules of her trade. She wanted to be one of the great correspondents, one of the great broadcast reporters. She got a good measure of what she wanted, and because she was decent and smart few people resented her rise. Now, a dozen years after we met, she is a network correspondent with a husband and three sons. And she hates to leave her children in the morning, hates it when they twine themselves around her legs and say "Don't leave," hates it when she gets home late or travels.

She doesn't hate it because they make her feel guilty, she hates it because she wants to be with them. She wants to be there, kissing their boo-boos.

Kids don't really need you for advice and counsel, though that's nice. They just want you there in the daily boringness, in the living room or kitchen or bedroom. They want you there while they watch TV. There's no such thing as quality time, there's only time.

Donna can't be there as much as she wants. Not because of her ambition—her ambition has changed, what's important has changed, or been modified by daily experience, by personal growth, by the changed realities of network news, by her own changed metabolism—but because she and Hugh in the early years bought a nice three-bedroom house in the Washington suburbs, and they've got to pay the mortgage. And preschool. And the clothes and the dentist and the birthday gifts and Bible school and Disneyland and cable. And she has to get her hair done, and colored, and Hugh could use a new suit and needs a laptop. (Hugh is in broadcasting too, and wants to be home more too.) It's all so expensive! They work and work and long.

Lately I keep thinking about what we have, what we pay for and give our money to. We pay for private schools because the public schools have failed, and they have failed for at least three reasons. First, they seem to exist not so much to educate children as to employ people; second, there is crime and disorder, which has been prompted in part by not giving educators autonomy in disciplining unruly

children, and in part by our strained society; and third, who teaches
has changed.

Teaching was once a revered profession dominated by women
who were held high, locally, as figures of respect and appreciation.
I was talking with a friend of mine who is a teacher on Long Island
about the uninspired teachers who'd taught the baby boomers, and
she told me some of the history of her profession: After the Korean
War the baby boom flooded the schools, and new teachers were
needed. Veterans were flooding out of the service; supply met demand. Men started becoming teachers in a big way in the public
schools—they became science and Phys Ed and English teachers. It
is nice that a stereotype was broken, that men could teach children,
but it was not nice that for many of these men teaching was not a
calling or a vocation but just a job. Their vocation became unionizing;
they succeeded, and made the teachers' union a powerful force. But
they also made teaching look like just another union job. They
increased the pay scale and decreased the respect in which the profession was held. In time, teachers came to seem like any other interest
group. The kids got lost in the shuffle. One of the most under-
reported stories around these days is the number of suburban communities that keep voting down school-board budgets. And they do
it in part because they've lost respect for educators. They don't trust
them as much anymore. They're just another union.

What else do we spend our money on? The house. And one thing
that is confusing here is the modern assumption that we should all
own a home. We all act as if this is a basic human right, but actually
it is something new in human history. I come from a long line of
renters; I grew up with renters; I am a renter. (I am admittedly
somewhat radical on this issue. I happen to think all ownership is an
illusion anyway: you're going to lose it when you die, so why make
a mania of owning a house or a car or a boat?)

I used to wonder why everyone thinks he or she has to own a

home, and it was the 1980s before I realized the obvious reason: for the tax protection to be had from writing off the interest on the mortgage. But this only points to the fact that the tax burden most of us face is too great, and has been too great for many years—certainly since we were children.

People talk about the eighties as a decade of greed, but I believe it is the failures of our governments that have forced people to become more "greedy"—more anxious to go the private-school route and the homeowner route. They're spending their money in part to protect themselves from government-run schools that don't work, and taxation that is too high.

I don't think we're greedier anyway, I think as a country we've grown more materialistic, which is not quite the same thing. Sometimes at night when I'm surfing I'll stop by *The Honeymooners*, *The Donna Reed Show*, *Make Room for Daddy*, *Father Knows Best*. What interests me is the sets. *The Honeymooners* was about a working-class couple, so the set was gray and bare. A table, a bureau, four chairs, a picture on the wall. Donna Reed was upper-middle-class—she was married to a doctor—but the set is still modest. A couch, a chair, a coffee table, two lampstands and two lamps, a desk, wall-to-wall carpeting, some pictures on the wall. On *Father Knows Best*, the same, with a big easy chair. When Robert Young takes off his jacket he puts on an old sweater with iron-on elbow patches. Beaver Cleaver's room is a modest wooden bed, a bureau, a mirror, pennants on the wall. No telephone, no CD, no television or computer, no Super Mario Brothers spilling out of a cabinet. Alice Kramden and Donna Reed wore cotton shirtdresses, though Donna's was nicer—Fashion by Ohrbach's, it says in the credits—and she wore earrings. Ralph Kramden wore his bus driver's uniform. Donna's husband sometimes shows up in a big white bib, as if he just operated on somebody over the garage.

When I grew up watching these shows, people had pretty much

what the people in the shows had. They got one or two weeks off a year, and they stayed home. They didn't go to Disneyland or the Bahamas, they went on day trips. They took the car to a beach and spread out a blanket from one of the kids' beds and they took the clothes off the kids and the kids ran to the water. Mom and dad sat with their arms around their knees, and watched the ocean.

We, their children, all want so much, have so much—so many food choppers, music-makers, golden things. We are materialists, and we try to cover our discomfort about this by putting forward political rationales:

I have to work to pay the mortgage after what Reagan did to the economy.

Excuse me but I'm working for something like security while Clinton tries to nationalize 14 percent of the GNP.

But we could all have smaller houses and fewer things. And our kids are wiser than we are—at least when they're young, before the culture gets them.

For women, though, I have this creepy feeling: it's feminism that put a lot of us in the office, but materialism that keeps a lot of us there. And that's not quite the movement we joined, not a movement we can be proud to be part of. We say it's deteriorating living standards that force us to live the way we live, but I think it's our wealth that's in our way.

—

And our culture. If you were in New York in 1993 you might have noticed the bus ads for VH1, the boomer rock channel on cable. VH1 wanted to communicate explicitly what differentiates their programming from that of other cable channels, and they came up with a print ad that was striking in its simplicity and clarity. On one panel there was a Renaissance painting of The Madonna. Underneath it said "Your Parents." In the panel next to it was a picture of Madonna in full concert-writhing mode. Underneath it said "You." You, it implied, are hip enough to worship the latter and not the former. Some Christian groups protested and the ads were eventually removed from the sides of New York's buses, which I thought was too bad because those ads were great: they said it all.

We are the inheritors of a coarsened country. My generation cooperated happily in the coarsening, of course, in the sixties and seventies, and contributed to it to the best of our ability. But at least we were young—children even, some of us—so it wasn't all our doing. Still, we went with it, and now we're stuck with it. The coarsened nation is what we're left to bring up our children in.

A coarse place is by definition anti-child because it is anti-innocence. Good parents these days go to great lengths to protect their children from the environment—i.e., the culture—spending their discretionary income on schools, scheduling them after school for Cub Scouts and music lessons and art lessons, anything to keep them from watching TV or hanging out with kids whose parents are not similarly keeping them from the culture. This last is inherently anti-egalitarian, because the children unprotected by parents are by and large not only less well loved but less well off.

There aren't enough good parents to go around. This would not carry such heavy implications if there were a healthy culture to pick up some of the slack, but there isn't. There is only the coarse culture, to make things worse.

A few years ago we were all talking about latchkey children, but the idea of kids being home by themselves after school isn't exactly new in human history. When I was a kid there were kids who went home to empty houses, and they did what kids do, put on the TV. There were game shows, cartoons, some boring nature show, an old movie, *The Ann Sothern Show*, Spanish lessons on educational TV, a soap opera.

Thin fare, boring stuff; kids daydreamed to it. But it was better to have this being pumped into everyone's living room than, say, the Geto Boys on channel 25, rapping about killing women, having sex with their dead bodies and cutting off their breasts. Really, you have to be a moral retard not to know that this is harmful, that it damages the young, the unsteady, the unfinished. You have to not care about anyone to sing these words and to put this song on TV for money. You have to be a pig. My friends complain about the decade of greed, and mean Michael Milken. I complain about it too, but I mean Def American Records, Time Warner, Death Row/Interscope—the entertainment executives, the record producers, the real den of thieves.

At night, in the old America, we had the famous family sitcoms on, all of them pretty much harmless, all of them portraying the same moral lessons:

It just doesn't pay to lie, Beav.

David, when you make a commitment you have to stick with it.

Donna, it's not nice to have homosexual affairs with the neighbors. I made that one up.

Anyway, these shows didn't exactly excite the baser instincts. They didn't sanction or encourage acting out. They didn't encourage violence, for violence, on these shows, didn't exist. And the fact that it didn't said to the kids who watched: Violent behavior is, simply, beyond the pale. This is not the worst message to give to children.

Rebel Without a Cause was on the other night. I hadn't seen it in years. The most touching thing about it is that the really wild bad kids had—drag races. They'd pick up a knife and say, "I'm gonna cut you," and they meant it—they'd cut your arm and run away. At the rumble Sal Mineo wore a suit. Natalie Wood wore earrings and pumps. Decorous delinquency. This probably says more about the director, Nicholas Ray, than it does about the fifties, but Ray had to operate within a framework of something approximating reality. He couldn't put the stars in tuxes because that would have been unrealistic; he couldn't have them armed with guns for the same reason.

(I said the Ozzie and Harriet shows were harmless, but I think they actually did some mild harm. Because children think what they see on TV is "true," a lot of kids who grew up watching them thought that down the street, next door and around the block there were all these normal families with well-adjusted parents who spoke softly and had steady jobs and wisdom. Few of us had exactly that, and we carried within us some shame for being different, when we weren't different, we were average. Some people didn't figure this out until they were adults and well into therapy. They howled with rage and resentment at having borne a shame that shouldn't have been theirs.)

One of the frustrating things about our culture is that it is impossible to talk about its decline without dealing heavily in clichés. Naturally, you talk about Hollywood. I just watched the dream ballet from *Oklahoma!* in which the Shirley Jones character dreams of Curly and the temptations of the world. It was on TNT this July Fourth weekend, part of TNT's salute to the American family. I looked up from the *New York Post* and there it was on, on channel 21. Elegant, sexy choreography by Agnes de Mille. Lush sets and costumes. A dream sequence of subtlety and intelligence based on the poignant assumption that the audience was bright enough to understand the symbolism.

Oklahoma! produced in 1955, was a big hit at the box office. But it wasn't considered in its time revolutionary or unusual. It was just an average very good movie. Now it would be an art-house movie if it were made at all, which it wouldn't be.

Hollywood had something like respect for the audience. It assumed it was playing to intelligent people with standards, or neighborhood hypocrites who wanted to act like intelligent people with standards. Also, the old Hollywood hands must have considered themselves artists, for there was such art in their output.

Now, as we all well know, an average Hollywood hit is an Oh shit! movie. The car comes careening over the top of the building toward the Mel Gibson character and he says "Oh shit!" to Danny Glover before, together, they jump out of its path.

They are coarse, these movies. Five years ago Hollywood producers, reacting to the charge of coarseness, defended themselves this way: "We just reflect reality—that's the way the country is now, violent and profane. At least we make it entertaining."

But they don't say that so often anymore. Hollywood seems lately, ironically enough, to be stuck in the same defensive crouch as the churches of America. Producers have stopped claiming they only reflect reality because it's been pointed out to them that they in effect admitted a few years ago that they know they helped shape reality when they started putting obvious political messages into the programs they create. The Bloodworth-Thomasons, producers, as we all know, of *Designing Women* and *Evening Shade,* have made a great point of having their characters give speeches that support the good (gun control, environmentalism) and oppose the bad (sexism, racism, ageism). One of the best anti–Clarence Thomas arguments I ever heard came from one of the characters in *Designing Women.* And there isn't much danger in any of this. It's just a show. It's not as if people don't know Hollywood is of the left and their shows reflect this bias.

Hollywood knows it encourages and discourages points of view, habits and social tendencies. And deep in their guilty little hearts filmmakers know they encourage violence in boys and men, and sexual acting out in everyone else. It's what they do for a living. They know it.

But in a way, the Hollywood defense of five years ago is right: their work really *does* reflect our culture.

Thirty years ago the people of America made the Hollywood people's jobs easier by telling them what we would and would not accept, would and would not pay for. We could tell them because we knew.

An example: To remember a Catholic childhood in the fifties is to remember the Legion of Decency. There was a Catholic Church and it was confident and big, and within this Church were tens of millions of regular moviegoers. The Church actually used to condemn movies whose content it deemed offensive. Once a year, as I recall, everybody would stand up at some point in a Mass and we would vow not to see any movie that was included in the Church's index of condemned movies. The index was, I think, printed weekly in the local Catholic newspaper. I think ours was called *The Tablet*, though I'm not sure because we didn't get it.

I only remember taking the pledge once. I was about ten. I remember standing there with everyone else and raising my hand. It probably made me feel good, as if I were a member of something. I wouldn't at that age have had thoughts about censorship, wouldn't have seen us as sheep. If I'd thought about it at all I think I would have thought: We're not censoring, we're just promising to boycott bad stuff. They can make it but we won't go. (It wasn't only Catholics. The South, still called in those days the Bible Belt, was full of people refusing to go to the same movies.)

By the time I was sixteen I would have refused to stand and make the pledge, or made a merry private vow to see every movie on that list, for by that time I was swimming away from the big ship.

But ironically, the condemned list was helpful to those in Hollywood, in a number of ways. I can't tell you what cachet a movie gained when it was condemned. It made it seem as if that movie must be powerful and fascinating and full of secrets. And, as it gained repute, some people would go see it for just those reasons. But, interestingly enough, when a movie was condemned, a lot of Catholics actually *didn't* go see it. And it suffered at the box office. And old Sam Goldwyn and old Jack Warner and even old Dore Schary would look at the week's receipts and think: It just doesn't pay.

The fact that a major portion of the American movie audience wouldn't go see a dirty movie gave the studio heads, and the writers and producers they employed, a kind of out. They didn't have to push the envelope, or rather they *couldn't* push the envelope, for if they did it would mean the studio would lose money. They were, in a way, artistically protected by what was impossible. And so, forced by commercial realities not to break new ground in such interesting areas as sex and violence, they made breakthroughs in the area of art. And Curly strutted in the dream ballet, and the Shirley Jones character high-stepped in full Freudian splendor.

Part of what I am talking about is the importance, for the artist, of having a vivid and genuine and self-confident society against which to react. A society of by and large good values, of general good health, that believed in the wholesome and believed *it* was wholesome. In such circumstances the artist has something—a real and authentic society with certain specific beliefs and habits—to look at, dissect, portray, react against. The artist can, in this atmosphere, locate and expose society's dishonesties, remind it of its unfinished business, spoof its ill-thought-out traditions and ways.

That old friction—the one between the genuine society and the genuine artist—made for great art. There was no *Ulysses* without an angry Irish populace to inspire and ban it. *Lady Chatterley's Lover* had power because everybody ran from the printing press screaming, "A dirty book, a dirty book!" To read it now is quite touching, because the dirty parts seem so quaint. Because people stopped running away from it, and stopped, and read it. And writers had to do more to make them scream.

In a way, in the past thirty years we, as a society, stopped being hypocritical; we stopped pretending we had no interest in the pornographic; we even stopped ordering in brown paper wrappers. In some respects this was good—honesty is better than dishonesty—but in many ways it was unfortunate. When a society elevates honesty as the highest virtue, over, say, kindness and decency, it can create quite a chilly place, and quite a chilling effect.

Hypocrisy is one traditional value our society might reconsider reembracing. Old America was full of grown-ups who were wonderful old hypocrites. They'd warn kids about the dangers of drink and then go out and quietly tie one on with the boys, they'd go to church or synagogue and not listen and forget to incorporate into their lives what they'd heard, they'd formally and even ostentatiously obey all the social rules and then discreetly act out their own sexual irregularities and dramas.

They were lying, but they were also, through their public actions and words, making proper bows to an agreed-upon ideal. They maintained a front, a façade. It was, I think, the price they all paid, perhaps without even thinking about it, to keep society going. Their phoniness caused some of them pain. But I wonder if more people are not in pain now, with the old façades gone, the structure of society weakened, and the neighborhood so much colder and forbidding.

I often think of wonderful old banned-in-Boston Oscar Wilde's famous observation, "Hypocrisy is the tribute vice pays to virtue." It was. And it wasn't all bad.

Anyway, I wonder if Hollywood doesn't see the idea of "society" as almost antique. I wonder if it doesn't see us as a loose collection of unaffiliated souls who are not so much immersed in life as saturated with movie and television imagery, people who have lost some degree of personal authenticity, as if we were sleepwalking through our days and waiting for the next Oh shit moment in the next Oh fuck movie.

Hollywood is left in the not entirely pleasant position of having to come up with even more outrageous violence and sex to get some attention, to grab and get an audience.

Imagine what that does to the soul. Imagine what it's like for a writer to look up from a PC and think, This is what I read Dryden for? This is the end product of all those years reading William Inge and Arthur Miller and Tennessee Williams and dreaming of opening night and the rave reviews and, like my beloved wicked Lilly, making a drunken phone call to Dash to ask which girl he's with? For this?

INTERIOR. PRECINCT BATHROOM. MEL STANDS AT URINAL, SHAKES HIMSELF, ZIPS HIS FLY, AND LISTENS. A TICKING SOUND. HE TURNS, FOLLOWS THE SOUND TO A STALL, OPENS IT, LOOKS IN.

INT. BATHROOM STALL. WE SEE SMALL BUNDLE OF PLASTIQUE AFFIXED TO SIDE OF TOILET. DIGITAL TIMER IS TICKING: 4 SECONDS TO GO.

CLOSE UP: MEL'S FACE

MEL

Oh shiiiiiiiiiiiittttttttt.

EXPLOSION RIPS ROOM.

This is how you earn your living? You wanted to contribute to the world, you wanted to make it better through your presence, you wanted to lift us a little further out of the muck. You poor man. You poor woman. And no amount of jogging, personal training, golf, no amount of rolfing, psychotherapy or ashram visiting is going to make you feel better or change this fact: you, with your Dartmouth honors and your good-natured, affluent, agnostic parents back East, you are a writer of Oh shit moments in Oh fuck movies.

What a thing to be.

—

But Hollywood isn't the only maker of the current culture. A much bigger day-to-day problem for most parents is the news, the local news on channels 2 and 4 and 7, which has long featured stories that include such phrases as "raped and sodomized" and "condom controversery." And, of course, Court TV, where the Menendez brothers have just finished graphically recounting allegations of their father's sexual abuse, and CNN, where penises are currently flying out of the windows of cars. It is strange to be a parent who grew up in a home where the news was always on, where Uncle Walter visited us each evening to tell us the latest happenings, and not be able to continue that benign tradition. It is strange to find myself saying, "No, not the news!" to a six-year-old, and insisting that if we watch TV this evening it will be cartoons or *Nick at Nite*.

The current culture is bad enough for children, robbing them of the uninformed innocence that is their due, but I also wonder, these days, if all the chatter that fills this sex-saturated society, all the trailer-park confessionals on Oprah and Phil and Sally Jesse, all the images and attitudes with which we are bombarded, hasn't taken the heat right out of things. I wonder if the cultural revolution that has swept America the past quarter century hasn't made this sexiest of countries a drier, colder place. You don't enhance a thing's power when you remove its sense of the forbidden, its sense of darkness. When you talk about it endlessly, chattering away about birth-control devices and performance enhancers, you render it, simply, banal.

—

I was at a dinner, and I was seated next to a fellow in his fifties, a charming and funny man, very alive to the world. And the talk—this is New York, in the nineties, and nothing is low enough for us—the talk was of "persistent rumors" that the president is having an affair with a certain movie star. This was before the Arkansas state troopers and the reports about womanizing.

Anyway, I was uninterested in the table talk for a number of reasons. One is, and I know this is unusual in an American, I don't care what the president does with his penis. I am much more interested in the adventures of that other arguably more antic organ, his brain. Also, these rumors are "persistent" only because people who couldn't possibly know if they are true persist in talking about them. They are doing this the way, when I was twelve, we read marriage manuals. We said, "It's good to know," but we meant, This is dirty, I really like it. Of course when you're twelve you have an excuse, at our age it's embarrassing.

And this smart bright man next to me just looked at me as the talk went on and everyone gave his or her nice, reasoned, groundless opinion, and he said softly, "Don't you miss the days when we were ashamed to talk like this?"

And I said, "Oh yes. The days when you had disgusting thoughts you kept them to yourself because society was better than that."

He said, "I miss repression and shame."

"Yeah. They were so sexy."

We laughed like children.

———

For me, 1993 ended with a pinched nerve in the neck that produced tight muscles in the shoulder which produced an arm that numbed and tingled. I went to the doctor, who said, "That sounds like a pinched nerve in the neck."

He gave me tests. We found I couldn't stand on my right foot with my eyes closed and maintain balance.

"Mmmmm," he said.

More tests, a few responses that seemed slightly off.

"I want you to have an MRI. Do you know what that is?"

"Magnetic Resonance Imaging. Boy, everybody's getting them."

"Not really. But I want to make sure it's what we think it is. It's not pleasant, but it's quick."

A doctor's office on the East Side, and a jolly technician.

"Are you claustrophobic?"

"No."

"You go in elevators okay?"

"Uh, yes. I take them and I don't have the classic claustrophobic illusion that the walls are coming in on me. But if it's a crowded elevator I get nervous, but I'm not afraid of the elevator, I'm afraid of the people."

He looks at me.

"Let me take you in and show you," says the woman who's standing with him.

A big room with a big beige plastic machine covering a wall. With a dark tunnel in the middle just big enough to hide a body.

"You lie on this little stretcher part and you put your head in this sort of basket part. Then we roll you in."

"For how long?"

"Two minutes, two minutes, and seven minutes. Then we take you out and inject you, then seven minutes. It's easy. There's a little mirror inside right above you, and you can see us with it. It makes people feel better to be able to see. But most of them shut their eyes."

"Okay."

"If it gets terrible you can crawl out."

"You can?"

"Yeah. Just kinda worm your body out the bottom of the tube, it's not closed off."

"Oh. Well, that's nice. Anyone ever crawl out?"

"No. We've had a few people who screamed and we had to take them out."

I lie down. She rolls me in. There is an intercom, with a little intercom buzz.

"You okay?"

"Fine."

"Not uncomfortable?"

"I wouldn't go that far."

"Okay, here we go."

They tell you about the claustrophobia but they don't tell you about the noise. It starts with a hollow knocking sound. *Bop. Bop bop. Ba ba boop bop.* You think of African natives beating out signals on a log. *Scared lady in the big tube taking pictures of her brain.* Then the *bop* turns into a drilling sound and it gets so loud it feels as if a guy with a jackhammer is right above you drilling down. *Hang on, lady, we're coming, hold on.* Whatever happened to that woman whose legs were crushed in the collapsed scaffolding in midtown? So brave, she kept bucking everybody up. And the teacher in the Trade Center elevator with the kids. CBS Radio, after the first blackout when radios were all people had to know what was going on, took a full-page ad a few days later in the *Times*—a lit candle in front of a little black portable, and underneath it said, "The light that never failed."

If you're free-associating your brain is unclenched, and if your brain is unclenched you're probably okay. The noise stops. They roll me out for the injection.

"Is it all right?" says a nurse with a soothing voice.

"Yeah, except for the trapped-in-a-noisy-coffin part."

"It will be over soon. Are you afraid of shots? Good, some people are. You'll feel a little prick, there we go, almost over, there we are. Bend it, please. Perfect."

Back in, I start to nod off.

As I say good-bye I see a picture of a brain on a screen. Is that me? Yes. Do I look okay? They look.

"We can't tell, but your doctor will see these soon."

The nice nurse says, "Are you afraid of what they'll find?"

"Well, you're always afraid they'll find a tumor. Or an empty spot."

She looks at the screen.

"I hope this helps your doctor help you."

Eeeeeeeee.

When I get home the phone is ringing. It's my friend Nicole. I tell her what the nurse said and she laughs.

"Did I ever tell you how my friend Ed found out he had cancer? I'll never forget him telling me as we strolled along a Washington street on a beautiful summer day. He told me he'd gone for X rays, and when they were done he got up and walked into a room where there were two technicians who sat facing away from him. And they were looking at his pictures and one said, "Oooh, look at this! You ever see one that big? And look at that one, wow!"

We laugh.

"Poor Ed. But he was so brave, and he beat it right up to the end."

The next day my doctor calls from his car. "How are you," he says.

"Fine, how's my brain?"

"Good."

"Oh, good-good-good."

"I found something that may account for the balance. A very small growth, we'll watch it, not to worry. If it turns into anything it will stay benign."

"Oh." *(Eeeeeeeeee.)* "Well, good, thank you."

"I was afraid, actually, that it might be multiple sclerosis."

"You're kidding." Boy, am I glad I didn't know that.

Modern life is funny. I am now celebrating that I don't have what four days ago it never occurred to me I might have. On the other hand, I now know what most people on this street don't know: I don't have an aneurysm or a dread disease in my head. At least right now this week.

I walk down the block to the gourmet place to get doughnuts to celebrate. It is dismissal time and the schoolgirls of Nightingale, the big grade school nearby, are laughing and elbowing each other at the counter. The sight of them actually brings tears to my eyes. So much ahead—life, love, time. MRIs. Thinking bulimia is a country.

But my brush with sickness got me thinking about certain kinds of death, both real and metaphorical, that I had seen the previous year, in 1992.

—

This mild brush with sickness became associated in my mind with a brush with a kind of political and professional pain I had experienced the previous year, in 1992. That is when I witnessed, with everyone else in the country, a death that was not real but metaphoric. It caused some mourning and reflection, some summing up. But it also, to my surprise and that of others, allowed a kind of liberation.

PART II

Liberty

*T*he great soup of New York is where I simmer. But two years ago, as the 1992 presidential campaign began to heat up, I almost left and rejoined old friends, old history, in Washington. I felt the tug, came close to the line, and ultimately resisted crossing it due to a combination of luck, instinct and unease.

One early autumn evening in 1991 I was at home, reading a news magazine, and my eye fell on a campaign-trail picture of Senator Bob Kerrey reaching up to shake a trucker's hand in some future primary state. There was nothing unusual about the picture—Kerrey was about to announce his candidacy for president, the photo illustrated a story on his plans, his prospects—but as I gazed at it, suddenly, for no reason, a thought that had been lurking in the back of my brain pushed itself forward: *Bush is going to lose.*

I was startled. Bush is going to lose, and they don't know it.

I thought about it for a few weeks, and then I wrote down my thoughts in a memo to the president's pollster, Bob Teeter. It was at the time—September '91—a particularly candid memo. But I had a hunch a certain toughness might be needed to pierce the haze of optimism that, I knew, had long enveloped this White House.

I include the memo here because it is about a time, and captures an urgency:

Bob, I'll begin with an image:

At the moment I see the electorate like a big old setter coiled in a corner, eyes half closed, watching the people come and go. And everyone thinks it's asleep but it's not; only it knows it's awake, and even it doesn't know it's about to take a big nip out of somebody's ankle.

Here's the analogy that haunts me:

It is 1945, and a triumphant Britain is done with war. The man who brought them through, Winston Churchill, is a national hero, part Wellington and part Disraeli. Just before victory in Europe was declared jubilant crowds took to roaming the streets; one massed in front of Whitehall. There Churchill came to the balcony bathed in the first early lights since the blackout, and the crowd roared. "This is your victory," he said to them, and almost as one they cried back, "No, it is yours!" in a wonderful moment of human gratitude.

The Last Lion was a politician, and he'd just looked at one happy focus group. Soon he called an election. He campaigned hard, followed by children waving the Union Jack and calling out his name. And when election day came he confidently cast his ballot, and by 6 pm that night the conservatives had been voted out and he had been defeated.

He reeled; the people of Britain reeled. People still debate how and why it happened. British troops were returning home in droves and opting not to return to the '30's, people were protesting austerity and years of want. And history itself loves to surprise, to take its zigs and zags; history loves to humble men.

But there was more.

Surely the British, having been through more than a decade of arduous and triumphant conservative rule (first Chamberlain, then

Baldwin, then Winnie) voted for change because a change of leaders would mean the war was really over—it would mean new headlines, new faces, new challenges. A vote against Churchill seemed a hopeful act.

But Churchill was really undone by his triumphs. He'd spent his entire mature political life warning of a foreign threat, fighting that threat, and finally defeating it. The removal of Nazism as an issue deprived Churchill of his political reason for being. His moment was over.

Britain in '45–'46 was on the precipice, about to lose its standing as an imperial power, unsure what it was about as a society, as a culture. It wasn't number one anymore. The playwright John Osborne soon captured some of this feeling in "Look Back In Anger" when he had Jimmy say, "How sad to be anything else in this American age." Churchill, I think, was partly a victim of his countrymen's intuitive sense that even though they'd just won a great war, the Empire was fading, the sun setting.

Labour promised change, offered visions of a better life, acknowledged Churchill's wisdom and said: But that was then.

You don't need a magnifying glass to find the parallels. Twelve years of conservative rule, a dispirited populace hungry for new headlines, and, most important, this: The Republicans, long seen as The Party of Grownups in foreign affairs, who warned of a foreign affairs threat, fought that threat, defeated that threat—the Republicans too may be undone by their triumph. Our victory over communism deprives us of one of the two primary themes of modern Republicanism—that the Soviets must and should be resisted for moral and practical reasons. And we have deprived ourselves of the other, for domestically our great message was We Will Keep Your Taxes Down and Cut the Size of Government—and the past four years we have done neither.

Really, there is no reason for people to vote for us now. Foreign policy is up for grabs, the Democrats' ideas seem as interesting and legitimate as ours. And we raised taxes and increased spending and raised the deficit. The prairie fire that started with Proposition 13 in the late '70's continues, and spreads—we've even helped reignite it—but this time we will not benefit from it, will likely in fact be scorched by it.

Unemployment is rising, the economy tightening and a growing personal austerity—a few less days at Disneyland, and let's rethink the car, the coat, the cab—is pervasive. (I talked with the CEO of the company that runs the Red Apple and Gristedes grocery stores a few weeks ago. He told me business is down 20% this year. I asked what people aren't buying. He said: steak, Evian water. I said, What sales are up? He said, "Kraft Macaroni and Cheese, 89 cents a box.")

And the American people as you well know feel that the sun is setting on the American empire, that Europe is rising as the Japanese continue to rise.

And twelve years of scandals. Triumphs come and go but scandals accumulate. Deaveresque influence peddling, HUD, Ollie, S&L, the den of thieves on Wall Street—the force accrues, adds up, rolls up into one big snowball that can knock you off the mountain.

Finally I sense, when I talk to people, normal Americans, a new dynamic. All you need is one trauma these days to change your mind. You don't get a bonus you expected, your cousin loses his job, there's an illness in the family and you can't pay the bills—one trauma and the whole world view shifts, and you get mad, and you vote no. Maybe it's always been like this, I don't know. Maybe I'm just talking to more people who lost their job and almost lost their house.

I'm thinking of my sister. She's a nurse in Jersey, works three days a week and is bringing up two children, her husband's a cabinet maker who's been weaving in and out of employment the past year, building is down. They both work so hard! And they almost lost their modest home last spring, and it was the temporary intervention of me and others that saved it, but the trauma—the shock of doing everything right and still not making it—has left her, and her Reagan-Democrat husband, changed. They are; they obeyed all the rules and still lost; and there's no way if I weren't her sister that they wouldn't vote Democratic in '92.

I'll tell you something else I think: people have politis these days. They all "know" Bush is going to win, they've seen the polls, and some of them will vote for the Democrat because they know everyone else is voting Republican and they just feel like protesting, scaring the incumbent. But of course if everyone does that, the incumbent's out of a job.

I forgot about Iraq. The good news is people bonded with the President during Desert Storm. The bad news is you bonded with your parents too, but you left.

I think people are going to feel that to vote against the Republicans is to vote for hope, for change, for a new headline and a new spirit. To vote against the Republicans is to vote against those country club sons of bitches who rigged the system, took care of their friends and left me at the age of 51 out of a corporate job and in the Safeway stacking cans of pineapples. To vote against Bush is to take a chance and start over; hell, it couldn't get much worse. Here's to the new era.

So Bob, I'm feeling down & dour about our prospects, a feeling I am not used to as I haven't thought since '76 and Watergate that our man was going to lose. I saw the President a few weeks ago, spent some time with him and got the impression he was feeling an appropriate concern about '92 but not a high level of anxiety— and I'd prefer to have seen the latter. Mary told me you have a good sense of the delicacy of our position, which made me feel better. I hope anxiety spreads among the President's advisors—if it hasn't already.

I'll end here with a semi-cheerful thought: If the Republicans lose it will be good for them, and as I think we'll only be out of power four years—the Democrats have no real ideas, are not an answer, and have little in the way of a competent and experienced human infrastructure that can run the government—it won't be so bad for the country. The Republicans are tired, they've exhausted their capital, both moral and intellectual—Henry Kissinger used to say government is all intellectual outgo, there's no intellectual income—they're out of step, out of touch and they don't know who they are anymore. They need to catch their breath, reorganize, re-gather and redefine—or fight out—what they stand for. Remember that line in Godfather II? Michael Corleone to the corrupt pol: "Come now Senator, we're both part of the same hypocrisy." That's how America increasingly perceives us; that's what we arguably are; that's what we've got to get away from.

But a Republican loss of the White House now will not do the country any good. An old time Democrat who is, like Mario, just peddling what is essentially the same old baloney—we'll get out of the slump with more taxes and more spending and more programs and more government and more officially sanctioned 'compassion'—will do the country no good. An untried and untested Bill Clinton, whose foreign policy impulses are vague and unformed at best and maybe zany and irresponsible at worst will do the country no good. They're not improvement.

So we Republicans are going to have to resummon our strength, redefine our reason for being, restate our beliefs—all with a sitting president who may not greatly enjoy the reflective process—and pull this one out. A task as existential as it is political.

Oh, one more thought: you may think, Churchill in '45 isn't necessarily the paradigm, what about Truman in '48? Yes, but we'll need two things, a stiff to play Dewey—oh where is the little man on the tank when we really need him—and a President willing to play Truman and do it.

I sent it.

And didn't receive an answer.

Maybe it was too tough; maybe Teeter didn't believe it; maybe he was besieged by memos and didn't have time to respond.

So a week or two later I sent a copy to a bright, open-minded man in the White House, who had one of his assistants reply. The assistant sent me a memo saying the Churchill-Bush comparison was not relevant; I had the order of the prime ministers wrong, and anyway Churchill had the beginning of a bad recession on his hands.

Oh.

But a few weeks later the Churchill analogy started showing up in unattributed quotes in news pieces, which told me either of two things: somebody read it and agreed, or someone is thinking exactly the way I am, drawing the same parallels, and getting nervous.

—

During the time I was writing the memo I saw President Bush, after not having seen him for a year. It was the fall of '91, and there was a message one day on my machine inviting me to attend a lecture in the East Room on George Washington. It was the third or fourth in a series on great presidents that the president and Mrs. Bush had been hosting; I had heard about them and longed to be invited.

The lecture was three days hence, and it was a long way to go for an hour in the White House, but I would see the president and get a sense of where and who he was these days. I called to accept, and the social office called back to say, "The president and First Lady would like you to stay for dinner."

There were about a hundred people in the East Room—Sununu and Dick Cheney, staff, friends of the Bushes. Most of the audience were there when I arrived, and an aide looked around and put me next to Alixe Glen—lucky for me, I hadn't seen her since the Bushes' Christmas party. She had been a stalwart in the press office in '88. We hugged and caught up.

The lecturer, a professor who had written widely on Washington, was excited to be there and gave it his all, but it was curiously flat. Washington, he told us, was no accident; he was an effortful man who made lists as a boy on how a gentleman comports himself; his natural and inherent modesty prevented him from encouraging a heroic and romantic view of his leadership and presidency; he did his two terms, retired, and the system evolved into a federal one not dependent on charismatic leadership. A good man and a great man; we were lucky that we had him.

The writer Chris Buckley, next to Alixe, leaned toward us. "Were you at the Lincoln? The guy spoke of the Lincolns walking out that door for the last time, hand in hand, and getting in the carriage for the theater. It made your hair stand up."

A reception line, then into the State Dining Room for a big buffet. The reporter Maureen Dowd had done her work: she had remarked in a book review in the *Times* that when she went to a Bush buffet it had been all Wasp parsimony, strawberry fruit mold and white wine. (Mrs. Bush, it is said, had answered, "If the food is so bad, how come I'm so fat?" A good example of how you can take the sting out of criticism by stinging yourself.) Now the food is good and plentiful and we stand around talking; I meet the head of a museum, who wants to talk about speechwriting, and the new head of the Peace Corps, and Paul Nitze, who talks about his book on arms control.

No one is moving upstairs for dinner. When the Bushes invited me to dinner two years before, it was forty people upstairs in the residence, in the long living-room area, with everyone balancing plates and glasses on their knees. The president joined clusters, chatted and moved on. But no one this evening is moving to go up.

Suddenly the social secretary is next to me saying, "Thank goodness I found you—they're upstairs, here's the elevator!"

It is the old FDR elevator, the one he had built so he could move on his own from floor to floor. It's easier to take the stairs one flight up, but I want to be in FDR's machine, and wait. It opens near the long living room, and to my surprise there are only a handful of people.

"Here's Peg!" says the president. He's in a chair in the corner, and as he rises to greet me I think: He looks pretty good, tall and lanky and fit.

To his left a couch, and Mrs. Bush sitting and chatting. She stands, I put out my hand to shake, she says in a big voice, "Hiya, pal! How are ya!" And embraces me as if we were old best friends. I'm so surprised I don't know what to say, and go "Hi!"

I am introduced to Grace, the president's cousin or niece—a young, twentyish energy-haired blond woman—and Nancy Ellis, the president's sister, and a couple from Omaha who are old friends of the Bushes, and Boyden Gray, and Dick Cheney. A small group. We sit on chairs and couches and talk. Cheney—grave, friendly, tidy-featured—says something sad. He mentions my book, and Mrs. Ellis says to him, "You, I hope, are keeping a diary so *you* can write a book."

Cheney makes that wince face he makes and looks down. "No, unfortunately you can't keep diaries in a position like mine anymore."

"Why?" I ask.

"Because," he says, "anything you write can be subpoenaed or become evidence in a potential legal action. So you can't keep and recount your thoughts anymore."

What a loss to history. It had not occurred to me but yes, Reagan's diaries were subpoenaed, and Bush's. (And now, of course, Pack-wood's.) Nothing good will come of this. People in government should not lose the right to write down and keep their private thoughts and observations; history shouldn't be denied the private conversations and disputes, the internal doubts that such diaries include. Such work should be protected.

We go into the private dining room for dinner. Thick, off-white place cards, engraved in pretty black-ink calligraphy. The president goes to his chair at the end of the table, picks up the card to his left and says, "Grace, can I move this if you don't mind? I see you, but I don't get to see Peg. Peg, get over here!"

There is a foot-high black plastic tube on a folded napkin in front of the president. "See my new toy? Gives you the right amount of pepper just where you want it; press this, and see the light? Lights up your food!"

He always has a toy. Three years ago as he planned his administration it was a big crystal ball on a black base; now and then when he had a decision to make he'd wave his arms over the ball and a deep Yes! or No! would come from its innards. He made people laugh by making believe the crystal ball was in charge.

We talk about New York. I tell him how much I like it, Willy is fine. How's the social life, he says. Fine, I say. Gotta get ya a husband, he says. That's okay, I say, and he laughs.

I tell him I'd recently seen his son Neil and Neil's wife, Sharon, and that they did such a gracious thing. I had a big luncheon speech in Denver, and they showed up to cheer me on. And it was right in the middle of the end of the S&L investigation, and not a great time to show up in front of the Denver establishment to cheer on not even a friend but an acquaintance. It was nice of them. They're terrific, I told the president.

The president looks down. He tells me the only personal sense of failure he has from his administration is that he couldn't help them. "Couldn't help him. And the pounding he took, every day, all sides."

His eyes are watery. His emotions can't be that close to the surface, can they?

"The pounding that boy took and there was nothing I could do and I'll tell ya—"

"Oh, but they survived so well," I say, "and the horror of what they went through really did bind them and make them stronger, don't you think? And now it's over."

"Yep. But—to see a member of your own family, one of your kids, and that stuff . . ." His eyes are full of tears.

I don't know what to say. We speak about Denver, and public speaking. A few minutes later the president says quietly, "I'm sorry about that emotional reaction a minute ago, didn't mean to tear up on you, get all emotional."

"You love him," I say. "You're a papa."

He turns to '92.

"The election," he says, "I just dread it, slogging through and all that stuff." He is pushing something on his plate. "We miss you around here," he says.

"I miss you all too," I say.

"D'ja think, some time, we can do it again," he says.

I smile.

He says, "I'm thinking, I'm not sure when or what but if you could come back and help us out sometime, you and me do our old routine, I'd appreciate it."

"I will try to help," I say.

I cannot say no to the president, but am conflicted, to say the least. I miss the White House when I'm there, feel nostalgia for it, but only until I've been there awhile. What I really like is to visit and leave. I'm never unhappy on the shuttle going north.

It's all such a balancing act. My presence will do Bush no good unless he's ten points down, in which case my presence will do him no harm, and could make a difference. Maybe it wouldn't hurt him, if he winds up ten points down, to replicate the group that helped in New Hampshire four years ago.

But oh, to go back to the infighting, the enervating to-and-fro. When I think of Washington I think of Elie Wiesel saying to Reagan:

"That place is not your place." They never understand, never really understand that there is no great speech without great policy. And where will great policy come from here?

I fly north thinking about the president's reaction when I brought up Neil, and about something John Chancellor had said a few months before.

I was in Washington in the spring of '91 for a task-force meeting on Radio Free Europe and Radio Liberty—the cold war is over, and should we redraw and redefine The Radios, as they're called, or pull the plug? The task force had been put together to make a recommendation, which, finally, was: Easy does it, pull no plugs before the drama is over, the wall is down but that doesn't mean democracy and a free press are entrenched, things take time, easy does it. A member of the task force wanted me to meet her friend John. We all met for a cup of coffee and Chancellor—fleshy, good-natured, and confident as he reaches retirement—chatted about what he'd seen around town lately, and then told me he thought Bush was sick.

"The thyroid thing, you mean."

"I don't know," he said, "but he's sick, and you know why I think so? Because he's cried twice, at least twice, in public recently. That speech where he told the religious broadcasters about the decision to send the boys to Iraq, and he choked, and the meeting with Billy Graham where he choked. A man like Bush crying in public, that speaks of a certain physical vulnerability, or frailty."

What he said struck me, and I thought: Yes.

I thought about another thing as I flew north. After dinner a group of us went for a walk, a few turns around the circle just off the south portico. The president had chosen a walking stick from a stand that was full of them, big brown wooden sticks with handles that were little duck heads and intricately whittled wood. He put on a cap. We walked in the dark and chatted, and then, noting that it was after eight and the last shuttle was nine, I began to say good-bye. He said,

"Do you have a car?" I said, "No, I can grab a cab there at the gate and be at the airport in ten minutes." He said, "No, gotta get ya there right."

He turned and asked an aide to get a car. As we waited we made small talk. We made small talk for ten or fifteen minutes. No car. He asked again.

"Yes, sir!"

But five, ten minutes later still no car.

It took almost half an hour for the car to come.

I've never seen a president ask for a car and it took a half hour to get there. It tells me that things at the White House are, at least this evening, a little too relaxed.

—

Three months later, in the winter of '92, I was at a local Italian restaurant on the East Side, surrounded by a mild dinnertime din, throaty laughter and smoke. Three of us, Jake, Esther and me. I tell them about Bush's State of the Union a few nights before, and how sad the experience was. For months the men around Bush had been pointing to the speech as the moment when all would be made clear, the "defining moment," as they kept saying, mantra-like. Stupid and pretentious phrase. And exactly five days before it was to be given, they didn't have a speech. Teeter had called and said, "We have a disaster on our hands. The president wants you to come down." I went down the next morning, the Friday before the Tuesday speech, saw the draft and realized that for once they weren't exaggerating.

I sat in Teeter's office at the Bush-Quayle campaign, and read. "The way this thing has been hyped and the shape it's in, this is a bullet coming straight at the heart of the president. I can't write a great speech and I can't turn this into a triumph, but I can push the president into the car and help him get away. That's all I can do, help him dodge a bullet."

"Sounds good to me," said Teeter.

I asked them to put me up in the Jefferson Hotel under an assumed name, in case it got out that a disaster was brewing and reporters started calling around to see if any New York writers happened to be in town.

An aide to Teeter called the hotel and then drove me there. At the desk he said, "We have a reservation for Miss Garbo. G. for Greta. Garbo."

The guy at the desk didn't lift an eye.

They set up a computer and I went to work. By six the next morning there was a clunky but serviceable draft. We met with the president at 9:00 A.M. He went through the draft, debated changes with Teeter and Skinner. I went back to the room, made the changes, got language from Scowcroft, put it in, got the next draft to the president Sunday afternoon.

We had a meeting—Teeter, me, the president, Dick Darman, Sam Skinner coming in and out—and I remember little save this. At one point the president asked if I'd like a cup of tea. I said yes. The president picked up a phone and asked for tea. An hour later it still hadn't come.

Nothing was working in this White House. If Ronald Reagan wanted tea and didn't get it, Nancy would have had a cook shot at sunrise. Here no one gets shot; here, it has occurred to me as I have absorbed the atmosphere, when you fail your boss raises his hand . . . and gives you a pat on the back.

The speech went all right. We pushed the president into the car and it sped away. I returned to New York. It was out that I'd been there and worked on it. I suspect the man in charge of the original draft, an attractive blond who played a solid game of tennis, told a reporter, who called me at the Jefferson. He even asked for Miss Garbo. Why would the blond tell the reporter? Because the speech wasn't great, wasn't a defining moment—or actually, unfortunately, was—and he wanted to make sure everyone knew it wasn't his fault. They farmed the sucker out!

To this day the thing I remember most vividly from the whole experience is this. The hotel staff, the room-service people and chambermaids from Trinidad and Barbados, saw that I was out all day during the day and writing all night overnight, and I don't know who they thought I worked for, but they must have thought it was someone quite demanding and maybe not so nice. Once I called room service for pie and coffee at 3:00 A.M., and the guy came and put it on the bed and said, "We heated it up for you. No check, just enjoy. And put the tray outside."

It reminded me of something we all know, and forget to notice. But there's a nice camaraderie that crops up among people who work strange jobs at strange hours and throw each other an extra egg on the grill. It's nice. I think when I used to work overnights I saw it as the main perk of the job. That, and not having to wear makeup.

When I left to go home I said good-bye to one of the room-service guys in the hall.

"Miss," he said, "can I ask you a question?"

"Yeah, you can."

"Are you the real Greta Garbo?"

"No. I wish I were. We made it up. No one's supposed to know I'm here, so we made it up."

"I didn't think so," he said, "but someone said yes."

He didn't ask who "we" was, and he wasn't surprised I was operating incognito. The things you must learn about life and people when you work in a hotel.

—

When I went home I wrote a memo to Marlin Fitzwater, who had just been told he was going to be put in charge of the communications shop.

I told him that I had never seen a White House like this. One thing you can count on with Republicans is a certain Germanic efficiency in the running of the institutions they control, but this White House is an exception. They didn't start writing the State of the Union until a week or ten days before the speech. Ben Elliott, who ran speechwriting in the Reagan White House, made the speechwriters have the first drafts in on December 26—it always ruined our Christmases. We rarely had timely policy or rhetorical guidance, so we always did our best and hoped. Then in the staffing process, which began about ten days before the speech was to be given, the revisions began, the rewrites were done in earnest. This speech was never even fully staffed out.

Five days before the speech, Reagan would have had a complete draft and be redrawing, memorizing, hearing about last-minute runs on this and that paragraph from Shultz and McFarlane, et at. In this speech, Bush didn't even have a usable first draft four days before the speech. He wasn't on TelePrompTer until the afternoon before the speech. He never got to adequately rehearse. He was fretful, frazzled, and had to reach outside at the last minute for a usable draft.

I told Marlin that if the staff in the White House I knew had failed on a crucial speech, this is what would have followed: painful and quite unfair leaks about the speechwriting staff in *Periscope* and *Washington Whispers* followed by the firing of at least one speechwriter and the possible firing of the head of speechwriting—and a real dressing down for the head of communications. Marlin, I said, we worked in one of the meanest and toughest of all modern White Houses, a bruising place, but—the job got done.

In contrast, in this White House, when the system failed everyone kind of walked around and said things like "God, the writer must feel terrible," and "Wilson must be feeling bad, let's call him in." There's a kind of cult of collegiality that on one level is good—people try to be nice to each other—but on another is bad—mediocrity flourishes unopposed. And there's a kind of smugness I found jarring. The people involved in communications seem proud of their loyalty to each other, without realizing their more immediate loyalty is to the president. They're proud of their institutional modesty without quite realizing that they have a lot to be modest about.

I told Marlin that it occurred to me that if I'd spent the past three years working there, I'd probably think by now that it was normal. But it wasn't. I told him to get back the gray heads, get in some veterans who've seen a war. "Mari Maseng [the former Reagan communications director] tells me that early on in the Bush Admin she tried to help, but the communications people made it clear they didn't need help from old Reagan hands. But she is a grownup, she is adept, she's taught me a lot about speechwriting and how things work, and she's a loyal Republican. Marlin, invite her in. I am sure she'd come in for at least a few weeks, scout the joint and tell you what works and what doesn't, what to do to fix things. Landon Parvin might be prevailed upon to come back and run speechwriting for a while—maybe get the President through the election. Landon is one of the great speechwriters—he got VP Bush off the Iran-Contra hook in a fine speech in '87. Bush likes him and Mrs. Bush likes him and Jimmy Baker loves him. Prevail on his patriotism. He's a good guy. You know who else Bush liked? Ben Elliott. Ben's up at IBM now, doing their corporate communications. Under him the [Reagan] speechwriting machine worked. He could be prevailed upon to run speechwriting too. Ben would be sympathetic towards Buchanan, I think, but he knows Bush will have the nomination and he knows Bush is much better than a Democrat.

"Marlin, I'm out of touch with all these people, talk on the phone now and then but that's it. My life has changed the past three years, I'm so out of the world of politics. I've pulled back from 'the world,' put off various outside-the-house endeavors. . . . I don't know who the bright young writers are in Washington anymore, I don't know who's up and coming, I don't have specific advice in that area. But Mari and Landon would know." I asked him to treat my advice confidentially, and I also offered an apology for calling him, well, a Washington asshole.

———

The Washington asshole part. I was sitting in Sam Skinner's office the afternoon of the State of the Union, and Marlin came in. I had always liked him. We hadn't seen each other in a long time. He said, "I really liked your book. It was really great."

"Oh, why didn't you tell me, I figured you didn't like it."

"I loved it. But I thought, Don't say anything, maybe she'll knock me sometime or say something critical about around here, and then I'll be on record saying something nice."

I looked at him. Marlin used to put people down for thinking like that.

"That's a real Washington asshole thing to say," I shared. "I never thought you'd turn into a Washington asshole, Marlin. Congratulations."

He laughed, but he was thinking. "I'm sorry. Don't be—"

I smiled and patted his arm. "I'll 'be,' Marlin. You better get up now because Skinner's watching us and you're on record as smiling."

"Ouch!"

"Teeter saw you kiss me hello. You better scurry over and tell him you mis-kissed yourself."

"Splat! Kapow!" He was laughing.

I punched his arm. "This is nice, ya know? Kinda like Tracy and Hepburn, if you had hair."

"Aaaaaaahhh!"

"I think I'm finished now."

"I have to go lay down."

"If you wanna chat anymore I'll be here, darling."

"Thank you, dear."

By the way, for all you politically ambitious Rogaine users, Marlin once told me something smart about men's hairstyles. He told me his hair began thinning on top when he was a young man, and had to decide whether to accept it or grow his hair long on the side and sweep it over the top of his head. He concluded that if he chose the latter, a lot of people on meeting him would think, Marlin's trying to hide the fact that he's losing his hair. Whereas if he didn't do the big comb-over, people would probably look at him and think, Marlin has nice eyes. So that's the route he took. And when you meet him you think, Marlin has beautiful eyes. (The problem for people in politics with trying to cover a bald spot with that hair-on-the-sides trick or with a toupee is: People look at you and think, That guy's got a lie on his head; I bet he's got other lies.)

—

But this started with dinner with Jake and Esther. I told them I was going to move down to Washington for six months to see if I could help. Jake listened, and then he kind of seized up.

"Peggy," he said, "you can go back to Washington and you can live there and you can work for the president—but you cannot stay there. The life is too easy. It's—seductive!"

"I know," I said, "don't worry."

"I'm serious," he said. "You'll wind up—on a talk show! It's not a serious place! It's too comfortable!"

—

A month later I was at the Palm in Washington, having lunch with a political reporter. He has been in Washington twenty years and seen it change, and he mentioned something I had been noticing more and more and forgetting to remember: Washington is rich.

"We're all compromised," he said. "I'm compromised too. There's a lot of money in this town, money coming in from Korea, from Japan. A young guy up on the Hill who's a top aide on a committee, he can leave the Hill after three years and become a lobbyist and open his own firm and the first year he makes two hundred thousand dollars. Lots of money. We're all compromised."

And then he smiled as if to say, Where'd that come from?

I told him the image that had been occurring to me: Washington is a big tub of butter, you gotta make sure you don't learn to love the lard.

When lunch was over he waited with me for a cab. As I got in he closed the door.

"Remember," he said, "don't stay!"

——

I looked for a house to rent in areas I thought I could afford, the more suburban areas of Northwest, and found I couldn't afford them. But I could afford chic and trendy Georgetown because it wasn't chic and trendy anymore. It's downright de trop. The reason, of course: crime. It's a rougher place than it was even a few years ago; people are moving farther out, to Northwest, and Virginia, and Maryland.

——

"Look," says the woman who shows me around. She is a real estate agent I'll call Marilyn. She's tall and dark, and everywhere she goes people know her.

"Zak! My darling! How are you?" She gives me a look. "Poor man," she says, barely moving her lips, "his wife just died. Alcoholic. So sad. I wonder if he's gonna sell his house! Ha ha! Aren't we terrible? But ya gotta earn a living!"

"Bobby!" They wave. We drive on.

"I sold him the one we saw on Thirty-fourth, steal of the century. In '89, when the bottom fell out. By the way, real estate would come back like a lightning bolt if we'd cut the capital gains, one thing your side understands!"

She is a Democrat. She loves her party, loves her Democrats, and she is lovable too. She calls me darling and tells me I love ya, kid. I like to be told this by big happy-looking people, so I love her too. We breeze happily along drinking Pepsis in the front seat. We drive by a big house. A caterer's truck is unloading. "The Bagleys are having a party! And they didn't invite me!"

"Then as far as I'm concerned they're finished in this town," I say, patting her arm.

The soft prettiness, the wholesomeness, still, of Washington on a spring morning. The trees, the sparkling light on the bridges on the river. People jog by soundlessly. There is such a feeling of health in this town, of physical well-being, and youth. When you visit Dublin you are struck that it is a young place, and indeed it is, the youngest city in Europe. In Washington too I am newly struck by how young it is, the young men in gray suits and trench coats walking along in groups, laughing, going into the Hamburger Hamlet.

—

One day years ago I met the fabled Edward Bennett Williams. He was near the end of his life, and wanted to talk about his memoirs. I was fascinated by him. He was a big man, tall, with a big head of gray hair shooting off his brow. He'd had such a life. Friend and adviser to the great, former Mafia mouthpiece, defender of corrupt union officials, president of the Redskins, mover in the Democratic party. And he bristled. Sharp eyes with thick lids, like a salamander.

I asked, "You have seen great people and small people, and known the most powerful and important men of your time. Tell me, what ruins men? What are the things that destroy a life, that turn success into failure?"

His face for a moment was blank with thought. After about five seconds he said, "Booze, women and money. Maybe not in that order, but pretty much."

Liquor, lust and lucre. Mood changers, undenied sexual urges, too great a want of material things. I rolled the list around in my mind.

That spring of '92 I couldn't stop thinking of what Williams said, for as I looked at houses in wealthy Washington, it occurred to me that the things that ruin men are perhaps the things that ruin cities. Too much Gimme, too much I want, I deserve, I need. Too much I'm hooked. Too much acting out.

—

I couldn't find a house. And I couldn't reach full resolution with the Bush-Quayle campaign on what exactly my role would be. They kept saying, "You'll be in charge of the message." I kept saying, "But what is the message? What does the president want to do the next four years?"

"We're talking about some ideas," said Teeter. But they didn't add up to much and they never connected to any discernible philosophy or point of view.

"We're going to create a new jobs bill," said Teeter one day.

Oh.

—

That night, sleepless, I fastened on all the Republicans with strangely eponymous names. Honey Skinner, Sam's wife, has a name like a farm implement. *We'll plow the lower 40, and then we'll clean the honey skinner.* French Wallop, Senator Malcolm Wallops's wife—her name is like a service you could buy at a Parisian whorehouse. *You want zee one girl, zee two girl, or zee French wallop?* Governor Wilson's chief of staff, Bob White, eats like a bird.

But there was something else. It has largely been my experience that when something big is supposed to happen, things click into place. I've moved a lot, I know how to find houses, it's funny I can't find one. No outside force is clearing the way here. It was in '91 and '92 that little by little I was returning, in a serious way, to faith and observance; and in any case I'd always felt that when I was on the right path I was put there by higher powers, as they say, and pushed forward by them. Those times that I was on the wrong path, going down a lane I'd chosen to take relying only on myself, my logic, my wants—those journeys wound up dead ends. Which happens, literally, to be the kind of street Marilyn and I kept turning into when we went on our jaunts.

—

There was a conversation the day of the New Hampshire primary. Teeter's most trusted aide and I were in her small office in the campaign. I hadn't been in Washington in a few weeks, and I was catching up. It was the afternoon, and there was no hard news, but Muriel had been in politics a long time and had seen the scene a few days ago, had seen Bush fly up to Manchester and say, "Message: I care." She had seen the Buchanan forces with their placards and jeers, and appreciated, as few around Bush could, the meaning of the lyrics of Pat's theme song, "We will we will rock you."

I had written Pat a letter the previous fall, when word first spread that he might run. I explored the possible repercussions for him, some quite good—a good showing by him would mean Quayle wasn't first in line in '96, Pat will have proved he could get votes on his own, and with guts, like Reagan in '76. I also told him that I didn't think he'd do well in New Hampshire, I thought he'd win.

But I urged him not to run—he'd never get the '92 nomination, and his efforts would take down Bush and put in a Democrat. So don't run, Pat.

And Pat wrote back ten words: "Beautiful letter, kid. I'll try to do it with class." Which is how I found out he was running.

And now here we were, Teeter's aide and I, and I tell her, "I just don't think it's gonna work for us this year, Muriel, I just don't think it's gonna work. . . ."

She studies me. She decides. "You want to know what I really think."

"Yes."

"Between-us-not-to-be-repeated-around-here I have concluded that there are two and only two camps in this campaign. One is devoted to justifying the decisions of the past three years and covering their backsides. Darman, etc. The other group is solely intent on the next nine months, and thinking up anything they can to win."

I nod, fascinated. Such candor in these precincts.

"And that," I say, "leaves no one thinking about such small but nonetheless interesting matters as, oh, which way the country should be going and what's right and what's good policy."

"Yes," she says.

"So one group's looking backward and one group's only looking down one narrow road."

"Yes."

"We lose that way."

"Oh yes."

"Being you, though, you have some kind of hope."

"I was hoping you could bridge the gap and make the difference."

"Oh, honey. Ih."

"Yes. Ih. Or ick, as the case may be."

I leave knowing that no one can bridge such a gap. Or, perhaps, should. I sink back in my seat on the shuttle, ignoring the apple and cheese spread, looking down at what will soon be the almost jungle-like thickness of the woods of northern Virginia.

Let them be what they are. Let history do what it does. Let it unfold unimpeded by your presence.

—

Another trip down, this one in the spring and this one decisive. A meeting in the White House, in the office of an assistant to Sam Skinner. Sam is there and Teeter and Darman and Kristol and Marlin. Teeter asked me down to discuss upcoming speeches. He announces that he envisions a series of three, all big and thoughtful and presented in serious places in a serious way. I nod. These will be important speeches, he says.

I wonder what they'll be about. I take notes. Before I can ask questions a noise comes from Skinner's direction.

"Aaaarumph," he says.

Teeter doesn't seem to hear.

"Aaar—Uh!"

I look at Skinner.

"We got a morale problem. We got a real morale problem here."

Teeter is looking at his yellow pad, refusing to look up.

"What is it, Sam," I ask.

"Well, the speechwriters aren't too happy you're here! It's a real problem!"

"Oh. Can we do anything about it?"

"I don't know what!"

"Oh."

I look at Teeter. He says nothing. I say nothing. Marlin inspects his cigar. Darman isn't listening. Kristol is smiling.

"Well, what should I do?" I ask.

"I don't know!"

"I don't know what to say." I look around for help, or elaboration.

"I got a meeting!" Skinner says. He jumps up and walks toward the door. "See ya, Peg! Hope ya didn't mind my saying, but—"

"That's okay."

Silence as he leaves. I am confused. No one likes to get bigfooted but—so what? That's not important at the moment. I have a certain history with Bush and he wants me here, it's not a big deal, we can work it out. No, that's not it. This is it: Bush is in terrible trouble, this is a fight to the death and we'll probably lose. This is like reinforcements coming to Custer and Custer's aide-de-camp saying, "Whoah, the presence of new troops could be interpreted as a reproach to our soon-to-be-dead veterans!" (If the Sioux were here they'd look at Skinner and turn to each other with delight: *White man real fool.*)

Still no one says anything. Until Teeter says, "Let's talk about the speeches."

And I look at him and realize that a war has been going on and no one quite got around to telling me, a little war between Skinner and Teeter, and I'm what they're fighting about.

And where is the president on this? The one time I met with him and Skinner and Teeter, the president told me he was happy I was coming back; Teeter nodded and the president said, in a mild aside to Skinner, "Long as it works out, Sam."

And Skinner nodded, mildly.

I thought it was politesse to a new chief of staff. Why wouldn't it work out?

But it wasn't politesse. Skinner didn't want me there because his head of communications, the hapless one who'd put together the State of the Union that wasn't, told him my celebrated presence would upset the staff. And Skinner's so dumb he figured Heck, can't have that. Worse: those thinking that way—Skinner, whoever else—don't know they're probably going to lose. They wouldn't understand the string of '80, '84, '88 would probably break. Why would they? They never understood why the Republicans won anyway. They all thought it was voodoo. Which, it occurs to me, may explain the past three years.

This all came not like three paragraphs you're reading but in three seconds of association.

So I put down my pen and looked at them.

The talk was of the speeches, but the speeches seemed unconnected to any reigning reality. And did not answer the question Why a second term? And when Teeter said, "Why don't you write the big domestic speech," I said, "I'll take notes on what it is you feel the president should say, but why don't we have one of the speechwriters write it, to improve morale." And when he said, "You'll do the big foreign affairs speech," I said, "Well, you've got a lot of good speechwriters here and if I write it, it could be a morale problem, so why don't you all be prudent about this and tend to that and work it out."

This made Darman testy. We were wasting his time.

Well, we were. But he and I were friends, or had been, for years, not daily or weekly or even monthly telephone friends but people who appreciated each other, and to a degree understood each other. Maybe he could sort of use his high standing in these precincts to say, "Looks to me like we're focusing on the wrong issues. 'Inevitable loss without great good luck and hard joint effort' is the issue, not 'Let's all worry about marginal matters that do not directly bear on the outcome of the contest.' "

But he was testy. We were wasting his time. And I thought, It's not just that maybe he's not my steadfast friend—maybe no one is his friend. All these men seemed to hate each other. Even Marlin just sat there twirling his cigar like the cynic in a Capra movie. And Kristol just smiled merrily as if to say, Welcome to the Bush White House.

The meeting ended and I walked.

—

Teeter and I bump into the hall, later, and sit in the Roosevelt Room, and I tell him some of how I feel and I tell him they're going to lose. And he says, "We're not going to lose!" And he adds, "We're going to fire most of the speechwriters, they can't cut it." And I tell him, "If you fire them it will cause more problems, what is this? You guys are—"

Kristol peeks in, walks through, grinning.

Why are they all smiling? Don't they know there's a war on? And why do they all hate each other? They didn't use to.

I fly home knowing: I don't want to be here.

—

Two days later I called a close friend; she cleared her schedule and we went to lunch and I told her, finally, as we left, how I felt and what had happened. She stopped on Fifty-eighth Street in the sun and said, "Wait. Wait. Don't they get it that you're doing them a favor?"

"No. I'm not, it's not a favor, I like Bush, you know how I feel. And I seriously prefer him to a Democrat."

"Don't they understand you're coming in to *help* them?"

"No. They think I'm a problem."

"Where is the president on this?"

"I don't know. It's hard to talk to him because they always surround him with a posse when anyone wants a meeting. And also I don't want to put him on the spot. He knows Sam's crazed over Sununu. Sam thinks Sununu's up there in the EOB giving interviews on what an incompetent his successor is, and he's probably right. Sam flips out. Bush is trying to show him loyalty. So if Sam doesn't want me there it puts Bush in a position."

"Who wants you there?"

"I thought everybody, but I think just Teeter. If I understand it right. And the president 'if it works out.' "

"What's your exact role?"

"I've been thinking about that. I feel like they think I misunderstood Bush in '88 and they want me to come back and misunderstand him again."

"Tell me what you want to do. Not should do, want to do."

"I don't want to be there."

She peers at me. The light changes and we don't move.

"You're just a little girl."

"What?"

"You're just a little girl."

"No I'm not."

"Yes. There's just you and there's all these guys and they're the White House and you're just a little girl."

I look at people passing. She means, You think you're the cavalry but you're a lone recruit, and it's worse than that, you're alone in pigtails. And they're sticking them in the inkwell.

"You don't need this. You should have walked out of that meeting, you just should have walked and said, 'I don't need this.' "

"That's how I felt."

"Why didn't you say it?"

"I don't know."

"Quit."

"That's what I want to do."

"Get out."

The light changes.

"Call me."

"I will."

"I mean it."

"I know you do."

—

I am a human ball of misery curled on the carpet of Jake and Esther's West Side apartment. Above me, a window. I imagine sunlight coming in and warming me in yellow glow. I imagine around me a chalk-mark silhouette.

I had seen Jake a few nights before and said, "I have woe, can I come talk to you guys."

He said, "What is it and how bad?"

"Work-related and full fetal position."

"Uh-oh. Come tomorrow."

And now here I am with a deranged monologue.

"I don't want to do what I said I'd do," I tell them. "I don't want to go. I've been up for nights trying to figure what to do and how to do it. I feel like it's just cynical down there and I don't want to be part of it. My hair will fall out."

They look at me.

"I have this image that it will be so ugly and enervating and meaningless that my scalp will constrict and all my hair will break off into these little more or less blond tufts."

"It's a look," says Esther.

"But how do I not go? If I declare I'm not going in, it's news. The press will speculate on my reasons and I can't tell them my reasons, so they'll make them up. Nature abhors a vacuum, Washington will fill it. No one leaves a job with good money and power for nothing. So Evans and Novak will say I'm talking to Perot. And someone else will say I had an argument with Bush and told him either he supports SDI or I'm out of here. Then a nice helpful aide to some idiot in the campaign will say, "It wasn't her decision, we didn't want her." Then someone will say, "No, she demanded more money, so they told her to take a hike.'"

"Mmmmmm. All sounds true," says Jake.

"But you know how I feel? Clinton won't be a good president but this White House doesn't deserve to win. I have no one to support this year, so I shouldn't be working in politics this year. So I have no choice. So I'm going to stay in New York, New York, the city so nice they named it twice, and write some essays and take some hits and eat my pork chop."

I have decided. No, I have admitted.

"And what I should do to minimalize impact is tell 'em I can't move down for personal reasons—this has the added benefit of being true, as Willy doesn't want another move. I tell 'em I'll help later in the campaign if they really need it. That will force them to rely on the communications people they have and get new ones. Then they need me less; then, in time, and if I'm lucky, when everyone's used to my not being around I quietly withdraw and no one cares and by then it's no story because I haven't been there."

"Okay," says Jake. "But tell your real thinking to someone in the campaign who you trust."

"I don't have someone I trust."

"Oh. Get out."

I send a letter to the president and Teeter and tell them I'm more trouble than I'm worth and the move is too much. I unplug the phone for a week. I get a letter from the president saying, Okay!

—

There were various delicate moments. One is a welcome-back-to-Washington party to be given at the Jockey Club by Robert Higdon, a smart, funny friend of the Reagans who is running the Margaret Thatcher Foundation in Washington. He is a generous and loyal man, and I told him much about my plight.

But it's too late to cancel the party, and we figure Heck, we'll have fun anyway.

And we did. It is a strange and delightful group, old friends and new friends, friends of Robert's, people I haven't seen in a while. Joan Rivers is there, my friend from New York who is also Robert's friend and who figured, Mmmm, think I'll go see the Washington types be stuffy. And two I hadn't seen in years, Clarence Thomas and his wife, Ginny.

He is seated to my right and I am struck by his eagerness to show good cheer and appreciation. America met, a year before, his stern and angry visage. But his friends know his sweetness, his intense kindness.

He says, "We never go out, Ginny and me, we're not very social, but we wanted to be here after what you wrote."

I had supported Clarence in his war. What strikes me more with time is the absolute certainty of the partisans on both sides of that war; it is like Alger Hiss versus Whittaker Chambers, arousing the same degree of undamped passion, the same amount of obsessed certitude; and, of course, so many people took sides based not on evidence but ideology. And like the Hiss-Chambers case, the Hill-Thomas case will never go away. They'll be writing doctoral dissertations on it in the year 2026. (I can understand. It was forty years ago and it doesn't matter anymore, but a part of me would be deeply satisfied if, on his deathbed, Alger Hiss said, "Forgive me—I'm sorry—I lied.")

I had watched the Hill-Thomas hearings like everyone else in the country, with fascination and horror. I felt a kind of horrified sympathy for her, walking into the lion's den, a lone black woman facing a row of tough white men in blue suits. And when her mother came in, frail old lady, and hugged her. And there was Clarence, his life in shards at his feet, lone black man in front of a row of white men in blue suits. I wanted to hold his hand and rub his back. 'Up straight, clear voice, win back your life.'

I don't know what passed between them. None of us will ever know. Maybe they don't quite "know." Memory is a trickster, moments fade, what grows more vivid with time is interpretation.

But we know other things.

I know how young men and women talked to one another in the office in the heady heyday seventies and early eighties. I know, "Who put this pubic hair on my Coke?" would have passed without comment in the editing rooms of CBS News. I know that rough gross talk was accepted from and by both men and women. My friends and I often talked as tough as the boys. That's part of what feminism was in those days, showing women were equal to men in their thoughts and comportment, showing we were no better and no worse. What I remember about the seventies and early eighties was that everyone acted like a jerk; everyone was insecure. Everyone did stupid things to show how secure he or she was. Now people run around denying they ever heard of the seventies. "I wasn't there, I took a nap and woke up at the Reagan inaugural!"

And most of us know something else: in an age when politics is everything, people will do anything. They will have no scruples, no compunction, no remorse. The left was fighting, it thought, for *Roe v. Wade*. Would the left do anything to protect it? Well, they just might. It just might get ugly, and vicious, and untruthful. But there are laws and traditions, and one is: the benefit of the doubt goes to the accused. And there were many reasons, especially in that atmosphere, to doubt.

One of the strangest things in the whole mess was the insistence by some that if you did not back Hill you did not believe sexual harassment exists, you are betraying women. I didn't, don't understand the logic. I believe that murder exists, but I am not sure even all those on death row are guilty. And I think as a tactic "If you don't back Hill you don't back women" backfired. People don't like it when they feel that on some level they're being coerced; and the more subtle forms are the most offensive. I know sexual harassment exists; only it didn't use to be called sexual harassment, it used to be called being a pig and a bully. Which is what I still think it is. But to know such people exist, such a phenomenon exists, is not to know Clarence was guilty.

I look at him now at this dinner and as he talks about books I think of what I wanted to ask him.

"Clarence," I say, "at the hearings. When you went into that hearing room with the cameras of all the networks on you watching you adjust the mike, scratch your face, touch your tie—the eyes of all the people of your nation were on you as you began to speak to clear your name. That moment—how did you do that? Knowing that any misstep, even blinking in the wrong way at the wrong moment, was about to enter the consciousness of every adult in the country. How did you go in there so strong?"

"I didn't go in there strong," he says. "I went in there a broken man. I had been broken. They had reduced me literally and figuratively to a fetal position. I was broken. And what got me through it was I prayed, I said 'Lord I am weak, I am weak, you must help me.' "

He tells me how prayer got him and Ginny through it, and is still getting them through it, for, a seat on the Court or not, when people hear his name they think of those hearings, and what was said.

At the end he said that what was so difficult for him was to be not guilty and imperfect. To be raised Catholic and always have such guilt over even the most minor human transgressions.

He shook his head. I thought: He means it is hard to bring the full concentration of your moral energy to bear, hard to defend yourself with the requisite high conviction, when you know you are not "innocent."

He isn't a Catholic anymore or, rather, does not practice as a Catholic. He and Ginny go to a Protestant church in Virginia.

A thought: good people are always at a disadvantage in the world because to be good is to be honest and the honest feel the weight of their misdeeds. Real bad guys don't, or not often, or not consistently, or not much.

—

Clarence was raised by the nuns. I have never known anyone of our generation who went through Catholic school who didn't rebel. That's not quite the right word. But people who went through Catholic school in the fifties and sixties and had to integrate what they'd learned into life in the seventies—they have many of them led tortuous intellectual and spiritual paths with regard to faith.

Some left and said, "No, enough, this is not life-loving." (A friend of mine who's in AA tells me you can always get a laugh when you say, "Hi, My name is Joe and I'm an alcoholic and a recovering Catholic.") Some became embarrassed, and absorbed through the culture The Right Way to Think. They sometimes spoof with real wit the Church's old emphasis on sin, and become modern, rational, humane. (I think this is not only spiritual, but has class dimensions: To stay a Catholic in the seventies and eighties was to identify with Aunt Tessy in Brooklyn and her superstitions, her unquestioning peasant's belief, her gossip, her chain-smoking, her mustache. Aligning yourself with her also carried political implications: Aunt Tessy called black people mullignones, which is some Italian dialect for eggplant.)

And some got the harpoon in their heart and exhausted themselves and exhaust themselves still, swimming away and being drawn back, swimming away and being drawn back.

I went to public school so I got to believe in anything, including the possibility of succor. Humans never spoiled it for me. No nun ever smacked me with a ruler, no brother ever belittled me for wearing the wrong shoes on First Holy Communion day, as happened to my father, who never really belonged to the Church after that.

They never hurt me, so it is not hard to miss them. For they're all dead or retired, those last of the old warriors for God, the priests and nuns of the forties, fifties and sixties. I miss their certitude, their renunciation of the world. Taking their place were the moderns—priests who'd like to help a parishioner trying to learn how to pray but, frankly, I gotta get to a 10:00 A.M. meeting with the homeless coalition, and their problems are a bit more pressing! And nuns who seem neither this nor that, neither worshipful and self-abnegating nor—groovy. A few years ago my friend Susan played for her daughter an old family movie of our confirmation. Her daughter, ten at the time, leaned forward and pointed as an apparition in a long flowing black robe with a big white headpiece entered the frame.

"Mommy, what's *that?*"

"That's a nun."

"That's what nuns looked like?"

"Yep."

"You're kidding," said her daughter, with wonder.

Everything's changed. Susan often visits a retired nun out on Long Island. The nun is in her late sixties. She answers the door in a jogging suit, with a Camel stuck to her lip.

—

At the end of the party Ed Rollins, Reagan's campaign manager in '84, and a man to whose destiny we will again return, motioned to me to join him at the bar. I hadn't seen him in some time, and always smile at his puckish face, puckish demeanor, rolly good nature. He wants to confide in me, and swears me to secrecy. I swear, knowing I'm probably the twenty-second, twenty-third person tonight to whom he's said, "Nobody knows this but you."

But he does surprise me. He tells me he's going to work for Perot. Ham Jordan's coming in too. He says, "There's another revolution out there." And he's right, but it is an inchoate one, not fully formed as the Reagan revolution was—not the same clarity of purpose. Later I think, No, Perot isn't a revolution, it's a revulsion. And an understandable one.

—

"Peggy, Barbara Bush."

I look at the clock. Just before eight. Willy snoozes beside me with an ear infection.

"Hello, Mrs. Bush, how are you?"

"Fine until I saw that thing. I just want you to know it's entirely incorrect, I've never said those things and wouldn't and it's just infuriating."

"Oh—I'm so sorry, but I'm not sure what you mean."

"You haven't seen it?"

"No. No. What does it say."

"Oh, it's a piece in *Newsweek* on me, one of those pieces that's supposed to be aimed at me but is really aimed at George Bush. They say that I've been criticizing your work and that's why you didn't come down here, and I don't know where they get this but it's just not true."

"Oh, Mrs. Bush, I'm sorry they wrote that, I wouldn't believe it if I'd read it."

"Well, as long as you know, Peg, it's not true."

"You're very kind to take the time to call. Thank you."

"Not at all. Take care. Good to talk to you."

"Thanks. Thanks a lot."

She is a gracious lady.

She had asked me in late January to help with her stump speech. I wrote some lighthearted stuff, strong woman good-naturedly stands by her man. I figured she rewrote it and used it.

Later I get the magazine. In a long article that argued that Barbara

Bush is increasingly the power behind the throne, I was put forth as a prime example of her influence. I had written a speech for Mrs. Bush, it said, and she hadn't liked it. She had complained behind my back, which figured in my decision not to come down to Washington.

The stupidest thing about it—aside from the fact that *Newsweek* never asked me and never asked her—is that no one ever accused Mrs. Bush of being a hypocrite. If she didn't like your work she'd tell you to your face, and not once or twice. Everyone knew this. Her power was her directness, not her subtlety. She was about as devious as a moose.

For weeks I'd been knocking down the story that I was jumping to Perot. Then I went through a round with—ahem—*Newsweek*'s Evan Thomas, who'd called to say his reporters had been told I'd decided not to go down to Washington because I was writing speeches and they were being heavily edited, and in a blowup with "top campaign staff" I had said— *"We have dialogue!"* said Evan: " 'It's my way or the highway!' and 'top campaign staff' had said, 'Then it's the highway!' " and I had stormed off, vowing that they'd never put my words through a "meat grinder."

I denied the story. Thomas said, "We'll have to go with it if we get corroboration." I said, "Don't go with it, no one can truthfully corroborate it because it didn't happen."

In the end, strangely enough, they didn't use it. A few days later I realized the dialogue he mentioned was in my book. I had likened the staffing process in the Reagan era to putting beautiful fresh vegetables in a meat grinder and rendering a smooth, bland puree. The little shits who made up the story used my book!

The sad thing is that *Newsweek* didn't make up lies and print them. *Newsweek* talked to an unattributed source who told *Newsweek* these things. I'm sure they went to another source who backed it up emphatically—or said, "I can't speak from firsthand knowledge but I have heard it's true, and believe it."

But why don't modern political reporters ponder the motive(s) of their source(s)?

Here's a typical unattributed-source interview. A reporter calls a mid-level White House shmegegge and says, "I'm hearing big complaints about Jones, he's turning a lot of people off over there." The mid-level source—Smith—has been waiting for this moment. He can't scream "Yeah!"—that might alert the reporter that there is a certain personal dimension. Instead the mid-level staffer grunts, and says, "I'm not surprised." He allows himself to be drawn out. His tone says, I don't like to trash people, but . . . He says, "Jones works hard, he's trying but—his judgment is poor, and it's a problem for everyone."

Again, the tone is important. You have to play it more in sorrow than in anger or it may not work.

Let me tell you why the mid-level staffer said what he said. In spite of a solid year of endless suckup his mediocre work is, he knows, about to catch up with him. He's about to be demoted again, or canned. He can tell by the way the chief of staff's secretary isn't quite maintaining eye contact the way she used to. Well, if he's going to get fired he wants the columnists to see it this way: WHITE HOUSE UNREST OVER JONES/LATEST FIRING RAISES EYEBROWS. The firing of Smith is not the natural result of his failures but another example of Jones's bad judgment.

And you know what Smith does after he talks to the reporter? He writes a memo to Jones, saying, "I just got a call from Bob Wilson of the *Times,* who says he's getting reports from quote White House staffers unquote that there's a lot of ill feeling against you. I told him it was bogus, the work of mischief-makers. I think I knocked it down, and I don't want to add to your problem list, but I think you might want to talk to a few of the folks in the communications shop and see if they can't help put a stop to this kind of nonsense."

A twofer! Smith hates the schmuck who runs communications.

There is such mischief among the ambitious underemployed.

But not all White Houses are quite like this. A friend of mine who knows says Democratic White Houses are just as creepy but not as cunning. "They're not as competent in their ability to manipulate," he says. "Same moral fiber, far more timidity in the execution."

Recently I was told by a guy I think of as a fine person, a veteran of bureaucratic wars, the following eighties story. I repeat it because it gives a sense of how a tough White House works.

My friend the fine person had a White House mentor, a gifted and devious mover named Mr. South, who was in constant war with a White House colleague named Mr. North.

North was a character and something of a rogue, but a pretty good fellow. Still, South hated him.

One day South found out that a soon-to-be-important young White House official—let's call him Mr. East—had answered, honestly, during his FBI interview, the one all White House staffers must pass before being okayed for full White House clearance, that in the sixties he had smoked marijuana. Not an unusual infraction, but East was a conservative Republican, a cultural conservative, and had some anxiety that some creep would get hold of the investigation and make trouble. Still, he told the truth. And went about his work wearing his temporary pass and hoping everything would be okay.

Well, South got hold of the FBI report. And pondered its implications, its many possibilities. Information is power, he always said.

In a few days South hit on a plan. He called East and said, "East, I'm a friend, buddy, and I gotta tell you, you got yourself a problem with that damn FBI thing."

East gulped. "What's the problem?"

"Well," said South, "that jerk North got ahold of it and he's telling everyone you're a drug addict. Now don't get upset—I'm gonna knock this bullshit down and if he tries to bring you down I swear the fucker's going first. Just know what's going on. And look—North seems like a nice guy but when he says 'Let's have some barbecue,' you just keep walking, okay? And I'll try to shut him down. Don't worry, be cool, I'm on the case."

To this day East, long gone from government, thinks North tried to do him in. He spent years avoiding North, who, sensing the lack of trust, the lack of ease, the—suspicion!—became, in fact, East's enemy. An enemy East had to expend considerable energy fending off.

South used to laugh about it.

But East never became close to South, either. South had something on him—the FBI report. And South, East knew, especially at 4:28 A.M., when he woke up with a start and tried to figure out the White House, just . . . might . . . have been playing a game. He knew this through instinct, and because of gossip: he'd heard, three months into his White House stint, that South hated North and North hated South.

Here's the most depressing part of the story. The man who told it to me—in passing, in a restaurant, as we discussed whether the eggs in the Caesar salad would give us salmonella—told it with a chuckle.

I said, "Oh, Jack, that's not funny, it's sick." And he paused and thought. "Yeah," he said, "but that was South—that was just him. And it's true, too."

—

But back to reporters, and their reluctance to consider the motives of sources. Considering such motives not only is inconvenient but might seem churlish. Because—well, fair's fair, and the reporter has his motives too.

First, some stories are, in the famous phrase, too good to check— too funny, too interesting. Check such a story and it may disappear. (Which causes another problem: no byline tomorrow. And you just spent seven hours on it. A day wasted.) And if it doesn't disappear exactly it might become . . . too interesting. Too shaded and layered, too ambiguous; it may become as interesting as truth. And you know what? It's hard to do truth in five hundred words in the nation section. You can only do—oh no!—gossip, buzz and the kind of brightness that you certainly wish would result in a screenwriting contract from TriStar. "Truth" sometimes takes a lot of words, thousands of them. And doesn't always have a hook. And isn't always bright. Sometimes it's dark as muddy water.

And there is simple fatigue. Deadlines, bosses, I haven't seen my kids in two weeks, I'm bushed, Smith is okay. The reporter is inclined to be sympathetic to Smith because—well, he was his best source in the EOB! Lose him and you gotta waste months taking some other mushmouth to the Hay Adams so he'll talk to you. And anyway—you owe Smith! He told you some things it wasn't even in his direct interest to tell you! He's helped you on deadline! You owe him. He always played.

And also and finally: Screw him, he's not the issue. The issue is, Screw 'em all. They all lie. Unattributed sources in the White House are like unattributed sources in the day-to-day gossip at *Time*. You want "truth"? Get a Bible. I'm outta here, my son's got a game and I haven't eaten anything that isn't room service in fifteen days. If my work contributes, however humbly, to the awareness of the American reader that it's all bullshit, then good. Because it is.

—

In Washington, unattributed comments are used like nukes: you can use First Strike, rely on Mutual Assured Destruction, try to put up an SDI ("We leak to *The Washington Post*, they leak to *The Washington Times*. Guess who wins?" said a man who told me how liberals and conservatives duked it out in the Reagan administration). Nonbelligerents inevitably get hit. They have to decide: Do I do nothing and nurse my wounds? Or do I join the war and fire, undermining my morals in order to protect my reputation for integrity?

Modern political journalism is a protection racket. Robert Novak once told one of his assistants, "In this town you're either a source— or a target." I always liked his saying that because it was true: Talk or die. It was like Don Corleone saying, "We're the Mafia and we kill people."

The press in Washington is like the old actor Edward Arnold as the mobster who tells the saloonkeeper, "In this town I'm boss. You own a saloon you pay a little tribute, or one night there's an accident. There's a gas leak and a spark"—he looks thoughtfully at the tip of his cigar—"and, boom, there's an explosion. People get hurt."

Everyone pays protection: everyone talks.

The only difference here is that the mobsters get to write essays on ethics, and turn them into the centerpiece of a collection, and invite their sources to the book party.

—

That summer I was at the Democratic Convention in New York for *Newsweek*, writing a piece called "Behind Enemy Lines," when I ran into Bill Safire, who said, "We must have lunch, or else we will be hungry."

Safire is a born encourager, a booster of the fortunes of his friends, and when we talked he told me something that helped clarify my situation.

He asked what my relationship was with the Bush campaign. I told him I was still sending them memos with advice and such, and he said, "Let me tell you a story." He said that one day years ago, when he was new on the *Times*, out of loyalty to his old friend he wrote President Nixon a memo on how to handle Watergate. Then, out of loyalty to his new colleagues, he went to his boss, Abe Rosenthal, and said, "Abe, I've sent a memo to the president, and there's nothing in it I'd be ashamed to have on the front page of the paper, but I just want you to know." And Abe said, "Bill, I have an idea for you. You write the memo, and then you give it to me, and I will take it and put it in the newspaper, and the president will read it, and we will give you money for it. Isn't that a good way to do it?" And Safire said, "Yeah, actually, that is a good way to do it."

"Write in the press," Safire told me, "and remember that your first responsibility is to yourself and your son."

—

That convention itself was strange.

Normally conventions strike me as very modern—all the vast media array. And when I first walked into Madison Square Garden and onto the floor it looked so vast and clamorous, as if something important was going to happen here. But this convention was post-modern. It did not satisfy, did not ring of experience. (Oh no, it was—another enactment.)

Anyway, you've seen conventions. What was interesting about this one to me is that there were no rubes, no hilariously innocent delegates from outside Sioux City. Everyone was purposeful and sophisticated, and as I watched them I realized as never before that we have become a nation of insiders. We all know everything now. No matter where you're from or what you do you've got the facts. We read *Spy* and *Vanity Fair*, know Irving didn't like to be called Swifty, know which film opened big last weekend and which network won the year, know the difference between a rating and a share, know who Michael Ovitz, Jeffrey Katzenberg and Binky Urban are, have an opinion on Paul Begala and Mandy Grunwald, have patiently explained to a grandparent what spin is, know Punch's son isn't really called Pinch, know what Q Rating, live pop and focus group mean.

We are all insiders. We are sophisticated beyond our intelligence, and cynical about things we haven't earned the right to be cynical.

It leaves a reporter—and that is what I am this week—without a role, without a costume to wear at the costume party. Reporters used to be the insiders. And at least they earned their cynicism! Now they put in their columns everything they used to say over beer at the bar. People read them and know all they know. More and more, reporters are stuck without a role. Because you can't play the city slicker when no one will play the rube.

I search for joy. I think of Dick Rosenbaum's New Yorkers at the '80 GOP convention. Rosenbaum, a Rockefeller loyalist, was trying to keep his liberal delegates' spirit alive. Suddenly, the big boisterous California delegation started a rolling chant. "Ray-*gun*, Ray-*gun*," they shouted, and then, at the end, "Olé!" Rosenbaum signaled his troops: the next time California started with "Ray-gun, Ray-gun" the New York delegation answered, "Oy vey!"

No rolling chants here. The delegates this evening are proper, businesslike, tailored. And these are Democrats. It is a painful thing to see politics become neat and tidy, instead of the big drunken slob it was when we were kids.

I see Maureen Dowd and Frank Rich of *The New York Times*, sitting quietly together in a long row of chairs. They are watching things with a kind of look on their faces, the not-quite-unconscious look of a sophisticated boomer couple waiting for *Guys and Dolls* to begin. What I think I am seeing is Boomer Irony, the detachment that saves the soul. You hope.

"I'll give you a quip if you give me one," she says. She tells me Frank's knowledge of conventions is derived almost exclusively from the movie *The Manchurian Candidate*. He is smiling in a glazed sort of way and looking at the ceiling, as if he were thinking Is that where they keep the snipers? I make a note to read their column closely.

I am taken with a sense that we are all acting out the fantasies of our youth. That just as Bill Clinton met John Kennedy in the Rose Garden that day, and puberty and ambition hit him at the same moment—and what a wallop that must have been—that that's when he decided, as children from troubled homes do, to "become someone." He met the person he would become, and is now acting it out. The journalists who as children saw John Chancellor being carried off the floor of the Chicago convention in '68—they are here because they decided back then that they too would, as adults, bring America the truth, be pummeled for their pains and keep their composure, publicly. And the delegates are acting out political happiness, and caucusing the way Mayor Daley and Mike DeSalle used to, in the middle of the floor, with people leaning in from the edges to hear. But you know that inside that huddle, in the exact center of that power, is a guy saying, "Do they have that $19.92 deal at dinner too, or is it just lunch?"

There is disappointment here, a palpable disappointment. The delegates—the more conscious ones, anyway—think: This is phony. We are acting. This is unauthentic. I didn't expect this moment to feel so thin and derivative. I thought it would be one of the great moments of my life!

Here's the problem: When Jack Kennedy was being Jack Kennedy he was—Jack Kennedy. When Bill Clinton is Jack Kennedy, and I, his delegate, cheer him on at least in part for the benefit of the cameraman from NBC who is in my face and will not leave, who is here to record my unselfconscious joy, I am taking part not in a convention but in somebody's unwell psychodrama. I am caught, helplessly trapped in the web of someone's neurosis! I am a walk-on in a crazed and inauthentic drama! And this, *this* is modern democracy.

And the reporters, the men and women who as boys and girls wanted to be Mike Wallace and Chancellor and Cassie Mackin. The poignant thing is that when they were kids Wallace and Chancellor and Mackin were big, they were the franchise. There's no franchise anymore, or rather there are thousands of franchises and thousands of reporters and outlets and cables and dishes. Here you are reporting

live from the floor of the convention and—you're not even important anymore! You're just part of the stage set, walking around with
your little headset on, feeling like a walk-on! And if some portly
full-Cleveland-wearing boss—wait, there are no more bosses, no one
wears a full Cleveland anymore!—has you thrown off the floor, no
one will notice! No one will care!

A few days later I am on the phone with Dowd. We are talking
about what we heard at the convention and I am thinking, as she
speaks, to tell her that I'd spent four days looking for the phrase or
word that would bubble up from the arena and become the famous
phrase of the convention. Something like "Ohio Passes!" or "Mr.
Speaker, give us back our delegation!" And I found the phrase and
it was "Virginia Beach, Virginia, you're up next." From C-Span. It was
to be the sound of the Republican convention a month later. It will
be the sound of the conventions of '96.

Maureen is talking about what she has discerned is the new
communications approach of the Clinton-Gore ticket, a decision to
wrap their rhetoric in tales of personal trauma, and in a kind of touchy
feely "I'm okay, you're okay" tenth-step psychobabble.

Maureen has a kind of low-affect chuckle when she locates something like this. She loves the false, especially when it is not untinged
by the disgusting. She is like a scout who comes upon a gross brown
glob on the clean moss of the forest floor; she wants to pierce it with
a stick and hold it up for all the children to see.

She reads me Al Goreisms on the chance I may say something
usable, i.e., something she thinks but cannot say because she is the
reporter of the piece and not an actor in it. As she speaks, as she reads
the things Gore says, I think of a conversation I'd had earlier in the
day with Lisa.

Lisa is my best friend, a brilliant wonderful person who has been
my friend since we were college guest editors at *Mademoiselle* magazine. We have been calling each other to share disgust and delight

for twenty years. This morning she called to share both at the morning talk shows.

"Did you see Roger Ailes on *Today?* He was evil and gleaming like a fat little devil as he did his little devil-spin. 'The Democrats may be unified, but it's too bad they had to leave out Jerry Brown and abandon a whole sector of their party to achieve it.' Squiers was with him, Bob Squiers. He did devil-spin too. With Bryant Gumbel, an-chor-devil."

Lisa is laughing. It's too small-time to be evil, it's just everyday spinshit, she says, but—in the cutaway she thinks she saw the devil behind the camera with his little ears poking up.

Maureen mentions someone in politics whom we both know to be a bad fellow, and I come awake. "Is he a devil, do you think?" I ask.

She snorts. "Not big enough. He buys Satan's cigarettes."

—

In midtown there was a media party to celebrate a political book. I wandered in, congratulated the author, said hello to people I knew.

"How do you like being a reporter?" said the journalist Ken Auletta.

I said, "It's fine, but it's funny, you walk up to delegates with your pad and your pencil and your credentials and say, 'Can I ask you a few questions?' and you see in their eyes this immediate war between vanity and prudence, between their desire to be interesting and their desire not to die. Because they're not naïve. They know who we are."

"Who are we?" he says.

"Oh, you know. The license to be mean."

"At least we *have* a license!" he says merrily, and walks on.

—

On election night I went to watch the returns at the home of Bob and Edith Bartley, in Brooklyn Heights. Bob runs the editorial page of *The Wall Street Journal*, was a supply-sider, a winner of the Pulitzer Prize for his independent, against-the-grain work. He and his band made ideas sing. Now fifty or so conservatives are gathered in his home to see the era end.

It should have felt strange to be in New York on an election night, after working in the '84 and '88 campaigns. But in '84 I spent election night on the outside, in a small party in suburban Virginia; in '88 I was with the Bush campaign in Houston, but the boys were in the hall feeling good and talking loud, and I stayed in my room talking to friends in New York on the phone. Now, in '92, I am on the outside with serious conservatives in New York and finally, on an election night, feel at home.

I had traveled over in the crowded car of a friend, a jolly journalist who was, this night, not so sad to see people in Washington who had patronized her become official losers. Do you think Bush is glad he extended unemployment benefits? she asks. She had missed part of the era, writing about it and not being in it, and now it was over. And she still had a job.

The talk in the car was like dialogue from *The Women.* "What about so-and-so, what's her life, does she have a husband?" asked a writer. "No," said an editor, "she has other people's husbands." I leaned over laughing and the editor patted my arm. "We call that a witticism up here in New York," she said pleasantly, in the same tone my son takes when he imitates a teacher. *And this is a robin. Do we see the red on its wings?*

—

When I walked into the Bartleys' house the first person I saw was Midge Decter, the essayist who won the admiration of many when, after Soviet Communism fell, she actually closed down the anti-Communist committee she chaired. We saw each other and put out our hands. "How do you feel?" I asked soberly.

"Liberated," she snapped.

I laughed and took her hand. "God, me too."

We no longer have to defend the stewardship of those who did what we asked them not to, no longer have to split the million hairs we split each day over questions of loyalty to everyone and everything—to the president, to a movement, a philosophy, a party, to people who had been good to us who later did bad things, to people who were never nice to us who fought the good fight, to young kids on the way up and old friends floating in the ether.

We can say anything now. We can try to determine a worthwhile truth and then say it. Freedom. The feeling of freedom pervaded the gathering, which became so loud that everyone missed the network projections, and no one knew who first announced Clinton the winner. They didn't care. They weren't sad. They had been liberated.

—

A presidential inauguration is a colorful pagan ritual, a celebration of and for the city of man, and why not? The city of man is a pretty wonderful place, or so it would seem on a bright, crisp day when the signs and symbols of man's oldest, greatest democracy strut before its citizens.

I am sprawled on the couch like a teenager, my feet on the Conrans trunk we use as a coffee table, the trunk that contains old papers—letters, drafts of articles, pictures of my family and a grinning president. I haven't opened it in two years. It is packed too tight and the top has bubbled, and when my son puts a glass of chocolate milk on it the glass falls over. I haven't opened the trunk in years because I don't want to see the chocolate stains. I sip a Pepsi and surf, looking for the best picture and audio.

One should approach the inauguration of a president as one approaches a Broadway show, with the same good-natured suspension of disbelief. It should not detract from the day to know it represents what Dr. Johnson called a second marriage, the triumph of hope over experience. In fact, to know that sharpens the poignancy. Man is a hoping animal; that's why when he gets up in the morning he looks out the window.

We are adults, have seen a bit of history, have few innocent assumptions about man's attempts to use government to improve his lot and advance the good. I think what Michael Novak thinks. Early in '93 I had run into the great social philosopher, who had just come from a room full of energetic friends of Bill Clinton who were busy planning Camelot. As Michael stood and watched them I joined him and said, "What do you think." He smiled and shook his head and said that seeing so much hope gave him a sharp sense of the tragic.

All man's wishes are broken on the wheel. And anyway—he didn't say this but I think he meant it—the problems of our country derive more from a spiritual crisis than anything else, and the Clinton people are not inclined by training or temperament to know this. In any case, many of them would not know there is little that government can do to solve it.

But maybe it's good to start out on such an adventure not knowing what is not possible. I don't know if it's true that ignorance is bliss, but I do think it keeps your energy level up. It keeps you trying.

—

All morning on inauguration day the phone rang. *Are you watching? What do you think of her hat? Call me after the speech and tell me what you think.* The Republicans who call are ironic and detached. My family, my sisters and brother, who as children watched Academy Awards shows and moonshots together, take the tone they've always taken at such events, and assume I share it, which I do. "Isn't it nice," says Patty. Yes, it is.

Kathy calls and says, "I always love these new beginnings. Do you think Clinton's cute? He's like a Parent-Teacher president in the suburbs, don't you think?"

I laugh. Yes, he's so eager. It's nice to have a president who seems fully awake, who'd wear a bomber jacket to the mall.

This is my family: they have a lot of Republican impulses in them and they feel personally connected to Bush, but they are Americans of the old school, and wish their president well. My mother has written Clinton a letter of support. Uncle Patrick calls to tell me that he too has written Clinton. "I said, 'God bless you in your work. We are all praying for you.' "

Almost everyone I knew that inauguration day hoped Bill Clinton would govern well and thrive in the process. They were patriotic enough to wish him luck, realistic enough to know he'd need it. The Democrats had earned their joy. After twelve years in the executive wilderness, if their joy that day was punky, or grated—well, tough. I don't remember we were always so gracious. And anyway, this inauguration day may be the last unalloyed happiness the Democrats will know for four years.

—

This is the way, in January '93, I saw it:

If Clinton plays a serious game—if he detaches himself from the demands of his interest groups and begins to speak of individual and not group rights; if he cuts capital gains, if he does a Nixon-to-China on values and sides with the people against Hollywood and Time Warner (it could work—they like him so much in Hollywood they'd listen), then the country will benefit from his leadership and the Democrats will have themselves a two-termer.

If Clinton plays a kid's game, caving in to the numerous demands of numerous pieces of his coalition, and accepting the government-is-the-solution assumptions of the woollier groups clamoring for change, he will fail. And the Republicans will roar back like a choochoo in '96, refreshed and recharged by four years in which they will—ahem—have reacquainted themselves with a fascinating country called the United States of America.

The Democratic House and the Democratic Senate have a Democratic White House with which to develop and pass new laws. Again, if Clinton stands up to the kind of people like the young Hill staffer who told *The Wall Street Journal,* "We just can't wait to start passing laws!"—if he thwarts their hunger for regulation and fights their antipathy to business—the country will be well served. And if not, the exact nature of what a modern Democrat is will be revealed: a confused and unknowing ideologue, still. Again, in the first case the country will benefit, as will the Republican party, for it will be forced to sharpen itself further in order to fight a worthy foe. And if the second case prevails, the country will take a momentary hit, and the Republicans will save the day in '96.

—

Four years ago I was there in the crowd in the cold. It was a bad seat, and I couldn't see. Now from a good seat in my living room I watch Bush sitting slumped. His chin approaches his chest as Clinton speaks. There is something good in Bush not being defensive about feeling bad. He is being himself in public, finally. He must still feel confused. Only eighteen months ago he was soaring, and the Democrats, sullen and resentful, were braced for another crash.

Only second-tier guys like Clinton rolled the dice, and they couldn't lose: it would give each of them a national platform, make them a national presence, increase their chances in the real race in '96. Not bad reasons to run. When Clinton told an interviewer that the day after the election he and Hillary woke up, looked at each other and started to laugh, you know he was telling the truth. They never expected it to happen. They didn't understand history better than anyone else.

—

As Clinton gave his inaugural speech I tried to listen to him, to stay with him, but my mind drifted.

For me, watching Clinton speak is like trying to watch soap operas. I've been trying to watch them for years because they're part of the culture, but I can never follow the story line, it seems to move so slowly, and the things that are said seem so airy. My mind drifts. Everyone's mind drifts when Clinton speaks. His words, phrases, thoughts, are so rounded, when every good thought has an edge, a sharpness that breaks through.

He is handsome and vibrant. My friend Wendy, who is twenty-three, came over inauguration night while I was watching TV, and when I clicked to a Clinton interview she looked at me and said, "All my friends think he's babe-uh-licious. So do I." It was the sound of a star being born.

But—something is wrong with Clinton's ego. All politicians have outsized egos, but with Clinton one senses a soft, doughy narcissism. The night he won the election he did a victory speech, and then he wouldn't leave the stage, insisting on walking around making fists and waving and showing the victory jaw. He even leaned down over the edge of the stage to touch the adoring crowd, and show more jaw.

Clinton's ego seems, to me, not big and strong but urgent and blubbery. I think of what Dorothy Thompson said in 1961 as she watched, from her sickbed, the Kennedy inaugural. "There's something weak and neurotic about that young man," she said, and though he was also other things, she was not incorrect.

—

I first met Clinton in December of '91, at a big meeting of mostly liberals who get together once a year to talk about politics and life. Our first night there, in the ballroom of a big hotel—I'd brought my mother, who was delighted at the chance to be surrounded by Democrats—there was a big dinner for all the three hundred or so attendees and their families. We sat at a table near the front. After dinner there were speakers—a movie executive spoke on the subject "Something That's Been Bugging Me Lately." It was pointed and funny. I felt someone looking at me from another table and turned. It was Bill Clinton. I looked at him, he looked at me. We nodded. He was listening to the speaker and thinking; he was also surveying the room to see who was listening and thinking. When the movie executive said one thing that had been bugging her was the high salaries paid to CEOs of ailing companies he took notes, scribbling intently. It was unselfconscious, or showy, or both. He wanted the speaker to know he took her seriously. He would also use this issue to his profit two months hence in New Hampshire, in the first big presidential primary of the year.

I was there in Hilton Head in part to get a sense of him, to take his measure. I thought he might be the Democratic nominee. As the head of the Democratic Leadership Council, a moderate Southerner who, I'd heard, was dynamic on the stump, it made sense.

Over a few days of beach walks and seminars I would see him—shaking hands outside the breakfast room, in the lobby on the phone, leaning against the wall, listening intently.

In the common area of the convention center where we held our seminars I saw him late one morning standing and talking to a group of adoring men in jogging suits. He was taller than most of them. They had known him for ten years, they were Democrats, and he was their hope. And Clinton didn't mind standing around talking about health care reform, welfare reform, politics, instead of playing tennis or golf. He loves it—a surprise in a politician because most politicians have some mastery of the arcana of public policy but few of them prefer such discussions to a quick nine holes.

I was asked to be one of the speakers at the big dinner to be held on New Year's Eve. Say anything you want, I was told, no more than fifteen minutes. The subject: "Sailing Uncharted Seas." What does that mean? I said. Anything you want it to, I was told. I spent a day writing and fretting. I am always nervous before I speak, in part because I am a public-speaking-phobe who managed to get through both high school and college without having to give an oral report. The first time since eighth grade that I stood and spoke in front of a group was May 1990, to a small gathering of IBM executives and their spouses. I was okay, no better. I've improved since, but the odd thing is that fifty speeches after the first, the level of nervousness is the same; it never diminishes.

"Don't worry," friends say, "people who aren't scared when they're up there don't do well." I never know if they say this because it is true, or because it is comforting. They probably don't know, either.

Five of us were to speak. Everyone was dressed up, and the ballroom was festive. I was to speak before Clinton. I had decided, the night before, that each day as we get up and put our feet on the floor and enter life we are sailing uncharted seas, so my subject would be: "Living." It would be brief and, because this is New Year's Eve, not about politics or policy, not about health care or the coming contest. I'd acknowledge who I am and then be a person.

When I was introduced I got up and they applauded nicely, and I told them that it was true, there were Republicans here, and we have been surreptitiously communicating with one another in code. When we say "Excuse me, where's the bathroom?" that's code for "I like

Dan Quayle." On the golf course, when one of us says "It's a gimme," that's how we say hi. We even picked Hilton Head as the site of the meeting because it's surrounded by bushes.

There was good-natured laughter, and my shoulders went down a little. It has occurred to me that one of my functions when I'm surrounded by those whose politics are generally of the left—at a seminar or a dinner party—is like that of a negro at a 1950s liberal cocktail party: I am an opportunity to show how broad-minded they are.

I cleared my throat and plunged in:

There are rules about sailing through life, simple ones. Be good to your crew, throw back the small fish, keep your hull clean. Scrape off the barnacles, but don't be rude about it, and if you don't have to scrape them off, don't. They just want to go for a ride too.

Remember who you are. On her maiden voyage the *Queen Elizabeth*, pride of the Cunard line, was steaming across the Atlantic when another liner appeared, came closer, and sped past. The liner's captain radioed his regards, and pointed out that the *Queen Elizabeth* is a bit of a slowpoke. The captain of the *QE* radioed back, "No, it's just that a real lady never travels in fast company." Be who you are, and have style.

Navigate by the stars, which are fixed and unchanging as the truths we were taught in childhood, truths which, like the stars, are unlikely to let you down.

As you live and work each day with your crew, try not to put too big a burden on them and yourself by pursuing the relatively modern notion that one ought to be happy. Jimmy Breslin was on TV last night, on C-Span, and Brian Lamb asked him, "Are you happy?" And Breslin was nonplussed. "We weren't put here to be happy," he said. He is Irish and Catholic, and no doubt knows that there are really only two moods you can rely on in life, anxiety and depression. But the key is to choose anxiety over depression—

choose scared over blue, nervous over sleepy. It's the more awake and so more hopeful choice.

We put a lot of pressure on ourselves and our kids thinking we have to be happy. I believe we should be told, when we are young, that we were put here to be depressed weirdos. If you think that and you wake up happy anyway, you'll think happiness is your tic, your own form of neurosis, and you'll trust it and have faith it will continue.

And don't try to be normal. I used to spend a lot of time in search of normal. Then Kathy Van Winkle, my best friend in high school, told me, "Normal is a cycle on your washing machine." I found this helpful. I don't even know why. I don't even know what it means.

Finally, as you sail, ponder the fish, and their magic. Children remind us of magic because that is what they see. They think magic is real. My son asks why the lights go on and I tell him about currents and circuitry and then I say, "Do you understand?" And he says, "Is it magic?" And, you know, I guess it is.

But the fish. On earth is man, and men and women look alike, no matter what their differences. Man is, always, the featherless biped. But below the waves in the vasty deep all the living things look so different, so rich and various. Fish the color of neon, octopi, giant crabs, fish that look like flying saucers—and way down deep the newer forms of life that have been discovered, like the giant pods that undulate in the currents, staring out into the darkness.

I go to the aquarium and the Museum of Natural History with my son, and we stare at the fish and the underwater creatures. And it seems to me they are like metaphors for man, for our virtues and failings; they "act out" what we are. The squid who rustles things up and then shoots ink to cover his escape; the kindly, intelligent porpoise; the stingray, elegant and sleek, with a deadly sting; the dutiful dolphins, who swim together in peace but can, when forced, pound to unconsciousness a hammerhead shark; the deceptive bubblefish, the innocent angelfish, the huge whales, powerful and impressive in spite of the fact that they don't really have much of a personality.

They are not only strange and wondrous, they remind us of how vivid life is, how full of possibilities. As if it's supposed to be. As if—Peggy Say would see Terry Anderson again, as if Yeltsin would wave the flag of free Russia from the steps where Lenin stood, as if a war could be swift and relatively bloodless, as if your friend could run for president.

This has been a great year for As If, and may it continue in this new year of our Lord, 1992, as we sail on together, aware of the magic of the sea and all its promising As Ifs. . . .

They applauded, and my mother waved. As I took my seat, Clinton congratulated me. "I feel the same way about New Year's as you do, I started coming here every year to hide from it. I'd stay home, put my feet up, watch the ball drop and get the blues. So I started coming here." He laughed. I realized: that's why I'm here, that's why most everyone is here, to escape the weight of "Auld Lang Syne."

Clinton's was the big and final speech of the evening, and when he was introduced he got a standing ovation.

He delivered an anti-Reagan-Bush rafter shaker that by the end had the crowd on its feet. He had notes, but barely referred to them. I realized: this is what will soon be his stump speech. We're going to be hearing this on "The Road to the White House" for the next few months.

The speech wasn't just good—pointed, and delivered with passion—it was, in its policy content, inherently moderate. He spoke about the family in a way any conservative could support, talked about how we're forgetting our children, the welfare system has to be redrawn and revamped, it's time to track down deadbeat dads. . . .

I thought: the guy's a natural. At the end, after the last ovation, I thought to myself that twice before with my own eyes I have seen great natural politicians: John Kennedy, when I was a little girl as his brown hair whizzed by in a cavalcade in Mineola, Long Island, and Ronald Reagan, the day I met him at the 1972 Republican National Convention and, as a college journalist, asked him what's wrong with liberalism. ("Well, it just doesn't work!") And now I have seen the third.

Reagan was great in part because he believed, understood and could persuade; Kennedy was great because he was a natural star. And this one—well, this one will bring back the word "charisma." He will be modern, and have charm.

You can move a country's heart with charm, you can use charm to achieve your purposes, but charm isn't a purpose, it isn't a belief, it can't tell you where you want to go; it can only help you get there.

I had a hunch: this man does believe in something. He believes in his charm. He believes in himself. He believes in his destiny.

—

The next time I saw him was seven months later, the following June, when he was campaigning in New York in the primary. He was to give a speech about foreign policy at a big hotel, and I wanted to see him again to see if anything had changed. As he scribbled at the dais before he was introduced he surveyed the room. When he saw me he nodded. The speech was long, diffuse; I remember only one thing: "I want to be the first president of the twenty-first century."

After the applause, after he left the dais, he crossed the room and put out his hand.

"Good to see you, Governor."

He nodded, asked how I was, asked, God bless him, after my mother.

There was a woman standing near us, watching closely. Her mouth was open. As he walked on she said to no one, "What is this, know your enemy?"

The last time I saw him was a few weeks before he was sworn in as president, at Hilton Head again, and everything now was different. Last year he was the dynamic man in the jogging suit, this year he was a silver nimbus floating through the room. The meeting was big, too big, fifteen hundred people, and there was a new self-consciousness. Two days in I was standing in the back against the wall, watching a panel, when I felt someone beside me. It was Clinton, watching the speaker and sipping coffee. He stood so close, our arms touched.

"Hi, Governor, how are you doing?"

"Well, get up each morning and put one foot in front of the other and just figure, keep goin'."

I tell him from what I've seen he's doing everything fine, it's a good transition.

"Thanks. Had a guy come to me the other day, said he was a Christian clairvoyant. Told me I'm gonna be as good a president as Dwight Eisenhower."

I can't tell from his face what he thinks of that, but he's smiling.

"What did you say?"

"I said, 'Well, sir, if you feel that is a good outcome I hope you pray for it.' "

We laughed and looked down. Clinton is a likable man, endearing even. He's like a friend of yours who maybe isn't the finest person you know but who's involved in a big endeavor, a very important endeavor, and who is trying hard to make it work. If I were a pundit I'd never go to the White House to see him, never go near him, because I'd never be tough enough on him afterward. This may be why he has pundits in so often. Anyway, the particular quality of effortfulness he has is endearing.

—

By the summer of '93, six months into his administration, I thought Clinton was over, a one-termer; I wrote down my thoughts, and wondered if, by '94, I'd feel different. I don't. I know it's too early to say it but—he's a four-year president.

A host of reasons. The voters remain, I believe, in a hiring-and-firing mood; they wanted to fire Bush and, having decided Perot was a screwball, hired the next viable candidate. They gave him 43 percent of the vote, wished him well and watched. I think they gave him about six months to show his stuff. In the first few months there were the famous messes—Zoë, Kimba, Lani, the homosexuals in the military flap, the foreign-affairs missteps, Vincent Foster. Then, later, Les Aspin and Bobby Inman. But more important than any of these, it seemed to me, was Clinton's first budget, unveiled early on when everyone was watching, and full of deep-fried crusty Grade A oinker. It was amazing. The day he was elected nobody went to the polls thinking, I hope our next president gives us higher spending, higher taxes, a bigger government and a lot more pork." Nobody voted for that in 1992, and yet that is what this adroit politician gave them. And—again, with everyone watching—it revealed a mind-set, it showed his assumptions, his understanding of the reality in which he is immersed.

I know he has three years to turn it around. He won on NAFTA, and he may win some sort of health care bill. The other night in his 1994 State of the Union speech he happily appropriated what have long been Republican issues, speaking with feeling on crime and values. People said he looked good, and I agreed. (In fact, it struck me that he is a better actor than my old boss Mr. Reagan—thoroughly engaged by the text, emoting with ease, showing that jaw, those glistening eyes. I can't tell you how much I enjoyed, in the days after the speech, telling Democrats, "Your guy, he's just—an actor!" It was fun. Made 'em crazy.) He is radiating a greater sense of competence.

But it won't save him. It was said of the Hapsburgs that their rule consisted of despotism tempered by sloppiness. Clinton's first year showed demagogic impulses tempered by ineptitude. My hunch: it won't make people feel better as he grows more capable, it will make them more anxious. And this, I feel, is connected to an unease about him that was there when he was elected, and that has not diminished but grown: they think his impulses are not toward truth-telling. They think he's an operator. They don't think of him as an honest person; they have a sense that he really is slick Willie. The Arkansas state trooper story, the Whitewater scandal, if it is that: they didn't create the unease, but they underscored it. And soon enough there will be a foreign policy challenge that is dramatic, and possibly frightening, and the unease will be underscored again. It won't go away.

So I think it won't work, and too bad, too. The country could use a good president. This is a big moment, America after the forty-year war with Communism is reconsidering itself. A president who could have wrenched his party out of its bad old ways—a president who could have questioned the system, considered new ways, respected the contribution of business and its needs, who would have had skepticism toward the idea of higher taxes solving things, who would have looked honestly at the entitlements—who would, in fact, have looked at that word, "entitlement," and considered what it has come to mean in our society—that president really would have been "the first president of the twenty-first century."

An operator like Carville might say, "Sure, if we'd gone down those roads we might have done some good, but they'd cart us out of here on a gurney in four years."

Maybe. But four years from now Clinton will have done no good, and he'll still be carted out on a gurney. (I happen to believe we're in for a slew of four-year presidencies, and that's not necessarily bad. Sooner or later someone will figure out you can walk out a four-year hero instead of a four-year bum.)

A note on political prognostication. We all know people who make too much of single events, who come to conclusions too quickly and announce, "That Pete Wilson speech on abortion, he's finished now." Young kids in politics sometimes do this because, why not? If they're right they're brilliant, and if they're wrong, hey, they're kids. But grown-ups know that one shouldn't as a rule allow single events to inspire dramatic pronouncements if for no other reason than the fact that life isn't that orderly. Life, like politics, is a big interesting mess. It's hard to call. A smart man I know, a businessman, once told me, as he spoke of a painful personal trial, that the important thing to remember when you have a problem is that reality isn't a painting. It isn't a static and unchanging canvas on the wall of a museum. Life is dynamic, the mural is full of movement—the wind blows, a central character leaves the frame, an unexpected group walks onto the canvas, leaves fall.

"As you consider your problems and their solutions, don't fix on the static picture," he said. "Just keep watching the movement, and figuring out what it means. Opportunity, changed circumstances. And maybe tomorrow you'll be in the picture."

Life be a strange old dog, and you always have to be open to surprise. Harrison Salisbury once wrote a great column in which he said, simply, Expect the unexpected. Be open to the idea that Stalin will make a deal with Hitler, that the wall will fall. Be open to the idea that a blowhard like Zhirinovsky will enter the stage, that Korea, which played a dramatic and surprising role in our history forty years ago, will, after long slumber, play such a role again.

But some things are predictable and have an unstoppable dynamic. When Bush rescinded his tax pledge, that day Bush was over. And he was over not only because he had gone back on his central pledge of '87 and '88—the informing pledge, the one that said, "I'm not an old-style liberal Republican, I'll hold the line as Reagan did"—but because in going back he signaled that higher taxes, higher spending and bigger deficits would continue, which threw a cold blanket over an already shivering economy, which, soon enough cooled further. So Bush was over, and the way I see it Clinton is over. Life just doesn't stop being interesting.

—

A talk with a friend in Congress. He asks what I'm thinking about, I tell him the above and he says, "My gosh, I had a conversation just like that yesterday. About Clinton, what I can't figure out is this: Is it that he's smart and has no philosophy at all? Or does he have a philosophy, a real North Star, and his party is in the way?"

I said I thought that if Clinton has, inside him, a real and fully thought out philosophy, then anyone as verbal and talky as he would have let it slip by now; he would have been incapable of not sharing.

Clinton seems to have a general philosophy—a kind of emotional liberalism. But the particulars aren't there, or if they are, they flow only from feeling, and manifest themselves in a moral posturing that may be personally satisfying but which leaves his audience hungry for more—for logic, for "what follows."

We must care about one another, we must include all segments and groups within our society, we must protect our environment. Yes, we must. Now tell us what philosophy, what logic, what shrewd long view you'll use to effectively care, include, protect.

—

Recently I listened to Carl McCall, a youngish comer in Democratic politics in New York—he is now state comptroller and wants to be governor. He was talking about our moral responsibility as a society to tolerate and accept homosexuals, and to understand the needs and realities of children who come from painful backgrounds and who become sexually active at a young age.

We all agree with his predicate: We must be tolerant and kind to one another, we must care about children reared in sadness.

But from that beginning he goes to That's why the rainbow curriculum in the schools is good, that's why schools giving condoms to twelve-year-olds, whether their parents approve or not, is good.

As I listen, it occurs to me that his political thinking is illogical (if I care, then I have the answers) and his way of communicating it manipulative (if you don't agree with my answers, you don't care). He is thinking emotionally. He is thinking the way men used to accuse women of thinking. This, it occurs to me, is what modern liberalism has come down to. "I care about the feelings of homosexuals, therefore books espousing their lifestyles should be read by your ten-year-old." And, "I care about children reared in deprivation, that's why giving them birth control is a good idea."

After listening to McCall I speak to a friend, a smart, thoughtful liberal. Why, I ask her, are modern urban liberals so sure that their answer flows from their question? I mean why, if they're so concerned about tolerance, don't they conclude, for instance, that children should be reminded of the values of kindness and decency—and a good way to remind them is to talk about the moral bases and traditions of the West, the Judeo-Christian ethic? And why, if liberals are appropriately concerned about troubled teenagers getting pregnant, don't they talk to those kids about not having sex?

"Yes," she says, "but you're missing something. It's what I call Fucking as an Entitlement. Fucking has become another entitlement to urban liberals. They think twelve-year-olds are incapable of not doing it, that homosexuals are incapable of any restraint, that little girls are ready, period. They think you can fuck without remorse, without responsibility, fuck yourself to welfare, fuck yourself to death."

What a speech. And she means it.

"You know," I say, "I believe liberals care. But if they care about kids and AIDS and kids and pregnancy, why don't they support a system that stresses telling kids why not to have sex? I mean, why not try to give them some kind of armor, some kind of moral protection, instead of just abandoning them to what we tell them is uncontrollable biological imperative? Why can't we try to influence them to hold off?"

"They do that in their own homes, and think everyone else should too. It's private, between parent and child."

"Whoa. Then why isn't birth control and giving out condoms private, between parent and child?"

"Because fucking is an entitlement."

"No, seriously."

"A lot of these kids don't have parents, or functioning parents."

"Most of them don't. Heather's lucky if she has one mommy. But why are condoms the answer? 'I know you don't have a father, so here's a rubber.' It's so disrespectful. It's so dismissive of kids' hearts."

We commune in silence.

"Well," she says, "at least it takes other organs into account."

—

A thought. When I was a kid I thought conservatives held a dark view of human nature, a crabbed view. *Those welfare types just waste their money, he's poor because he doesn't work hard, you know how they are, we have to control them.* But now it's liberals who hold the dark view. *People can't make responsible decisions for themselves, they have no self-control, no self-respect, we have to control them.* It is so ironic that this is what liberalism has degenerated into. This is a country full of people trying to be decent, trying to give each other a break and hoping they'll get one. People trying to do right, live right. Funny that this crop of forty-ish post-yuppoid urban liberals doesn't see this, or respect it. Their parents did.

—

Some thoughts on Clinton, the age, and the media.

When you talk to people who are successful in television news these days you're often aware of an unspoken subtext to their conversation. It is "People don't respect the media the way they did when I started out, and neither do I. Which is embarrassing, because I'm a star. I have been yielded up and crowned by a system that is crass and corrupt. And yet I myself desire to do good, to do work that is a contribution and not an embarrassment."

The star—powerless to change things, and frustrated—secretly blames the producer, the producer secretly blames the executive producer, the executive producer secretly blames the president of the news division, who blames the president of the network, who blames (a) the affiliates, (b) the audience, (c) the dunderheads who own the network. Not necessarily in that order.

Many of these people are in therapy. I suspect a lot of them are trying to reconcile who they are with what they do. This is probably a fairly common theme in therapy these days.

Everyone knows the television network news divisions lost their standing, their place of high national respect, in the eighties, but not solely because cable came in and changed the realities. The real beginning of the end was Paddy Chayefsky's 1976 masterwork, *Network*, which by the eighties had fully sunk into the national psyche, providing not only the famous anthem "I'm mad as hell" but a new vision of those who give you the news.

By the mid-eighties, *Network* had gone from great movie to revealed truth. Its message was reinforced in 1987 in *Broadcast News*, when Holly Hunter barked intelligent ad-libs into anchorman William Hurt's telex.

Politically the long slide of network-news power could be traced in the rise of Reagan, who sailed to two terms over the correspondents' handsome heads. They disagreed with him on everything and could not stop him. Nor, twelve years later, can they keep Clinton from crashing. In 1968 Lyndon Johnson said, "If I've lost Walter Cronkite then I've lost the country." Twenty years later, when George Bush lost Dan Rather he won the election. (A week ago, staff members of *Entertainment Weekly* gathered to watch the debut of Rather and Connie Chung on the *CBS Evening News*. Someone said, "The set's different. Is the set different?" No one knew, because none of them watched it, or the other network news show. In the office they keep CNN on in the corner, sound low, like a constant, muted telegraph service. They look up when they hear a Mayday or an SOS.)

Sometimes I rue the diminution of network news power. They were, at least, the grown-ups of the game. And it's at least partly good to have powerful, relatively independent people on TV nattering to the nation, in part because their power helps break up and defuse other power centers in America. And diminishing power is, in general and as a rule, not a bad thing. Why shouldn't Tom Brokaw, elected by Arbitron, have as much power as Mark Hatfield, elected by Oregon? You can vote with your feet, the conservatives used to say about leaving high-tax states. You can also vote with your zapper.

Then I see something like what I saw this morning. The *Today* show. Bryant Gumbel did a live two-way with Senator David Boren, who had broken with the White House to fashion a compromise budget with another Democratic senator and two Republicans. All moderates, all grown-ups. Their idea is insufficient—it includes a series of tax hikes, though not as steep as Clinton's. Still, it ought to be discussed and, by thoughtful people, dissected.

Gumbel comes on, looks at Boren's round and sleepy face, and says, first question, You've said in the past that you want to support this president—how is it helping him to get into bed with senators from the other side?

Nothing like starting the day with a little elevated discourse. And at eight in the morning, just in time for the kids to get a lesson in comportment before they go to school.

It was so vulgar. He should have been picking his teeth. *Howya feel screwin' with the enemies of the people?*

You might say Oh yes, but he's a ridiculous person. Perhaps he is. But you know why else Gumbel asks questions that way? Because he thinks he's bigger than a senator and bigger—more famous, better paid, has lasted longer—than a president. So why shouldn't he be arrogant? Who is he supposed to respect, you? (I can hear the future Bryant Gumbel *Playboy* interview: "If I'm arrogant, then so be it, but I would argue that it's arrogance on behalf of the people." If my brother read it he'd look up and say, "Bite my shorts.")

—

An irony. There are people who say Ronald Reagan's presidency was delegitimized by the Iran-Contra scandal. But I think it was network news that was finally and ultimately delegitimized by that scandal. In the mid-eighties the television news shows aired, over and over, moving and dramatic stories about the plight of the American hostages in Iran. These stories built up and made inevitable public pressure to do something, anything for their release. Nightly the steady drumbeat—why is the administration failing to act? And then, when the administration did something, anything—and made one of its worst blunders—the networks blithely castigated the administration for an unseemly and unhelpful obsession with the hostages, and doing anything to get them out.

And the people of the country noticed. They're not stupid. They noted that once the scandal blew there were no more TV pieces about the poor hostages because the poor hostages weren't the story anymore. The jerks in the White House were the story.

It also may partly explain why the American people have become essentially bored with TV network news, with the predictability of it. It wasn't just Rather and Brokaw who lost numbers, it was all the network news shows—and people were going elsewhere not just because options were available but because they wanted options. But there's something else happening. My generation, the aging boomers, the famous basketball in the python, the demographic king—so many members of my generation are tired of the news. They don't watch it because it doesn't seem to be what's happening. *N.Y.P.D. Blue* is happening, Helen Mirren is happening, Letterman is happening, HBO is happening, even reruns of *M*A*S*H* are happening. But local and network news shows now seem more and more like an old show you've already seen and from which you learned nothing. (There was a John Prine lyric on an album many of us grew up with, Bette Midler's first album, that anticipated this. It was from "Hello in There," a song about the thoughts of a woman in late middle age. She says, "And all the news just repeats itself / Like some forgotten dream that we've all seen." It had then, and still does because I just got it out and put it on, a haunting quality.)

Part of it is simply the accumulation of years. We've watched thirty years of news shows. There are only so many times you can hear "A Brooklyn shootout ends in tragedy," and want to look up. And part of it is more metaphysical. Thoreau said of the daily news that it is essentially uninteresting because if you are familiar with a phenomenon, you are familiar with its numerous applications. If you're familiar with the principle that fire destroys, it's not really news that a barn burned down. (Unless, of course, it's your barn, in which case the "news" is personal tragedy, family crisis and, perhaps, How do I handle the sufferings of Job?)

And part of it is maturity. This is what I think my generation increasingly knows: the news is just a recitation of the daily "facts" of a flat and foolish world. The eternal things—the eternal mysteries—are more interesting. The day-to-day blends into larger themes, and it is the themes (the self-destructive impulses of man, the odd way individuals have of repeating the same mistakes, man's search for meaning) that are compelling. And they find better, more interesting treatment in books, on the stage, in old movies, than they do in the oeuvre of your local anchors, of Michelle and Ernie and Chuck and Sue.

—

At the start of the last century the idea of the news was itself still news. When, in the mid-nineteenth century, Darwin's work challenged the teachings of the Bible, creating a major intellectual crisis for thoughtful believers, it was exciting that you could read about it in the daily press. You could also wake up to reports of the carnage in the Crimea, and see it given a certain context, a certain meaning in, interestingly enough, a poem printed in the papers and inspired by a report in the London *Times* about the charge of the Light Brigade. The idea that big things could happen and you could read about it the next day or a few days later—that was still relatively new in human history, and so exciting. You could wake up into a day empty of history, and the facts in the paper would fill it up.

A hundred years later, in the middle of this century, we found something even newer and more splendid in televised news, televised events, a box that brought live pictures of your country, your president, right into your house. It must have been exciting to see the first Murrow *See It Now*, in which he pointed to two monitors, one showing, live, the waves of the Atlantic Ocean and the other the waves of the Pacific. Young Don Hewitt sat there with his hands on the monitor switches, as if he were assisting in some kind of creation. The oceans rose up for your inspection and you were sitting there in the living room in your Bermuda shorts, with Hewitt—or, as a wry young journalist would later call him, God—performing the miracle with his hands.

But now, almost half a century later, we think: That's not news. That's just pictures.

But also, in a sense particular to this era, the news is ultimately frustrating because fewer of us have a sense that we can change it. An abused baby is taken to a city hospital and will, they say, survive; you'd like to be its foster parent for a few months and hold it close, because you've been a parent and know what a difference simple physical tenderness makes—even if it becomes only an unconscious memory it might, someday, be helpful in the pursuit of other forms of succor. But by the time your request got through the bureaucracy the two-year-old would be four, and lost. You'd like to do something about crime, but what really can you do beyond "define deviancy down," as Moynihan puts it, and put a NO RADIO sign on your car window. You'd like to change the system, but the courts and those who use them will not let you. The most active thing your mind can do about justice is have fantasies about it.

In my city, in any big American city, this is just one more way that you are a member of the ironically disfranchised. You're a member of the middle or upper middle class, you are educated, are capable and have many interests. You are, moreover, the taxpaying backbone of this city—you *support* it—and yet you are excluded from its power centers. Union leaders run the town, City Hall runs it, the political grid runs it—and none of them want you messing with their city. You could gain power as a journalist, but you're not a journalist. You are locked out of power, which is funny, since you provide the money without which the people who've locked you out can't operate.

All in all, a good reason to stay home and watch reruns of *M*A*S*H*. At least remembering how much you liked it, feeling that old warmth is, since you're feeling something that feels good, "news."

—

I still think not the most important but the most memorable story of Bill Clinton's first year was his famous LAX haircut.

When I was first told about it on the phone, by a reporter breathless with amusement, I thought: Big deal. Presidents are busy. If I were president and had gone awhile without a haircut and I could get one on Air Force One, I'd do it. Good economic use of time, get there and get a trim at the same time. Only problem would be turbulence, hit an air pocket over Omaha and you could wind up looking like Boy George.

"No, no," said the reporter who called me, "he did it on the runway at LAX."

"Oh." (So?)

"He sat," explained the reporter, "in Air Force One on the runway at LAX, and we all had to wait for fifty-five minutes while he got a cut and blow-dry!"

"Oh. He put out the press."

"No, no! You've forgotten! When Air Force One is on a runway the airport gets closed!"

Oh Lord, of course. Now I get it. Three runways were closed, planes were circling and 747s couldn't take off—all because meathead wanted a trim before the next town meeting with gangsta rappuhs.

How oafish. Putting everyone out like that. Later I learn about Christophe, the two hundred dollars, the personal-services contract. What would the press have done to Ronald Reagan, or Poppy from Kennebunkport, if they'd done something so imperial, so ill-mannered? (Later still, we would all learn that no air traffic had, in fact, been diverted. But it doesn't matter, it's "true" forever anyway, as it will be "true" forever that George Bush didn't know what a super-market scanner was, when in fact a reporter simply made a mistake; Bush knew what a scanner was. But it will always be "true" that he didn't.)

As the days went by and criticism of Clinton mounted, I think I detected among journalists who had been supportive of Clinton a kind of survivalist class snobbery. They see him failing; they see the pallbearers coming over the ridge; they don't wish to get hit by the mud at the grave site. "Clinton isn't *my* fault, dammit!" They detach over issues of personal style. *It's all so Dogpatch! It's a redneck's wet dream, getting your hair cut on Air Force One. Watch it, I'm telling you, soon it'll be Fiddle and Faddle!*

This line is not completely new. *The Wall Street Journal,* a few months into the administration, likened the Clintons to a hillbilly couple. From the *Journal,* because it opposes Clintonism on principle, it was funny. ("Is it true, do you think?" asked a furrowed-browed essayist at a newsmagazine. "No," I said, "it's not 'true,' it's 'an insult.' It is true, however, that their sophistication is greater than their intelligence. They know how to use a mike, they just don't know what to say." He sighed with relief. A least they're not hillbillies.)

—

Some thoughts on class and the problems of comportment:

There is a thing in Clinton that I suspect elicits the unconscious sympathy of a lot of Americans. It is that no one taught him how to do things. He didn't have parents who taught him How To Do It. He had to learn by himself, through observation and imitation and through the promptings of instinct. When you learn that way you learn mostly by mistakes.

A lot of members of my generation have spent the first half of their adulthood learning how to do it. I don't mean the small silly stuff like which fork to use, I mean the more difficult things that have to do with relationships both professional and personal and what's the right thing to do or say or think. How to comport yourself in the world. How, for instance, to be warm and nonjudgmental with the new friends at lunch but not join in the gossip; how to protect yourself in various situations without becoming like your adversary; how to react when someone inappropriately says something wounding; what you have a right to ask of a boss or a teacher or a colleague, the difference between a fair sense of what you deserve and a snotty sense of entitlement; how to show thanks for a note, a boost, a party thrown in your honor. There are people born with an instinctive knowledge of these things, and I think their knowledge comes from a kind of grace. But most others grope and look around and wonder, Is this right? Am I doing this right?

An example. A woman I know, a lady of great attainment, was, at one point in her career, targeted for abuse by a well-known male colleague, who saw her as a threat. He was awful. He tried to undermine her with the boss and in the press; he was provocative in his comments to her face when others were in the room, and ridiculed her when she left. She suffered. In time circumstances changed, and she no longer worked with or near him. And when she sees him now on social occasions she smiles and pats his arm and says hello and sweetly accepts his kiss.

One day, talking to a friend of the lady of great attainment, I said, "Is she right to be that way with him? So nice to him after all he did?"

"Yes," said the friend, "she is."

"But—when you're so creamily nice to someone you know is bad, when you're dishonest to him and yourself about your true feelings, doesn't it sort of undermine your own integrity? And isn't it disorienting? He tried to kill you, so you kiss him. If you treat everyone the same nice way, don't you get confused, and seem less authentic to yourself?"

"First of all," says the friend, "she's a very nice woman. She actually tries to incorporate in her life the very decent values she was taught as a child. And one is, be nice, forgive. But she is also shrewd. She would never waste time disliking that jerk. She'd never delight him with the knowledge he'd hurt her. She'd never give her energy to hurting him. She just sails by. He's a fish she barely sees."

"A shark she barely sees."

"Exactly. So, Peggy, when you see someone who's not been nice to you, just smile and say hello and sail by."

This was the best advice on How To Do It I received in 1993. It reminded me of a saying someone told me a few years ago: When you think about your enemies you're letting them live in your head without paying rent. (The same person told me, When you worry, you're paying a deposit on trouble that may not be delivered.)

A thought: One of the American nation's first best-sellers was Ben Franklin's *Poor Richard's Almanac.* Chock-full of homey and practical advice. Maybe Americans, rejecting Europe's corrupt guidance, and living in a wilderness, always had an appetite for sage sayings and books of advice because that was the way they could learn How To Do It. Ben Franklin, Dale Carnegie, Norman Vincent Peale. This was always an unparented country. Maybe we all learned reading by firelight.

A lot of people learn how to act from religion. They go to church or read the Bible, and some of the things they absorb are "Do unto others . . ." "Love thy neighbor as thyself," "Let he who is without sin . . ." These are not only good moral guides, of course, they're good social guides.

But remember Lord Chesterfield's letter to his son? We need a new such guide, for young men and women whose ambitions about life—to seize it big, and right—were not anticipated or accommodated by their backgrounds.

Anyway, what I keep thinking when I see Clinton is what Pamela Harriman said: He had no one to guide him. I had met her at a lunch in '93, and asked her if Clinton was at all like her old friend John Kennedy. She said, "Oh, Jack was from an elite—Harvard, the British embassy, old Joe to guide him. Clinton had no one to guide him, he had to do it and learn it all himself."

I don't think young George Bush sat around at Andover reading Chesterfield. But he didn't have to. He had old Prescott Bush with his big bushy eyebrows, just in from the Senate, to show him, by example, How We Do It. How we old-line Protestants on the East Coast do it. Where you put the rug, how you knot the tie, how to react when the waiter is rude. And Bush had his mother shooing him out to the tennis court and teaching him, later, through a curt wave of the hand, Score, don't spike. Reagan didn't have a father to teach him but he had his mother's good-natured rectitude and ambition for her handsome son. And then in Hollywood they taught him the fork stuff.

I don't know if any of this applies to Bill Clinton and the haircut. But if he didn't know it wasn't the thing to do, he sure knows now.

—

Clinton, his beliefs and background, were one preoccupation that spring of '93. More important to me was a search to which I've referred, and about which more will be said. But there was a weekend that spring when a mild breakthrough occurred, for me, unbidden; a weekend when I knew that a kind of spiritual rebirth that was happening within me was changing the way I experienced the life around me, both the daily things and the special things.

It is hard to explain, but when I look back on this weekend in Washington I have a sense that it was informed by the idea of distances—a greater appreciation of certain kinds of distance, and a sense that other distances, some of them around me, were collapsing, enfolding.

—

The New York I left that Thursday afternoon in late April was cool and colorless, but the Washington I entered was blooming. When I arrived the trees were bright but incomplete; by Friday you could almost hear the buds burst. *Pop pop pop*, from Virginia to Maryland. Now it was Sunday morning. The dogwood and lilacs, the rhododendrons, white, pink and scarlet, had burst into sweetness and beckoning around the front doors of Northwest, across the lawns of Great Falls. Chevy Chase and Silver Spring were awash in their smell, Capitol Hill was alive with their color. It was angelic.

I was in Washington for three days, the purpose of which was fun, and getting a sense of Washington in the first spring of the Clinton era. I was staying with friends in Silver Spring, out far enough to be truly suburban.

Coffee and the *Post* on the porch. We pad around, clear our throats, tease Tom about the natty piping on his robe—with his sleek leather slippers and trim mustache, he looks like the cad in *Cass Timberlane*. A portable phone purrs, wicker creaks. Birds sing on the other side of the screen. If I put my hand through I could touch their wings.

—

When I was in my teens and twenties little in nature held my interest. All that perfect beauty (meadows in sunlight, hillsides ablaze) seemed insipid, or a rebuke—*Why can't you just relax and enjoy life?*—and I looked away. What interested me was people and their conversation, their dialogue. (A few years ago in the National Museum in Dublin I walked among dark, bland nature studies— *This is a hill. This is a hill in gay profusion. Any questions?* But then I turned a corner and saw the portraits. They were so alive with energy and tribute, rendered with such knowingness and soul. It was as if Ireland's artists were saying, Come on, only people are interesting, all the rest is just religion.)

But now this brilliance strikes me as a gift, a clue. It is orienting, like an old pirate map with North/South. I am heartened and surprised—for three days I have been heartened and surprised—by my delight. As I associate being transported in this manner with retired ladies tooling in the yard in floppy hats and stiff gloves, with a mental picture, in fact, of a stout gray lady shooing a bee and leaning back in satisfaction, her soiled hands curled on her khakis, I am startled, and try to imagine the lady being me, the compensation being mine. I bend into a rhododendron, feel its wet petals on my face, inhale.

In the bathroom upstairs I shower and dress. It is small and old, and the smell of soap and the thickness of steam cling and do not dissipate, even with the small creaky window opened wide. The curtain is thin lace, and moves gently. It is like 1957.

In the front yard I wait for my friends. We will go to an afternoon lunch and book party. I sit on the stoop and absorb. The toddlers in the house in back laugh and squeal in the pool. A car goes by. Someone is knocking on a door.

I am in my early–Katharine Hepburn suit—periwinkle blue, sleek slacks, broad shoulders, snug at the waist. It's like the suit she wore in *Woman of the Year*, when she says, "Hewwo, Daddy."

The car comes. Hugs, oohs. I rub Walter's back. As I hug Meryl our earrings collide. We're color-coordinated, she says. We run down directions. It is Safire's house we will journey to on this beautiful day.

In the car—we are writers, after all—I tell them the words of the morning have been "When lilacs last in the dooryard bloom'd," but Whitman's lament is not right for this day, and anyway I can't remember much, and there's no poetry in the house. The song of the day, on the other hand, is from the old Davy Crockett show with Fess Parker. "Green grow the lilacs all sparkling with dew."

Walter and Meryl begin singing and remember half the words, and

I can remember the last line: "And they changed the green lilac to the red, white and blue." None of us can remember why the song would have taken a patriotic turn.

We catch up. Meryl is doing a magazine piece on a journalist known, in her younger years, for her cutting and merciless profiles. The journalist is afraid that Meryl will do to her what she has done to others, and is attempting to disarm by showing her vulnerability, her fears and concerns. Meryl knows she's being spun; she also knows the journalist's vulnerabilities, fears and concerns are real, and even poignant. What should Meryl do, give the journalist a taste of her own Prozac, or show mercy? She will show mercy, to her credit and disadvantage. (The journalist, reading the piece three months hence and seeing she escaped in spite of the three unpleasant facts unavoidably included in the fifth graph, will get on the phone with her friends and say, "It's okay, but she's not really very—sharp, is she?" And the journalist's enemies will get on the phone and say, "What a puff, did she miss the headline or what?")

"Is it a right on Georgia? Is this Georgia coming up?" Walter is hunched at the wheel, peering over the dash.

I have been back to the White House, I tell them. It was so strange and touching. I walked the huge halls of the EOB and my heels on the tiles sounded just as they did eight years ago, that echoey sound. I was on the first floor—I was surprised how disoriented you get in that square building after just a few years—trying to find my old office. From down a hall I saw a door to a suite, and it was the right one, and as I approached I thought of the triumphant picture of Reagan that had been on the wall. When I walked in I looked. In its place was a gauzy, smiling picture of Hillary and Bill. I laughed.

A secretary—young, black, purposeful—looked up. "May I help you?"

"Hi. I just used to work here and wanted to visit."

"Oh, how nice."

"It's this office here. Can I look?"

"Sure. Nobody's in. It's Mrs. Clinton's task-force room."

"She's doing health care in here?"

"Yes."

I walked in. A long brown conference table and chairs. In the corner where my desk used to be there were file boxes, but this was my old air conditioner and this my old window and nothing had been painted. My old paint. I put my hand on the sill. I used to watch Reagan cross into the EOB from here. Someone put an oak pedestal in the office years ago, and it was still here. I kept a toy for Ben Elliott's children on top, a battery-operated ski lift on which little plastic penguins rose and fell.

I asked to see Ben's office, but was told I could not. The First Lady's chief of staff had it now, and she was holding a meeting. For a moment I thought, I could tell them Pat Buchanan had a lot of happy moments in that office, really ruin the karma.

The secretary asked my name, I told her, she asked me to spell it so she could tell her boss who had come by.

"Well, do come back again," she said pleasantly.

I smiled and said I'll no doubt be back. They always come back.

I found the speechwriters in a rutty warren of offices down the hall. David Kusnet, the chief speechwriter, was red-eyed with fatigue but sweetly said, "Come in." They were making do with three speechwriters (every modern president has had six) and they shared a few researchers with other offices. I thought: This won't work; the writers will tire and write something stupid and Clinton will say it and a round of "Blame the speechwriters" will begin. Kusnet knew this. I offered to write the president reminding him that this most important of offices must be fully staffed and treated well. (I wrote this to Sununu once. He called and told me the reports the speechwriters were being treated badly were the work of rumormongers who resented not getting jobs. It wasn't true, but I don't think he knew it. He didn't understand that denying writers something like mess privileges is denying them the chance to see and hear the reality of the place in which they work.) David smiled, explained the 25 percent staff cut the president is adhering to, said give it a try.

As I left I met an exhausted young man from the press office and asked if he was having any fun. His bearded face was thoughtful. "The way I see it," he said, "even when this place is pretty awful it's pretty great." He'll be okay.

—

We have left the highways now and drive through leafy streets. We talk more about what has become for me a preoccupation, thinking about being in your forties in the nineties.

I'd long thought thirty is the age of ambition, forty the age of fruition, but this doesn't feel like fruition, does it, it seems more like a settling in and a casting about. You're not making decisions now so much as living with them. And life seems so real and earnest.

On a tender spring day there are a lot of people with whom one wouldn't go straight into Oral Thinkpiece, but Walter and Meryl are intellectuals, and happily live in their heads. They like topics and are capable with them. And they like to talk about living not only because they think about it but because talking about living is a good distraction from the anxieties of life-at-this-second.

"In part it's the age," says Meryl, "where you know that if you haven't gotten married yet, you are probably not going to marry."

"Yeah, and that wasn't in the plan, that's not what you imagined when you imagined the picture of your future. It's also I think the first age when if you're married and it's not working you're stuck. The marriage seems dead but you don't have the assumptions we had in the seventies and eighties that divorce is definitely the answer."

"That 'This will fix it,' " says Walter. "It's also the age, when you first see with your own eyes and in a personal way 'when bad things happen to good people.' "

"You mean Meryl's friend who died of cancer."

"Yes, but also even down to seeing people who haven't been lucky in their careers, through no fault. They just didn't have any luck, and they're stuck."

"I think it is the age," I say, "of the first powerful reckoning about what works in your life and what makes you happy and what your purpose is."

We ride in silence.

"You know what else? Just to be shallow. You even have to finally figure out where you belong in the summer. Are you the Hamptons or the Litchfield County crowd or the Jersey shore, and if you're one of them, which crowd, which group, which one you won't tire of."

"And which one won't tire of you," says Walter.

"Yes! Where to make the sound investment."

"Well, I am up nights," says Meryl, "going over my life and driving myself crazy regretting things. This that I did wrong, this thing that didn't work out. And during the day I'm fine and I live my life and it's a good life, but then it's three A.M. and I wake up and start torturing myself—"

"Does it make you feel better to know others are up and anguishing too?"

"Mmmmm, no."

"How about some of them are saying, 'If only I'd done what Meryl did, why wasn't I more like her'?"

"Mmmm, okay, I like that one. Honey, this is Colesville coming up and it's a right. And left at the light."

"Can I do a last morbid summation?"

"Sure," says Meryl.

"At the dinner last night I sat next to Barry Diller and he said he wished someone had told him when he was in his forties that all the books that said 'This is the reaping, this is the joyous reaping of thirties effort' were wrong. The forties for him were difficult, and it made it worse for him to know it was supposed to be great. He looks like he's enjoying his fifties, though."

The dinner last night was the White House Correspondents Association dinner—huge, black tie, twenty-five hundred people in the Hilton. Vulgar and fun. I was with *Vanity Fair* at a bad table that gave us a lot of freedom to get up and walk around.

Donald Trump was with us, at the next table. A halo of sprayed hair, a face still round with subcutaneous fat. When we were introduced I looked into his eyes—small, bright, thoughtfree—and was surprised to think: He's crazy. He was seated next to a beautiful young woman named Vendela, who someone whispered is a famous model.

About an hour into dinner there was movement—someone leaving our table, Vendela joining us. She was composed but looked as if she'd endured something, like a swimmer. Trump, I was told, had spent the meal talking about her breasts and other women's breasts and who has good legs and who's probably good at sex. It was all so vulgar, so comically crass, that it was a surprise. People don't usually act so exactly like their reputations.

Elayne Boosler was the entertainment. She was funny, but seemed not to have been fully briefed on who this audience was. They're not exactly stuffed shirts—they like humor that pushes the edge a little and gives them a chance to give each other knowing looks. But they don't, two weeks after the fire and the dead children, enjoy witty references to Waco, and they don't use phrases like "get laid" when the president of the United States is up there on the dais. (At "get laid," which was part of a funny joke about John Tower, Clinton seemed to redden, and drew laughter by putting a hand in front of his face.) It was all part of—dare one say it?—the lowering of standards that continues to level our land, that we take for egalitarianism but which is really a corruption of that spirit. The egalitarian spirit wasn't supposed to translate into "Everybody, back in the mud."

Clinton spoke, not successfully. He ad-libbed a reference to Boosler's wild hair, saying, "She stuck her finger in an electric socket and that's how it got that way!" Mild groans. He made a reference to Waco, saying even Rush Limbaugh defended Janet Reno but that's just because at the hearings she was attacked by a black guy. At this, startled silence and oooaohs that were almost boooaoos. At the end he spoke heartily and approvingly of his administration, and his motives.

—

Clinton I see for the first time is like Carter, the same tone deafness, the same misunderstanding of the character of his office. Like Carter he is diligent and intelligent, but there is a lack of internal grace, a lack of inner elegance.

After a joke about his budget director, Leon Panetta, who a week before had indiscreetly told reporters that the president's initiatives are in real trouble, Clinton noted, to laughter, that Leo's a Catholic and I gotta remind him when not to go to confession! Then Clinton says Catholic again and makes another Catholic reference, and by the third time you kind of got the sense that Clinton has a little Catholic problem. He probably doesn't dislike Catholics, he's modern and so can't dislike anybody, but he is a Southern male who grew up in a somewhat Baptist culture, and no doubt he feels Catholics are— different. As in, they kiss rings and pray to Franco. They are dark like Mario Cuomo—like Leon!—and enjoy quoting Augustine while they stick the shiv in you.

—

We get to Safire's big white house on a friendly green street, walk in and are guided to the back by a handsome young man in a tux who deposits us in a sunny room that has been turned into a bar. Outside and below us, in the tree-lined backyard, a chattering of Potomac royalty, Journalism Division. I think of Tom Wolfe's Sherman McCoy walking into the benefit at the Metropolitan: "Those swimming teeth."

"You go first," I say to Meryl.

"What?"

"I'm afraid. You go, I'll follow unobtrusively."

She laughs, we descend and mingle, nod and kiss.

Lunch in the brilliant sun in the courtyard of the house, trees and bushes all around us. Nature is here again, holding up standards.

Beef, salad, cold salmon in a light cream sauce, white wine, thick bread. A happy murmur of voices. So bright. A network correspondent pretty as a movie star is wearing black sunglasses.

We talk at bright tables. To my right a stranger, a childhood friend of a friend, a soft-spoken doctor who is pleased and slightly intimidated. Me too, I tell him, and I've been here.

"This isn't really my world," he says. He tells me what he does, explains why he's in town. He is a researcher working in prostate cancer. Dole has been really great about speaking about his own experience, he says, "He's saved lives."

"Point out the luminaries for him!" says the lawyer to my left.

"Ah. Well, that is Charles Krauthammer the incisive columnist, and that's Hugh Sidey, we read him as kids in *Time*. Great writer, and a great man. There are the Shultzes, whom you met. He's proud of his new book, and should be if for no other reason than the size. What work! His wife is named Obie and is Irish. Katharine Graham of the *Post*, great lady of journalism, Walter Pincus of that paper. Maureen Dowd of the *Times*, who in the eighties changed political reporting in America, broadened the parameters, allowed sensibility in. Alan

Greenspan, who runs the Fed, as you know. Let's go ask him for money. Let's go say Hey, I could use a few dollars. Andrea Mitchell of NBC, made herself into a correspondent with real will and grit. Safire and the beautiful Helene, elegant lady. Evan Thomas of *Newsweek*, runs the Washington bureau. Leon Wieseltier of *The New Republic*, with the long white hair. I love to see him because he looks the way senators looked in the Civil War. He's very witty. Catherine Crier, formerly of CNN, now ABC. Lloyd Cutler, longtime Democratic party mover and member of Safire's lexicographic irregulars. Before, he was telling Bill the derivation of the term "bugger," which comes apparently from a nickname for Bulgarian and is connected to what he delicately characterized as what was rumored to be their favored form of birth control. Michael Beschloss, wrote the recent book on Bush's Soviet policy, Russian policy, with Strobe Talbott, now of the State Department."

"A lot of very accomplished people."

"Yep. And some of them are nice, or nice within this context, which is quite a context, *n'est-ce pas?*"

He laughs, and tells me more about cancer research.

Lunch over, we stand and say good-bye. People who've been sitting with someone interesting rise and busily seek out someone else interesting. All part of our need for stimuli, our desire to see and hear, connect, exchange. All part of being there. (If our mothers— ethnic, raised in the old America—were here they'd stick with the person they'd eaten with, afraid he or she wouldn't find new friends.)

In a bright cluster with bright people. Someone mentions a bestseller, *The Bridges of Madison County.* Sidey smiles and says, "You know, I never knew a photographer who didn't see himself like the photographer in the book—the most sensitive and silent, the most wonderful lover."

"What is it about?" says a writer. No one answers. I have read it but hate to let them know.

"It's about a woman who meets a man and falls in love and sleeps with him once and mourns for twenty years and dies," I say.

"I don't have to read about that," she says, and my laugh is so abrupt I spill Coke on the cobblestones.

Katharine Graham joins us and is asked about Barbra Streisand, whom she'd seen at last night's dinner.

"Oh, the poor woman. She was in the middle of people who were there to protect her, and people were jumping over their arms to talk to her and get her autograph. And they kept saying, 'I'm nobody, but I admire you so much.' She was just surrounded by people saying, 'I'm nobody—' "

"Yeah," says Leon. " 'Who are you to say you're nobody, buddy?' " He is amusing himself this afternoon making believe he doesn't quite understand anything.

Someone mentions Trump and Vendela, that he apparently gave her a hard time. A woman says, "Now he's claiming she wanted to sleep with him and he turned her down." We laughed. It's ludicrous.

Someone says something about Elie Wiesel, and the opening last week of the Holocaust museum. "Six million!" says Leon, who shakes his head and moves on.

We stand in clumps and clusters, gesturing and talking in our blazers and flowered dresses. Suddenly a breeze comes up, sweeps in, and showers us with dogwood petals. They swirl in the sun and fall softly on our heads, like a blessing. We laugh, brush them off, and continue our spirited talk.

—

A year and a half into the Clinton administration, and the Republicans who will run for president are in a busy wilderness—planning, jockeying for position, having their people call the Manchester, New Hampshire Kiwanis to ask if they need a speaker anytime soon, sending Christmas cards to thousands of close friends, keeping up on the issues so they're not caught flat-footed by a foe and, of course, raising money. That is when I see them, because that is when they're in New York.

—

In early '93 I went to a dinner for Jack Kemp in the home of a rich New York financier. Old word, financier, but due for a comeback. I had asked a friend, What exactly does our host do? and was told, "He's a principal in the main financial entity of John's investment group."

Oh.

This could mean he runs money. I heard that phrase from the wife of a man who works at Goldman Sachs who was describing one of the members of a board she is on. He's a nice guy, she said, works downtown, runs money.

Runs guns, runs dope. Is he a smuggler?

No, he runs people's money—"invests it, finds opportunities." Funny how people who work downtown are drawn to the kind of phrases you would hear in rap songs. Anyway, financier: a more elegant vague term.

The dinner is not a fund-raiser for Jack but a way for him to meet and befriend future contributors. And for me, a chance to see Jack and wonder if I am seeing the next president.

A small elevator opens silently and deposits me in the entrance-way of a sprawling apartment. I step into a beige marble foyer. Beyond, a huge room with long Trumeau mirrors and pale antique rugs.

A beautiful young man, the caterer's assistant, approaches. Blond hair gelled and slicked back, bright teeth, handsome tuxedo. An Armani angel. "Welcome," he says, softly, with a smile. "Hello," I say the same way. "Please come," he says, as he gestures toward a room full of people.

"May I get you something to drink?" says another tuxedoed angel carrying a silver tray. Flutes of blond champagne whisper and humm. "Water, any kind, or a Coke, thank you."

"Surely."

He zips away. On rollerblades, his small silver wings beating like a moth's. I made that up.

The caterer's assistants. They are all so trim and beautiful, so full of creamy competence. They don't mind, at this point in their young lives, being the help, taking the coat, getting the drink. It's just a stop on the way to a career in acting, writing, as a great chef or restaurateur. The job is a funny anecdote they'll tell someday on Letterman. Also they're getting a free education: they get to observe the powerful and celebrated up close, and now and then catch each other's eyes. At the end of this evening, when Jack speaks, they lean against the wall in the foyer, listening intently.

To my left, a sweeping staircase that leads to a room full of clinking, chuckling sounds. Ahead of me, groups of murmuring men in crisp tailored clusters.

"Peggy! Oh, I'm so glad you could come."

Our hostess. A warm and saucy woman, quite beautiful, with sweeping gray hair. She detaches from a cluster, her hands out. I wonder what expression is on my face, try to arrange it into happy and friendly. The cluster opens. Everyone smiles. I smile back happily and have nothing to say. One of the nice things about life is nobody else does, either.

"You look wonderful," she says.

"Oh, thank you."

"You really do." She winks. "What's happening in your life that you look so good?"

They look at me expectantly. Do I have a modest triumph to share? No. A witty, self-deprecating deflection? No. I fall back on the truth.

"I got all new makeup the other day."

She laughs, squeezes my hand. *You're great, kid, I'm gonna teach you how to do this because, listen, you don't know.*

She is the kind of sixty-, sixty-five-year-old woman to whom you want to say, Tell me honestly—don't be modest, modesty is the most boring virtue—how beautiful were you at your height, how big a knockout and what did it mean to you, to your life. Was it part burden? Did all the options and possibilities it gave you cause confusion? Do women have it all screwed up now, do we misunderstand everything? And please—as you near the big sunset and consider the strain and delight, tell me about men.

But you don't because—well, you'd scare her.

The cluster. Larry Tisch is being congratulated on CBS's triumph, number one network this year. Ed Rollins is talking about the upcoming Jersey gubernatorial race. Don Marron talks about possible Republican presidential hopefuls.

Someone mentions Bill Weld, the governor of Massachusetts. I say I've never met him, he seems smart, is he that hungry?

"He's hungry," says a woman. "I've never seen so much ambition."

I peer into my Perrier.

Ambition is a funny word in modern life. It comes with a disapproving sniff—*He's so ambitious.* But no one great became great without ambition, it's a must, a crucial component. Lincoln sitting in his Springfield law office, legs thrown across a corner of his desk so the mud on his boots wouldn't get on a brief, head cocked back, staring at the ceiling as Billy Herndon whittled. He was a good small-town lawyer in 1857, a former one-term congressman and failed Senate candidate who wanted to be the next president, and thought he would be. Talk about ambition.

It all depends what you're ambitious for. It all always comes back to Nixon's formulation: Some men want to rise in order to be big, and some want to rise in order to do big things. The problem with a lot of modern politicians is that they know they have to appear to want to do big things, and so they talk about them and convince others—convince themselves!—that that's what they're about. When that's not what they're about, it's just a coat they put on. Themselves is what they're about.

"Well," says a woman, "you wouldn't believe what Weld said to me the time I met him. I sat next to him at a lunch and we were talking about being from New York or something and he said, 'You must know my wife, she's a Roosevelt.' Can you imagine?"

She looks at me and blinks insistently, blink blink.

"That he said his wife was a Roosevelt?"

"Yes!"

"Oh. Is she?"

"Yes, but that's not the *point.*"

What is? That he sees his wife in a niche under Roosevelt Relative? That it's vulgar to say, "You notice that like many successful men I married well." But in what way is marrying a Roosevelt marrying well? (I'm sorry but . . . you know, the socialist wing, the dipso wing? In what way are they better than my family? My family's dipsos put theirs to shame.) Maybe he just meant, My wife's family is from New York, like you. No, he meant, My wife's family is from New York, and since you're obviously a well-heeled Protestant lady of a certain age you probably know them.

I don't know what to say, so say nothing.

At dinner I am seated with a journalist. He is young and wry. We talk about the paper where he used to work. I am a fan of its editorial page, he a veteran of its news pages. We laugh, knowing that means we're enemies. *The Wall Street Journal* is split in two by the ax of ideology. The news pages are put together by bright young liberals, the editorial page by bright young conservatives. The two groups communicate, he tells me, in a most interesting manner. When news side hates a particular editorial on a particular issue, they will, soon enough, run a front-page feature on the issue, careful to offer facts and viewpoints the editorial writer did not include. When news side runs a story on an issue that subtly or not so subtly reflects the assumptions and language of the left, editorial side will soon enough offer an essay on the issue, including information and arguments page one left out. If this is true—and I have worked there and am not sure it is—it might be one of the secrets of the *Journal*'s success. It bristles. Everyone's on their toes.

We talk politics, about America's unease. I mention my preoccupation with the suburbs whence our generation sprang, my hope to spend more time in the town where I spent my girlhood and find where and how it is, and why it seems so lost.

"Actually," he offers, "I think some of it has to do with God."

Not religion, God.

"That we have lost God as a people?"

"That he is not what he was to us. We don't give him the same place we did, as a society."

"I think that too."

"And it's hard for the media to report this story because they're writing about the competition."

"I'm not sure what you mean."

"The media compete with God," he says. "Because they're God too."

"Their prevalence and power?"

"Mmmmm. And the worship of the people on it."

The holy trinity of anchormen, the gospel according to Peter, Thomas and Daniel. And all the angels and saints on *Rescue 911*, *Baywatch*, *90210*. The Word revealed by Letterman. This is what Paddy Chayefsky was suggesting when he had Howard Beale go into ecstasies and almost speak in tongues. And the William Holden character—he's so tired because he's the one who knows all is vanity. The Pope once made a speech to broadcasters—it was at the end of his first visit to New York, and as he left he spoke to the journalists who had covered the story. He told them they have a mission, a duty to try to add to the life of man on earth. You are servants of truth, he told them; you promote unity among nations by sharing truth among peoples. "Do not grow discouraged," he said. "Be faithful to the truth and to its transmission, for truth endures; truth will not go away; truth will not pass or change. And I say to you—take it as my parting word to you—that the service of truth, the service of humanity through the medium of the truth—is something worthy of your best years, your finest talents, your most dedicated efforts."

A friend of mine was there, and wrote it down, and still keeps it, so moved was he to realize that a pope saw his job as he does.

Edward R. Murrow once said that just because you have a microphone doesn't mean you have anything to say. This is, in a way, a growing leadership problem in America—big mike, no message. It is also the modern media problem: fifty-seven channels and nothing on. Funny, since we all hunger. This is one area of business in which supply is not equal to demand.

—

The sound of silver tapping softly on a crystal goblet. We become quiet, and look to our host. He stands and thanks the Kemps for coming, thanks his friends, old and new, for coming to meet and see once again Jack and Joanne, asks everyone to enjoy the dinner, promises interesting talk at the end of the evening. He has a soft Southern accent. He does not enjoy speaking, but enjoys being host. He is slim, black-haired, but soft and un-edged. Like the rich Kentucky ringer in *The Hustler*—"Dyew know billyuds, Mistuh Felson?"—who asks George C. Scott if he'll take a check.

We eat. Grilled vegetables and a big white fish stuffed with spinach, proffered on a silver tray. To my right is a pleasant, mustachioed young man who tells me he is head of a fashion house. They make the perfume I am wearing. Do you like it? he says. Yes, it smells pretty. Will you wear it long? I don't know, last year I was wearing Boucheron, this year this. Why did you try Boucheron? I was walking through Bloomingdale's and somebody sprayed me. Why did you choose this scent? A man gave it to me and I liked it.

He shakes his head. That's the problem with the perfume business, he says. Women used to be loyal, they'd pick a scent and wear it twenty years. Now they just go from scent to scent, and I could strangle them!

—

Jack speaks. All over the place as usual. Taxes—jobs—empowerment—genocide—Bosnia—capital gains. Earlier, upstairs in the cocktail-party part, when I had first seen him, we went through the usual awkward moment. I never know if he'll hug me or shake hands, kiss me or nod, and he doesn't, either. I just sort of square off softly and let him do what he wants. But self-consciousness keeps one from moving the right way at the right moment, so when he puts a hand on my arm to draw me closer I put out my hand to shake, and when he sees the hand he becomes confused and winds up kissing me next to my nose. Hello! we laugh. He launches into how Dick Darman ruined the Bush administration. What is interesting is how freshly he feels it, as if it were still happening.

I am aware as one always is with Jack that he sees you not as a person, or even a small audience, but as a blackboard on which he, with his chalk, his experience—*I've been on the playing field*—can write out the next play. A blank slate on which he can write his Jackness. I have known him almost ten years and we have never had a conversation. Only Jack either writing on me or throwing quick questions. Sometimes I drop them. "Ah, she's fumbling for an answer!" he says, good-naturedly, and walks on.

What to make of Kemp. He was a hero, a great man of the party in the seventies and eighties. He had the courage to be unpopular with the men who ran the Reagan White House and the Bush White House. He stood tall against taxes and against Communism. But in the past few years he seems to have become—crabby, irascible. His friends complain that he never listens to them, respects no counsel, if you don't see it his way he puts you down and keeps walking. There is—what. A lack. "Ever young," we used to say of him.

I spent two hours with him on a dais at a gathering just after this dinner, and afterward I thought: He doesn't want it. He doesn't act as if he wants it. He groused about Irving Kristol, an intellectual hero. Kristol respects what the press calls the religious right, says that in their concerns you can discern many of the legitimate themes of the future. But Kemp talks as if he's removed himself from those old sympathies; it's all economic issues, it's all capital gains.

Our dais conversation took place at the yearly dinner of East Side Manhattan's conservatives. It is not, therefore, a large dinner. A few hundred people show up, elderly ladies in strange hats and fusty old gentlemen who used to be lawyers and some younger ones, journalists, who come out of loyalty to Tom Boland, head of the club and former law partner of Roy Cohn. Tom is a wonderful example of sane loyalty. He knew Cohn, he knew everything about him and he knew his good points too, his loyalty and irreverence, and he'll tell you about the good and bad of Cohn and then shrug a small undramatic shrug that says: He was my friend, and I'm not going to put him down for you. He was a member of my troupe.

Kemp said hello to people who came to the dais to shake his hand and wish him well, and fussed that tonight is maybe the last night of the Knicks-Lakers playoff and I gotta see it, how long will this go. He turns to me.

"What should the Republicans do to come back?" he asks.

"Well, they have to get back to basics. They have to start with taxes and spending, and then—"

"See? The economy! You said so yourself."

"Oh, Jack. You start there. It's not just 'the economy, stupid.' "

"What else is it?" He's throwing short passes tonight, boom boom.

"The social-issues stuff is serious, Jack."

Tom Boland gets up and the speeches begin; Jack speaks and it's okay and insufficient, and he leaves in a whirl of handshakes, back pats and imperatives: "Call me!"

More important, Kemp seems to have removed himself from the old instinctive conservative skepticism toward government. He is so eager to use government to help people that he acts as if he's forgotten that it is not the federal government that is the prime helper of the poor in America, it is freedom. Freedom to build, freedom from excessive taxation, from regulations and lawsuits that can ruin your dry-cleaning business because someone says you don't employ enough of this race and that gender. Freedom to work as a kid off the books and learn and get good habits and not have the guy who runs the candy store be buried under tax and medical forms.

Right now this, I think, is where Kemp is: drifting, and damning the captains of the other ships.

The Jack question: Can he snap out of it? Can he refind himself?

Cab home, up the stairs, into my son's room. Asleep, his pale face is round and pink. He sleeps so deep. His lashes are so long. I put my lips to his head, his ear, whisper "I love you" and wonder if it will go into his dreams and make a monster go away.

—

There are many splits in the Republican party—left, right, social conservatives on one side, libertarians on the other—but one has been insufficiently noted, which is odd because it is probably now the most significant. It is the split between old and young Republicans.

Old Republicans came to politics and power during and before Vietnam and Watergate; they understood their job to be not winning, but limiting loss. They were outnumbered in Congress, the mood music of the culture was against them, and their president was Nixon, who, domestically, decided to accept the assumptions of the welfare state, which he allowed to grow at great speed. (We tend to forget, but the size and scope of government services increased at almost Johnsonian rates during Nixon's years.)

Young Republicans came to politics and power in the age of Reagan; they never felt defeated, never thought limiting loss was their job. They do not accept the assumptions of the welfare state, they have no special respect for the Washington establishment, they are not cowed by the media. By and large their feeling about taxes is possibly reflected in this: When they were in college and read Oliver Wendell Holmes's famous observation that taxes are the price we pay for a civilized society, a lot of them thought: That sounds right. But in their lifetimes the taxes grew so much higher, and America grew far less civilized. They find it hard to rationalize taxes now.

Old Republicans had their good points: they supported civil rights. Young Republicans have good points too: they do not suffer from racial embarrassment, and think race is a stupid basis on which to decide much. Old Republicans watch Jay Leno; young Republicans listen to Rush. Old Republicans go to the Gridiron; young Republicans go to think-tank meetings. Old Republicans come from guilty Greenwich; young Republicans have less gelt and so less guilt. Old Republicans are liberal to moderate; young Republicans are conservative. Old Republicans are yesterday; young Republicans are the future. Old Republicans are often but not necessarily old; Dick Darman, still in his forties, is an old Republican. Young Republicans are often but not necessarily young; Irving Kristol, in his seventies, is a young Republican.

If the Republicans pick a young Republican as their nominee for president in '96, they will not only win, but win with meaning.

—

A talk with Frank, former Bush administration official, serious thinker and affectionate friend. He is on the scene in Washington, moving among think tanks and symposia. He is one of those friends with whom one can have long, free-associative conversations full of jump cuts and comfortable silences. Now and then I worry because ideas are more important to him than politicians, and so he has not aligned himself with this or that group of supporters; this leaves him un-protected by a tong and, paradoxically, open to charges that he is a self seeker. He worries about me because I am not aligned even with a think tank. ("People find it hard to reach you," he says. "Oh, good," I say, and he laughs.)

Our talk today is of the other potential Republican candidates, where they are and where they're going.

Me: I've figured out this. What the Republicans need in their next candidate is a fellow who can navigate between the various demands and desires of the anti-tax, anti-big-government, liberal-on-social-issues wing and the anti-tax, anti-big-government social conserva-tives. A guy who can steer among the rocks, a great navigator who through his very bigness can bring together the old Reagan coalition.

Frank agrees, sort of. In his heart he feels it mostly comes down to the economy; on the social issues he is ambivalently liberal. This, he believes, is the winning side, the right side, and also the realistic side: a government, especially a federal government far away in Washington, can only do so much. Let the president get the economy straight and undertake the first serious post–Great Society reordering of government.

Well, yes, I say, *but.* But the welling social movements of the future are about the sourness of our culture, the fraying bonds of our society, the sense of being bullied that people have by pressure groups, by the p.c. movement. Everyone is worried about the country we're bringing up our kids in.

Frank: Well, the next guy has to be a new conservative in that he is, in a modern and sophisticated way, a man who understands that the federal government must be changed in some of its essentials, judged and operated by new criteria. And the moral and intellectual reasoning behind his actions must be explained—not his emotions but his reasoning, the philosophical underpinnings of his positions.

Me: Yes. And tell me this. Am I right? This is the thing that's so frustrating. Everyone knows the government spends too much. And every political leader we have, both parties, they're all afraid of naming the things they would cut if they cut the budget. They're afraid they'll be unpopular if they're specific about entitlements, whatever. And this has been going on for decades. But people would be just so relieved and heartened by a politician who would be honest about what he'd cut and why he'd cut it. I know he'd take some hits, but he would gain respect as a truthful and courageous person. It's just *time*. Am I wrong?

Frank: No. If anyone asked my advice for what to do in New Hampshire I'd say "Go up there and tell them you're going to eliminate two or three specific cabinet agencies." I'd tell Kemp, Go up there and tell the truth, tell them HUD does little good. The thing that hurts the Republicans now is they're the only alternative to Clinton but you can't trust them because they won't tell you what they really think and what they'd like to do. And everyone knows.

Me: Yeah. But more. I'm not getting it right but listen. Republicans no longer argue with the assumptions of the welfare state. We're split over whether to cut or whether to grow and if we grow that will take care of the cost of everything. But it's time to again challenge the assumptions of this huge overblown state. Should government be doing everything it's doing? I don't think so. Why don't we question the very assumptions that built this state once again.

Frank: Because a pollster will tell you not to.

Frank is having a despair day.

He is in despair because he knows all the potential Republican candidates, has seen them over the years up close. The famous old saying about laws and sausages—that if you want to continue enjoying them you don't want to see them being made—applies here. You don't want to spend a lot of time in politicians' offices if you want to continue enjoying government. They will force you to make the transit from skepticism to cynicism, a truly pointless journey. One must always remember that politicians, most of them, are no more or less noble than anyone else, and it has always been thus. You don't want to know what Harry Truman was telling the Pendergast machine as he rose in politics, you don't want to know what he said to Tom Pendergast on the phone. You don't want to have heard Jack Kennedy on the phone, either, or Eisenhower. You've heard Nixon. You don't want to know, as Michael Barone noted, that Adlai Stevenson died with one book by his bed, the Social Register. Anyway, propinquity is the enemy of hero worship. Quick, go tell your valet.

Frank hasn't found someone to believe in; Frank can't find a packhorse for the philosophical ideas that will bring progress.

We run down the list.

Pete Wilson. If he survives in California, and I think he will, he will make a run in '96, but—where is he on taxes? On the social issues he is—what? A careful incrementalist, a prudent survivor. But he made a very good and unremarked-upon speech at the Republican convention in '92, showing up on a live feed from Sacramento, where he was fighting with Willy Brown and the Democrats over state spending. He talked with clarity and intelligence about governing and belief. He has grit. He's like an army captain in a tent in the

Korean War; you don't know if this dry, by-the-book kind of guy could be a general, but in a battle he'd throw himself on a grenade to save his troops.

The Wilson question: Will he throw in with the young or the older members of the party? And who is he, really?

Bill Weld of Massachusetts. Everyone says he's very smart, the Republicans in New York talk about him all the time, and he'd have an edge in the '96 New Hampshire primary because New Hampshire gets Massachusetts media; they all know him. But to survive in Massachusetts he has been a government-cutting, tax-cutting, social-issues liberal. A modern yuppy Republican. Frank knows him, I do not. I ask: If a high school valedictorian wanted to devote her graduation speech to how God has guided her through her life, and the local school board told her such a speech was a violation of church-state provisions, would Weld speak out against the school board? No, says Frank, probably not, the Harvard part of him would come to the fore. Would he talk about what's coming out of Hollywood and into our children's minds? No, says Frank, he's young, Eastern and modern.

Oh. Then, who needs him?

Dick Cheney—an adult, calm, measured, sophisticated in the best sense. And his wife, Lynn, is a genuine intellectual and writer about social and cultural issues. The delightful thing there is that Hillary Clinton will have paved the way for what would be, in Lynn Cheney, helpful activism.

Cheney's had many big jobs that he's performed so well—secretary of defense post–Soviet Union and during Iraq, chief of staff for Jerry Ford, party leader, longtime congressman. But, says Frank, he'll bring back the guys who got us in trouble, he'll hire Teeter, who'll go to his polls and tell him to go moderate-liberal, forget that young-conservative stuff, how soon can we raise taxes?

Is that true?

I think so, says Frank. Where else would they go, and where else would he?

Oh. No good.

Fact: Three years from now a guy with peerless foreign-affairs experience is going to look good. Fact: No one really knows what Cheney would do or think domestically.

Phil Gramm: One of the best minds in the Senate, a man of belief, with a wonderful Asian American wife. Started out as a Democrat, went Republican out of principle. A man I know, an activist who spends all his time gathering information on the Hill, shot me down recently when I expressed my enthusiasm for Gramm with this: "His best friends don't like him." He did not elaborate. Gramm has a big broad face and big eyeglasses and his Texas drawl is kind of—well, yammery. Not pretty and soothing like John Connally's. People say you have to be good-looking to run for president, but that's not true. But I do think it probably hurts to be odd-looking. And there is perhaps something too distinctive, or odd, about Gramm. He loves ideas. He's genuinely thoughtful. I wonder if he likes people.

I throw in a wild card. Frank, I say, how about a guy who not only talks the talk but walks the walk, a man who has governed statewide, successfully, for a good many years now, and who has successfully and intelligently and idealistically turned ideas like welfare reform into realities like state welfare reform and renewal. He's down home, smart as anything, highly sophisticated, and with another terrific wife who's a schoolteacher and a normal human being. I'm talking about—

You're talking about Tommy Thompson of Wisconsin, who told the Hotline the other day that he is not running for president in 1996.

Oh.

Bill Bennett? A man with a wonderful mind, a man who is genuinely thoughtful about the nation's problems. But—the first office you run for should probably not be for president. Colin Powell? If he announces he is a Republican, the party will dance with delight. But if he enters a primary his views will come under scrutiny, and I suspect he is, domestically, an Old Republican, a low-budget liberal; and that won't work. However, if he is a Republican and he enters some primaries, he is probably your next vice president.

We saved Dole for last. We're both fascinated by him. Frank says, Obviously he has to be taken seriously as a real contender, he's out there every day on TV as minority leader. He is, at the moment, the man who speaks for the party.

I saw him recently at a small dinner. Tall and witty, he was something I had not expected: warm and relaxed. I had met him only once, years ago, in his office, and he was intense, and brittle-seeming.

He has, I think, been changed by a near-death experience. When he lost to Bush in '88 it was a blow, it was painful, but he knew he might come back in time. The wheel turns, you never know. But when Bush lost in '92 and a boomer came in and ended forever the almost uninterrupted forty-year reign of the men who won World War II—and Dole saw that history's pendulum had swung, and would not likely return for some years, and he reckoned with the fact that he would be seventy-two next time out, when Clinton ran for reelection. . . . Well, he knew it was over. He'd have to go through the rest of his life bereft of an animating dream.

Just around Clinton's inauguration day Dole flatlined and his soul left his body and hovered over the operating table, and he saw the light and moved toward it and then—*a crashing noise. It was the sound of Clinton collapsing dramatically, prematurely, fatally.* And Bob Dole's soul was yanked back into his body.

Recalled to life, and feeling great. He's out there every day as Mr. Republican, and maybe he'll be seventy-two next time but he's young in his head and vigorous, and what was Reagan in 1980, seventy? And Dole knows something else: after four years of the reign of children, seventy-two is gonna look pretty good.

At the dinner I asked Dole if he was having the time of his life. He said Yes! When he was majority and minority leader under Reagan and Bush his life was waiting for the White House to call and tell him what he had to do, whether he agreed or not. Now he has autonomy and independence again—"And I see George Mitchell walking out of his office with his head down and his back bent and I say, 'George, been there, good luck.'"

I asked him what constitutes the presidential temperament. He's seen the last six presidents up close. What did they have to have in their temperament, their personality, that is necessary, and what is desirable?

He interpreted my question to mean: Do *you* have the presidential temperament. He said he has given a lot of thought to this question since '88 and the charges—"Stop lying about my record"—that he'd come across as dark and angry. He said he learned you just can't seem to lose your temper in public, at least over your personal fortunes. He brightened. "I saw Reagan lose his temper once, though, and it was great." It was during budget negotiations, and Reagan had been told some bankers were opposing him on some issue. "He threw down his glasses on the table and snapped, 'I've had it up to my keister with these guys.'" Dole laughed. He suggested it's fine to show your temper now and then over policy, where it can be not a flaw but a tool.

The subject that was on his mind and that he introduced to his end of the table was immigration. He was newly back from California, and everywhere he went—big groups, small groups, every ethnic group—he was asked, "What are you going to do about immigration?" "It isn't xenophobia," he said; the Mexicans and other recent immigrants were coming up to him and asking about it, they're taxpayers and they're seeing California sink under the weight of illegals who come into the state and go on its services—medical services, schools, welfare. California's going broke.

A spirited conversation ensued. A young woman to Dole's right said softly but with spirit, "I'm pro-immigration. I'm a bleeding-heart conservative, and if you see these people come across at Brownsville, in Texas, and you see that they've got nothing and they're coming here for the same reasons our parents did, for the dream—it's very hard to be against them."

"Oh, you can't be against them, we're all of us children of immigrants, but we've got a problem," a man said. But he said it wearily, in a hunched way. It was the defensive crouch of the affluent when they talk about the immigrant. Yes, his people came here from someplace else, but now he's rich, he's made it, and he's ashamed. He knows that if this conversation were a scene in a book he would not, with his good suit and rounded well-fed features, be the good guy. And yet—he has given this issue fair and serious thought and feels he is right: we must regain control of our borders.

I jumped in. "Something important," I said, "has happened since the last great wave of immigration this big, the one that brought our grandparents. Then, when they came here, they had to survive together, helping each other and being helped by churches and settlement houses, but pretty much without the money and services of government. They got free schools, and that's about all. And a lot of them made it and some of them didn't." I turned to my dinner partner, an Irish Catholic, and said, "Jimmy, a good number of our people went home and groused about America for the rest of their lives." He laughed and nodded yes.

"Now," I said, "we have changed the equation. We have arranged it so that we can give immigrants a great deal from the coffers of the state, which is to say, from the money we take from taxpayers. The fact that we offer services encourages people to come here and partake of them. Now the cost is growing insupportable. And it is not wrong or morally incorrect to say, 'Wait a second, let's take a breather, hold up for a while, let things settle down and see where we are.' This is what we've always done after periods of great immigration. And by and large it's worked."

"But they work so *hard*," she said.

"I know, I know"—I straighten, so as not to go into The Crouch— "and they have always been a plus in our history and will continue to be, but—easy does it."

Dole talks about "the delicacy of the whole matter," and veers off to Pete Wilson trying to survive with his budget problems.

—

On a table in my living room I keep in a plastic frame the Ellis Island tag of my aunt Jane Jane, my grandfather's sister, who helped bring me up. Jane Jane came over around 1910 on the *Californian*—not, as I once thought, the *California*, which two years later played a dramatic role in history by sleeping through the night as a few miles away the *Titanic* sent out distress calls.

Jane Jane went through Ellis Island like all the other steerage passengers, and wore on her coat the tag I keep. It is five inches long and six inches wide and faded yellow. On the top it says, "To assist inspection in New York Harbour, Passengers are requested to attach this Card to their Clothing." Below, there is a length of string tied by my aunt's then-young hands that was used to fasten the tag to the button of her coat.

In big letters near the top it says INSPECTION CARD. Below that, in parentheses, "Immigrants and Steerage Passengers." Then the data: "Point of Departure, LONDONDERRY. Name of Ship: CALIFORNIAN. Name of Immigrant: Mary Jane Byrne. Last Residence: Glenties." There are a series of no longer decipherable stamps, and then, at the bottom, the ship surgeon's daily inspection record of the health of beautiful, somewhere-in-her-twenties Mary Jane Byrne, who each day of what appears to have been a nine-day crossing showed negative for typhus, smallpox and tuberculosis.

She went from New York Harbour to Brooklyn, New York, where her brother Patrick, my grandfather, and her sister, Etta, lived. Grandpa worked for Consolidated Edison. We don't know what he started as, but he wound up wearing a suit. Bridget was a cook in Manhattan. She may have been called Cook, or Cookie, which became my older sister's nickname. In later years Mary Jane Byrne became Jane Jane when a child, my oldest sister, Barbara, couldn't pronounce her name.

Jane Jane became a chambermaid and an elegant lady who knew a good suit and fine gloves from common things. I think in her young days she was a bit of a snob, the kind of person who would call rougher, newer immigrants greenhorns. She considered herself refined, and was. When I think of this part of her life I see her standing in the bedroom of her less beautiful mistress, a kindly-of-her-type woman in a robe and gown. Jane Jane stands in the yellow glow of the small lamp that lights the mirrored vanity. The mistress sits, taking down her auburn hair and shaking it, shaking out the waves. Jane Jane stands ready with a Spanish comb, watching and thinking, That is a good brush, that's what a good brush looks like. The brush would have been tortoiseshell and silver. Things like hairbrushes in those days were beautiful and made with care, as if their purpose—going through a woman's hair, untangling it, soothing it—necessitated art. And the mirrored trays they kept them on. What does it say, I wonder, that now such things are made of utilitarian plastic, and not made for celebration at all?

Jane Jane worked and learned. She and her brother and sister, they all worked and learned. They loved America. They felt lucky to be here. They were grateful. Only years later, when I was in college and attended for a semester a school in England and went on my vacation to Ireland, the first of my family to return, did I understand finally exactly why. I journeyed to Donegal town in County Donegal and found my cousins. The older of them remembered my aunts and my grandfather, had been children with them, and told me of what they had been like long ago.

They had lived in a white-walled thatched-roof cottage that sat alone in the middle of a hollow in the middle of dark green hills. They kept sheep and farmed. The house is still there, the summer place now of a professor from Trinity College in Dublin. He uses it to get away, and, you know, you can get away there. It's a faraway place. When I went to the house I walked around and stood in the rooms and looked out the windows my grandfather and great-aunts had looked out and saw what they saw—empty hills, silent dark or bright. And an insight came and I knew: they left in part to escape loneliness. But they were more loyal than they intended: they brought the loneliness with them. That's why, when I knew them in Brooklyn, they were up all night talking, talking, playing the radio, avoiding the silence. They would have loved zappers.

I was taken to the small cottage of an old, old man named Paddy Kennedy, who had been in boyhood my grandfather's best friend.

"I was with your grandfather the day he left for America," he said.

"Please," I said, "tell me what you remember."

He told me Grandpa walked out of the house and down the lane to the road with his father. They waited for a truck, standing together. When the truck came my great-grandfather shook his son's hand. "Go now, and never come back to hungry Ireland again," he said.

What a sentence. I pondered it, and asked Paddy Kennedy, "Did they kiss and hug?" And Paddy blinked in alarm—"Of course not." *Why would they kiss and hug?* I thought then this was about being Irish, but now I think it's about another era. Men didn't, then.

My grandfather never did return. He and his sisters lived in Brooklyn as Americans. Bridget, dour and thrifty, saved enough money in fifteen or twenty years to buy a brownstone in Brooklyn, on Clinton Avenue. She moved her family members in one after another and, as they suffered reverses, let them live free.

They loved each other, were dependent on each other, fought with each other. They were each other's main drama. When Grandpa married—old, about fifty, to a young Irish immigrant named Mary, who was big, sweet, kind, had an innocent face and an innocent mind—Bridget and Jane Jane viewed her as stars view walk-ons, necessary to the action but not central to the story. When discussing her background they would sweetly note that she came from a house where they kept sheep in the kitchen.

The first child of Patrick and Mary was my mother, Mary Jane, who was dreamy and a good drawer and liked to read. What her friends always tell me when they talk about her youth was that she was the most popular girl in the neighborhood, and the best dancer. "She could *Lindy*," her friends Angie and Tessie always say when we gather at weddings and funerals.

Their second child was my uncle Johnny, who was funny and shy and smart. He had a terrible stutter well into manhood, and he went bald at eighteen, and from that time on he wore a hat in the house. (It was testimony to his courage, and to the endless possibility of human change, that in his middle age Johnny, who had fought in Korea, decided he wanted to become head of a big veterans' organization. To do this he would have to make big speeches, and he was ashamed of his stutter. But he ran anyway, and won, and when the time came to give a big speech he decided, They'll just have to hear my stutter, they can take it, they took Pork Chop Hill. Having decided the stutter didn't matter, the stutter wasn't so bad, and there were people who didn't know it had ever been an issue.)

After that came Peggy, the prettiest and most dynamic—she wanted to grow up and work in Manhattan in a big business office, and did, and Patrick, the sweetest and most sensitive, who became a marine. He was assigned for a while to guard Eisenhower while he played golf at Camp David. Then Patrick went to work for a bank. When you came in with almost no collateral and knew you didn't have a chance of a loan and surveyed the faces of the men at the desks, he was the kind of loan officer you'd go straight for. He'd smile and blush and tell you a joke and try to give you a break.

This is my favorite story about Patrick and my grandfather. When Pat came back from the marines and went to work in the bank, he fell in love with a girl with big eyes. Her name was Emily. She was, as Grandma and Grandpa noted, a German, meaning her parents had come over from Germany many years before she was born.

This was in the late 1950s, and Grandma and Grandpa were old, in their sixties and late seventies, which isn't so old now but was then. Grandpa had been retired for years from Con Ed, and had been sick for a long time with cancer. He had a large wound in his face that was cleaned and rebandaged each day by Grandma. I remember her standing above him—she stood painfully, on legs swollen by high blood pressure—and chatting as she cleaned his face with soap and water and peroxide. He couldn't speak anymore, or rather he could make sounds, grunts, but the only one who always understood was Grandma, who understood so well they could still talk politics and what was in the news together.

Didya see what that Dewey did?

Eh buh jer.

I think so too, the old woman.

Bridget had sold her house by this time and retired to a little cottage she had on Long Island, and Grandma and Grandpa lived in a walk-up, a railroad flat in Brooklyn, on the third or fourth floor. Twelve feet from their bedroom in the back the El roared by day and night. When I was a little girl I'd visit them, coming in on the Long Island Railroad from flat, square Massapequa. I'd lean out the window to see the trains roar by and watch the people on the street and look

over at the other buildings where old Italian ladies were leaning out
the windows watching the street, and they'd nod or wave to me and
I'd think Boy, this is great, this is like being on the set of a Dead End
Kids movie.

My grandparents lived on a small pension, what their children
gave them and Social Security. They didn't have much money, and—
there is this. It used to be said of the Irish in America that they were
somewhat inattentive to certain physical realities around them. Such
as the fact the floor could use a wash, and this window could actually
use a curtain or two. Once a friend of mine, an Irish Catholic who
worked in the press office in the Carter White House, was talking to
a reporter from *The New York Times*, an impressive young man, and
as they were talking he saw a small cobweb up in the corner of the
ceiling. He pointed and said, "Ah, Irish lace." She laughed, but she
burned. And when she told me we laughed and burned together. She
waited for months for him to come and say "What can I do to get
a few minutes with Jody Powell" so she could say something friendly
like "You could kiss my Irish ass," but she never got the moment or
never took it. "The timing's got to be perfect," she'd say, "the rhythm
has to be right."

Nothing was new in my grandparents' house, everything had been
jumped on by children. The couch was threadbare, the linoleum in the
kitchen and living room was cracked. They were old and unwell and
couldn't see, but there was more. It wasn't only the diminution of
human energy, it was an abstractedness, a preoccupation with the
particular music they were hearing. They didn't see the dullness
because they were thinking about other things, bigger things, stranger things. You have only so much time; you can read Pascal, talk
about the old days, watch the news and then Jack Paar, or you can
tidy up the house. This is not a contest.

Patrick, wanting to be an American just like the other Americans,
wanting to be modern and hygienic, and wanting most of all the love

of Emily, came up with a plan. She would meet his parents. She would come to their home. She would be impressed. Then she would marry him.

So this is what he did. He bought paint and painted the entire apartment, he bought linoleum and laid it from the front room to the back, he bought a toaster and a tablecloth, he hung curtains, and he brought Emily home. And of course they loved her and she loved them, and Patrick was proud, and a year later it was a wonderful wedding.

Only one thing had gone wrong. Grandpa had gotten all dressed up when Emily came, but he hadn't shaved, which surprised Patrick because he'd just bought him a brand-new Remington electric shaver, the plug-in kind, so Grandpa would no longer have to lather up his face. Patrick took Grandpa aside and said, "Pop, aren't you using the new shaver?" And Grandpa was abashed and apologetic and said it hadn't worked. Pat felt bad and went into the bathroom, found the shaver on the sink, picked it up and saw that the head was encrusted with soap and lather. He started to laugh, and when they said good-bye that night Pat kissed Grandpa, who was so moved he kept hugging.

But the point, which started many, many pages ago: My grandfather and his sisters loved America and never rejected Ireland, and communicated to us, their grandchildren, a sense of being Irish, the great pride and embarrassment and distance of being Irish, that never left us but also never left us feeling less American than anyone else. For practical reasons you spoke English and not Gaelic, but so what? English is the language of America, whose citizen you hope to be, whose life you hope to join. Gaelic was always a secret language anyway, you learned it in case the ever-interesting English decided to ban the saying of Catholic prayers. Irish food they continued, the hams and potatoes and vegetables and puddings. Irish dress—please. Irish dress was the tradition of looking poor. Here they could look not-poor. Irish ways—talking, judging, joking, reading—you had no choice about, and why would you want to? Irish faith—this you continue and never drop, and if they ever try to keep you from being Catholic in America you leave because more than you are an American, more than you are Irish, more than you are anything else, you are a member of the Church. Catholic is what you are; Ireland, or America, is where you live.

They never said these things. They communicated them the way truth is communicated, by how they lived, by what they blurted out without thinking and gave their time to, by what they shook their head and went "Whhiisssshhttt" at, by what they laughed at, by the Mass cards they kept on the bureau mirror. You didn't discuss whether to go to church on Sunday, you got up and got dressed. You didn't talk about whether your work was satisfying, you did it and brought home the cash. You didn't read books about parenting and discuss its joys and fears, you brought up the kids. You didn't discuss the merits of Roosevelt, you voted Democrat unless you were a fool.

They were so much less self-conscious than we! They were not crippled by the habit of observing their actions and dissecting their meaning. They acted. They crossed an ocean.

They stayed up at night and gossiped and their gossip was mostly remembering people and things they knew long ago. And they also on Saturday night, at the oilcloth table, as they sat and sipped beer and sherry and the women smoked cigarettes or took snuff, made observations about the people of the city, the politicians and social figures and titans of industry, and the movie stars they saw in the papers. They discussed their actions, statements, scandals and professional decisions and had opinions about them. They watched the whole parade with interest and never lost the sense, so deep they didn't have to say it, that they were everyone's equal, no one's inferior. They knew an equality deeper than that bestowed by democracy, the equality of belief: We'll all wind up in heaven or hell and

Rockefeller may wind up flying beside you, so don't look down on him because he's rich. Then again he is not only no more likely to wind up in heaven than us, he is possibly more likely to wind up in the other place, so feel for the man.

When you know this it is very hard to think less of yourself because Mr. Rockefeller has a better car. It is hard not to think more of yourself when you're so fully evolved that you know cars don't matter. Which is not to say a nice Ford wouldn't be nice, and we mean to get one.

They had another reason for pride or, rather, a reinforcing mechanism for their respectful vision of themselves. It came from the popular culture. Hollywood, seeing a huge new untapped market, gave the immigrants of Ireland what they thought they'd like: depictions of themselves that showed them to be, simply, indomitable—or at least really interesting. Heroes were Irish, heroines were beautiful colleens. Jimmy Cagney finding his soul and dying with the Fighting 69th, Pat O'Brien leading the boys across the Marne, Spencer Tracy helping Mickey Rooney through Boys Town, Bing Crosby telling Ingrid Bergman to dial O for O'Malley. Scarlett O'Hara was Irish, and George M. Cohan and, more to the point, John Ford. You could go to the movies in the 1930s and '40s in America and think, The Irish must be pretty terrific people. Everyone knew Hollywood was giving a highly sentimental view of the Irish, but still—it was not unhelpful to us.

My grandparents and parents knew these movies in the theaters, the big Loews in Brooklyn, but my mother's children grew up watching them and absorbing their message on channel 9 in New York, on *Million Dollar Movie*. Channel 9 in the fifties and sixties had no money for programming, so they'd run the same old movie once every afternoon and twice every night for a solid week (triple showings on Saturdays and Sundays). It was, as someone once said, the first VCR. This is part of how the New Yorkers and Jerseyites of my

generation—growing up thirty and forty years ago when the old
ethnic sense of the turn-of-the-century immigrants was getting thin-
ner—received a sense of blood.

It was how we got a sense, when it was not always communicated
to us, of Irish spirit. I have read, and believe it, that young Mafia guys
get their tradition now not from old capos but from the *Godfather*
movies. This in a way is how we were.

An insight for those of the liberal persuasion:

Those of us who complain about the ugliness of the current culture
fear, among other things, for young immigrants from Latin America
and the islands. They don't get what we got, a cultural presentation
of their people as the hearty backbone of a great nation that was, God
bless it, just a little bit sissier until we came along. Stupid dull people
who say words like "positive role model" and "uplifting message"—
this is part of what they're talking about. And they're not stupid, they
just don't know how to find the right sensitive words because they
have actual lives, they do things for a living, they're not communica-
tors.

But my immigrants. I thought of them at the Dole dinner as the
tone turned guilty. I wanted them to be there. I wanted them to be
unselfconscious and just and tell us what immigrants know. That all
immigration should be legal, that the INS should be respectful, that
it's right and good for immigrants to preserve their culture and their
tongue but that English is the language of America, and if we are not
bound by language, if we take to speaking different tongues, we will
start to break apart; that America has gotten soft but that immigrants
are still tough; they can take it, they can learn the language. That it's
okay if you have to go on welfare for a little while but only a while,
because welfare in time corrupts the spirit. That if you continue to tax
everyone at the high rates at which Americans are taxed, you will
slow the immigrants' upward rise. Bridget would note that if she had
come here when taxes were this high she never would have been able

to buy the house in which she ultimately sheltered three generations of her family. They would say to be protective of America, not only for its sake but for the world's.

—

The Dole dinner broke up early, at least for me. Later, thinking about it, about him, I realized that what is interesting is that Dole is so obviously running for president only six months into a new president's four-year term. This is something new. He hasn't announced, but he's not being coy and everyone knows what he's doing.

At the dinner he had been asked about taxes. He lost to Bush in New Hampshire in '88 for one big reason: he refused to vow not to raise taxes, while Bush took the vow. What about now? "I've never seen taxes make the economy take off and create jobs, at least not in American history." I perk right up.

"Not in human history either," says Ted Forstman, to laughter.

But what does this all mean? What *is* Dole on taxes now?

Near the end, a conversation at the other end of the dinner table reaches ours. What, someone wants to know, was the definitive and great changing moment of your life? Liddy Dole chooses to interpret the question as being limited to professional matters, and says, "The airbag." Bob Dole is told what his wife answered and smiles innocently. "That's sweet. She means me." He says his was what happened to him in World War II—"and it wasn't all bad, there were good things that were part of it"—and the Reagan years' agreement on Social Security, which, he says, turned it from a system operating at a deficit to a system in surplus.

Anyway, Dole: he's tanned, rested and ready. But what about the reflexive cynicism? It is delightful in a purveyor of one-liners and puncturer of opposition balloons, but it is disheartening in a leader. Cynicism is as bad as sentimentalism, it's just another way of protecting yourself with something that isn't true. And is he not one of that generation of Republican leaders who came to power during Watergate and Vietnam, and who understood the job of a Republican to be low-budget liberalism? He has a firm sense of the possibilities. But maybe now is a time for someone who doesn't know what is possible, whose "ignorance" can expand the boundaries.

The Dole question: Can he, at seventy, after an entire adulthood of life in a capital city that is a moral septic tank, smack himself on the head, reach out to the young conservatives and embrace progressive ideas? Can one become, in old age, a realistic idealist? Or will he be, this time out, a more moderate exemplar of the old tag: tax collector for the welfare state.

It will be interesting to watch him, and the other presidential prospects, over the next two years. C-Span has already, in this winter of '94, begun *The Road to the White House, '96* to the shamefaced delight of those of us who can't resist watching who's running and why and how they're doing.

But, an irony: In a nation with a political class that is more than ever obsessed with the presidency, one senses that the presidency is not where the real action is taking place in America right now. The real action, the real things that will shape our future, are taking place in the country—in the culture, in the winds of intellectual fashion (multiculturalism, political correctness), in the schools, in the cities as they wrestle with unions and in the suburbs as they wrestle with budgets. And in churches. A lot of action going on in churches, and a lot of people there.

PART III

The Pursuit of Happiness

Through these past few years of motherhood, politics and writing another thing was happening to me. I spoke earlier of a search, a spiritual one. It loped forward in the earliest nineties and then gathered speed in starts and stops, but mostly starts.

One day in 1992 I got on the phone to talk about it with my friend Tim, a former priest, who is, I think, the holiest person I know, even though he is the last commie, a liberation theology socialist who doesn't think America should have a defense budget. (He was a Jesuit.) But he's my commie and I love him, as I love his wife, the second-to-last commie, who works with unbecoming fervor in the Clinton administration.

Tim loves God. He loves him in the tenderest way. And so he works as a bureaucrat but functions, for friends and family, as a kind of spiritual counselor. I told him that something was happening with me and Christianity, that I wasn't feeling the mild engagement I'd felt the past few years but a kind of desire. It felt like a hunger, or a thirst. He listened, and said, "That's the language of conversion."

Conversion. What a surprising word. And wrong, I always believed in God. "There are many who see Christianity, and any religion for that matter, as a process of constant conversion. That if you take it seriously and seriously incorporate it into your life the nature of your belief and worship and the level of your comprehension will naturally grow, and change. As will you."

There was something exciting in this, and something disheartening. For as he spoke I realized I'd had conversions before, and they had gone away.

"Think about what faith has been for you," he said.

Well, it's been a presence. But I think I usually kept it apart from me, over on the side, as if belief were a nice bag I carried, a bag I valued and would talk about if you asked me where it came from or even, if you were rude, what it cost, which in my case was nothing. But I rarely opened it and looked inside, and when I did I quickly let it shut.

And now, I said, that wasn't enough. Now I felt not like a person reading C. S Lewis and writing "This is true" in the margins, but like Anne Lamott in *Operating Instructions*, who kept taking her baby to church and crying.

So this is different. Maybe it will stick. Maybe I am converting from person who approves of Christianity to Christian, from person who agrees with something to person who seeks to be animated by it. Who seeks to live it.

Which was not the plan. The plan was that after years of delicious and delightful experience in the world, of a real full wallow, of pursuing the low and ultimately empty but at the moment pretty delightful pursuits, I would, being old now and facing the big end, straighten up. In time—in my seventies, at ten minutes to death—I would become religious. Until then I could be my loathsome and disgusting self.

I could see the demands of deep faith, but not the joy. The joy was unknown to me, and yet at the same time I knew of, or had had intimations of, its existence.

Once, in a religious phase—and that is what it was, a phase—I was standing in the kitchen of my basement apartment on Thirty-third Street, in Georgetown. It was about eight-thirty at night. I was putting on water for tea. I think I was just standing there holding the kettle when something happened—a peace descended, a profound peace, a peace that I had never felt before. It was as if I understood something, but didn't understand what I was understanding. But it was something about bigness and spaciousness and grace. It felt like a good promise. A few evenings before, I had spent three hours with a priest in a small, lively Christian community in Maryland. We had talked about belief and prayed, and at the end he took my confession. It was the mid-eighties and I hadn't been to confession in about twenty years, and it was the first time I ever saw a priest take a confession sitting in a chair in a living room and then get on his knees and pray with you. And it took a long time because every time I'd get to the end and he'd begin to absolve me I'd think of last-minute sins and add them on, so he'd have to start all over again. Afterward I took a train home and fell asleep for twelve hours. And now, a few nights later, here I was with a kettle in my hand. I remember looking at the deep-blue tiles that covered the walls of the kitchen, with bright crisp lines of white spackling between. And I stood there and felt peace. I don't know now how long it lasted—I think maybe only five or ten or fifteen seconds. But I was sure I was being told something, being given a taste of something I could have, if I wanted it.

Which I didn't. Or at least I didn't do enough to pursue it. Why wouldn't I take steps that, this moment seemed to suggest, would make this thing, this peace, a part of my life? I don't know. Because it was the unknown, because it would be rigorous, because it would deny me joys I knew, because the compensating joys would be— wholesome. And there is the burden of an ardent nature: I could become good and ruin my life.

But there was something new or, rather, growing in me now that would effect this latest conversion— No, no, that was spurring it: I wasn't enjoying the distracting joys of the world as much anymore. The joys of the world seemed less vivid than they'd been, less whole and able to fool. Any number of examples. Professional success. Success is nice and I've had some and enjoyed it, but—so what? It isn't sufficient reason to get up in the morning. It's not good enough to live for. Success for me has been, essentially, getting invited to things I don't want to go to but like saying I went to. And one of the reasons for that is that I found I wasn't as drawn to and charmed by experience anymore—at least the kind of experience that is being at the party, the convention, in the hot-air balloon. All that now seemed mostly fine but basically overrated. Oddly enough, whenever I have been at the center of things—in the White House, at the party, in the studio—I would enjoy them and have a great time and notice things, but I would also think, and it wasn't only a detaching mechanism, a self-protecting way of not being there, I would also think: This is all an illusion. This is a lovely, tender illusion. We're all running around being busy and doing important things but this has nothing to do with anything. Up there God and the angels are looking down and laughing, and not unkindly. They just find us— touching, and dizzy. We are touching and dizzy, all of us, with our big plans to raze the slums and find a caterer and get junior into Yale.

—

Tim told me to read, think, pray and get a regular spiritual counselor.

I'd go into the Paraclete bookstore, a religious bookstore off Madison Avenue, and books would almost fall on me, strange books, wonderful books, a strange and eclectic mix. The poetry of Thomas Merton and Gerard Manley Hopkins. Then Merton's prose, which is the best of him and deeply poetic. A skeptical history of Marian apparitions. A chronology of the early Church. A history of Christianity in Victorian England. The memoirs of mystics. Essays by theologians, by people who've seen angels, by priests in the Peace Corps and nuns in the slums. I didn't know what to look for, so I took whatever looked interesting and all of it was and some of it was exciting. A woman who worked in the store started calling me and saying things like "We got a new one in from St. Ignatius Press."

But the most exciting thing was that the Bible started to make sense to me. Catholics of my generation don't know the Bible the way the other Christians do, we weren't as schooled in it. The Bible always seemed to me like something written in a foreign tongue. The prophets, the arcane references, the unexplained ecstasies. I loved some of the psalms, as everyone does, or at least as everyone did until· they changed "He leadeth me beside the still waters" to "He takes me to a verdant place"—but beyond that the big black book was, for me, opaque. Bible-study class opened the door, but one day, and this still feels like a small miracle, one Saturday morning in the spring, as my son watched Ace McCloud and the Centurions in the next room, I took my Bible, the new Protestant one from Bible class, and turned for no reason I remember to Acts of the Apostles. And I burrowed into my chair ready for a nice frustrating read and the closing of a book. I had never known what "acts of the apostles" meant, what the phrase meant; I had never thought about it. And now I read—and understood. This is what the apostles did after Jesus died. This is how they talked to the new Christians and the Jews and the Gentiles and the Greeks and the Romans—this is the evangelization that took place after the Crucifixion. In a panic of loneliness, at the bottom of an empty cross. They found each other and found Him again and received the spirit, the amazing grace, and went into the world and started the Church. Oh. *Oh.*

It is hard to explain how exciting this stupid and obvious discovery was. But it all made sense to me for the first time. It was history and revealed truth, and it was wonderful, fascinating. Peter and Paul said wonderful things, they had thirsty, brilliant hearts, they were great rhetoricians. I started to read it all in a new way and with a new comprehension, and one of the things I realized is what everyone else who cares about such things knows but I didn't really: They were brave. They were all surrounded by miracles every day and they were afraid and brave.

I started to do something new, too. I wanted to start to pray, and I realized I didn't really know how. I knew how to ask for things and I knew how to say the prayers of childhood, but asking for things is not a dialogue, or is at least only the beginning of one, and I didn't know how to move it forward, deepen it. As for saying prayers, the Hail Mary and Our Father, that seemed more reciting than engaging. I read that the Pope had recently taken his rosary beads and held them before a group of pilgrims and told them, "This, *this* is the answer." And I thought, It is? How?

—

Tim had told me: Find a priest or a very spiritual lay person to talk to, to meet with. This was hard. There was a good monsignor who talked to me once, but he was overworked and understaffed. The fact is, of course, that there aren't enough priests to go around anymore, and the ones you meet are rushed and busy, and when you take their time to discuss your soul you know you're taking them from the meeting of the homeless coalition, the visit to the hospital, the school administration meeting. You can't just walk into a church anymore and look for a priest because the churches are closed, locked up against crime. They're only open for an early morning Mass, noon Mass and evening Mass. Otherwise they're locked all day. This is one of the saddest single facts of religion in America—the synagogues and Protestant churches are locked too—and sadder for the fact that it is so obvious a metaphor. The doors are closed.

When I told my friend Michael I couldn't find a priest to help me with prayer, he said, "Then you must pray for one." And so I began.

And even though the process was imperfect and unknowing, the attempt itself was good, as if I were at the beginning of a potential, and to my delight and surprise, I started to look forward to it.

I also began to tell my friends about what was going on with me, and found that something like it was going on with a lot of them, too. Nancy is on her own quest, trying to reconcile her modern convictions with the Church she knew as a child, fled, and longs for. Lisa sees the old men in synagogue rocking back and forth with prayer, and she wants it too, feels it too, and tries to pray each day, but it is hard because the prayers are in Hebrew and not immediately accessible to the heart, and the translations are—flat. But she prays every morning, and is looking for a rabbi to guide her. We are each other's support group. And there are more. But I started truly seeing at this time that society in general is not supportive of such pursuits; it is no longer animated by the old habits and ways. It had it more when my friends and I were kids—a boring thing to say, everyone's a cheerleader for the age that formed them, but we were better off then, as a country, weren't we? And I mean all of us, even the most abused of us.

I was thinking about these things in the spring of '92 when Steve Forbes of *Forbes* magazine called and said, "We're doing a special issue to mark our seventy-fifth anniversary, and our theme is Look, for all our troubles, we have never in the history of man had it so good. We're wealthier, smarter and healthier than we've ever been. Why, then, do we all feel so bad? We want you to write an essay, as long or short as you want, that thinks about that."

This is precisely the kind of assignment I always turn down because it takes me away from my real work, which is not doing other things that don't seem right.

"Yes," I said.

And for two months, for that is how long it took, I thought and wrote:

It occurred to me, first, that the life of people on earth is in many ways better now than it has ever been—certainly much better than it was five hundred years ago, when people beat each other with cats. This may sound silly, but now and then when I read old fairy tales to my son and see an illustration of a hunchbacked hag with no teeth and bumps on her nose who lives by herself in the forest, I think: People looked like that once. They lived like that. There were no doctors, no phones, and people lived in the dark in a hole in a tree. It was terrible. It's much better now.

But we are not happier. I believe we are just cleaner, more attractive sad people than we used to be.

There are serious reasons members of my generation in particular are feeling a high level of anxiety and unhappiness these days, but it is interesting to look at how we "know" this: the polls.

I used to like polls because I like vox pop, and polls seemed a good way to get a broad sampling. But now I think the vox has popped—the voice has cracked from too many command performances. Polls are contributing to a strange new volatility in public opinion.

A few years ago, when the Gulf war had just ended, George Bush's approval ratings were at nearly 90 percent. Within eighteen months they were at 30 percent. This was a huge drop and, in a way, a meaningless one. President Bush didn't deserve 90 percent support for having successfully executed a hundred-hour ground war; Abe Lincoln deserved a 90 percent for preserving the union. Bush didn't deserve 30 percent support because the economy went into recession; John Adams deserved a 30 percent for the Alien and Sedition laws. It is all so exaggerated.

The dramatic rises and drops are fueled in part by mass media and their famous steady drumbeat of what's not working, from an increase in reported child abuse to a fall in savings. When this tendency is not prompted by ideology it is legitimate: good news isn't news. But the volatility is also driven by the polls themselves. People think they have to have an answer when they are questioned by pollsters, and they think the answer has to be "intelligent" and "not naïve." This has the effect of hardening opinions that haven't even been formed yet. Poll questions do not invite subtlety of response. This dispels ambiguity, when a lot of thoughts and opinions are ambiguous.

And we are polled too often. We are constantly having our temperature taken, like a hypochondriac who is looking for the reassurance no man can have, i.e., that he will not die.

I once knew a man who was so neurotically fearful about his physical well-being that in the middle of conversations he would quietly put his hand to his wrist. He was taking his pulse. When I was seven or eight years old, I became anxious that I would stop breathing unless I remembered every few seconds to inhale. This mania was exhausting. At night, on the verge of sleep, I would come awake in a panic, gulping for air.

People who take their pulse too often are likely to make it race; people obsessed with breathing are likely to stop. Nations that use polls as daily temperature readings inevitably give inauthentic readings, and wind up not reassured but demoralized.

But there are real reasons for our national discontent. Each era has its distinguishing characteristics; each time a big barrel of malaise rolls down the hill there are specific and discrete facts rolling around inside. Here are some of ours:

Once in America if you lost your job—if you were laid off from the assembly line at Ford, for instance—you had reason to believe you'd be rehired. Business cycles, boom and bust—

sooner or later they'd call you back. There was a certain security in the insecurity. Now it's different. Now if you're laid off from your job as the number two guy in public affairs at the main Jersey office of a phone company, you have reason to fear you'll never be hired back into that or any other white-collar job, because employment now is connected less to boom and bust than to changing realities, often changing technologies, in the marketplace. The telephone company doesn't need you anymore.

You are a boomer, and obscurely oppressed. But there is nothing obscure about your predicament. So many people are relying on you! You and your wife waited to have children, and now they're eight and ten and you're forty-eight—too late to start over, to jeopardize the $75,000 a year you earn. And if you tried, you would lose your medical coverage.

Your mother and father are going to live longer than parents have ever lived and will depend on you to take care of them as they (as you, at night, imagine it) slide from mild senility to full dementia. Your children will have a longer adolescence, and expect you to put them through college just as mom and dad are entering a home.

Your biggest personal asset is your house, which has lost value. You have a hefty mortgage, your pension is underfunded, you don't think your Social Security benefits are secure and you do not trust the banks.

The last may be the most serious in terms of how people feel. In the years since the Depression we have been able to trust that the institutions we put our savings into would be there tomorrow and pay us interest. We don't know that anymore; most of us are afraid that all of a sudden a major bank, strained from its own feckless loans to middle-aged mall builders who make political contributions, will fold, taking the other banks with it.

We wonder: If there is another depression and the banks fail, how will I and my family live? How will we buy food and gas and pay for electricity? We don't know how to grow things! What will we eat if it all collapses?

I think the essential daily predicament of modern, intelligent, early-middle-age Americans—the boomers—is this: There is no margin for error anymore. Everything has to continue as it is for us to continue with the comfort we have. And we do not believe that everything will continue as it is.

It is embarrassing to live in the most comfortable time in the history of man and not be happy. We all have so much, we have so much more than mom and dad that we can't help but feel defensive about feeling so bad, and paying off our charge cards so late, and being found in the den surfing from channel to channel at 3:00 A.M.

And there's this: We know that we suffer—and we get no credit for it! Sometimes we feel the bitterness of the generation that fought World War I, but we cannot write our memoirs and say good-bye to all that, cannot tell stories of how our boots rotted in the mud, cannot deflect the neighborhood praise and be modest as we lean against the bar. They don't know we're brave. They don't know we fight in trenches too.

I find myself these days thinking of Auden's words about the average man in 1939, as darkness gathered over Europe—the "sensual man on the street," barely aware of his emptiness, who promises he will be true to his wife, that someday he will "be happy and good."

Auden called his era the age of anxiety. I think what was at the heart of the dread in those days, just a few years into modern times, was that we could tell we were beginning to lose God—banishing him from the scene, from our consciousness, losing the assumption that he was part of the daily drama, or its maker. And it is a terrible thing when people lose God. Life is difficult and people are afraid, and to be without God is to lose man's great source of consolation and coherence. There is a phrase I once heard or made up that I think of when I think about what people with deep faith must get from God: the love that assuages all.

I don't think it is unconnected to the boomers' predicament that as a country we were losing God just as they were being born.

At the same time, a huge revolution in human expectation was beginning to shape our lives, the salient feature of which is the expectation of happiness.

It is 1956 in the suburbs in the summer. A man comes home from work, parks the car, slouches up the driveway. His white shirt clings softly to his back. He bends for the paper, surveys the lawn, waves to a neighbor. From the house comes his son, freckled, ten. He jumps on his father; they twirl on the lawn. Another day done. Now water the lawn, eat fish cakes, watch some TV, go to bed, do it all again tomorrow.

Is he happy? No. Why should he be? But the knowledge of his unhappiness does not gnaw. Everyone is unhappy or, rather, everyone has a boring job, a marriage that's turned to disinterest, a life that's turned to sameness. And because he does not expect to be happy the knowledge of his unhappiness does not weigh on him. He looks perhaps to other, more eternal forms of comfort.

Somewhere in the seventies, or the sixties, we started expecting to be happy, and changed our lives (left town, left families, switched jobs) if we were not. And society, that tough old galleon, strained and cracked in the storm.

I think we have lost the old knowledge that happiness is

overrated—that, in a way, life is overrated. We have lost somehow a sense of mystery—about us, our purpose, our meaning, our role. Our ancestors believed in two worlds, and understood this to be the solitary, poor, nasty, brutish and short one. We are the first generations of man that actually expected to find happiness here on earth, and our search for it has caused such unhappiness. The reason: if you do not believe in another, higher world, if you believe only in the flat material world around you, if you believe that this is your only chance at happiness—if that is what you believe, then you are more than disappointed when the world does not give you a good measure of its riches, you are in despair.

In a Catholic childhood in America, you were once given, as the answer to the big questions: It is a mystery. As I grew older I was impatient with this answer. Now I am probably as old, intellectually, as I am going to get, and more and more I think: It is a mystery. I am more comfortable with this now; it seems the only rational and scientific answer.

My generation, faced as it grew with a choice between religious belief and existential despair, chose . . . marijuana. Now we are in our Cabernet stage. (Jung wrote in a letter that he saw a connection between spirits and The Spirit; sometimes when I go into a church and see how modern Catholics sometimes close their eyes and put their hands out, palms up, as if to get more God on them, it reminds me of how kids in college used to cup their hands delicately around the smoke of the pipe, and help it waft toward them.) Is it possible that our next step is a deep turning toward faith, and worship? Is it starting now with tentative, New Age steps?

Finally, another thing has changed in our lifetimes: people don't have faith in America's future anymore.

I don't know many people aged thirty-five to fifty who don't have a sense that they were born into a healthier country, and that they have seen the culture deteriorate before their eyes.

We tell pollsters we are concerned about "leadership" and "America's prospects in a changing world," but a lot of this is a reflection of a boomer secret: we all know the imperfect America we were born into was a better country than the one we live in now, i.e., the one for which we are increasingly responsible.

You don't have to look far for the fraying of the social fabric. Crime, the schools, the courts. Watch channel 35 in New York and see your culture. See men and women, homo- and hetero-, dressed in black leather, masturbating each other and simulating sadomasochistic ritual. Realize this is pumped into everyone's living room, including your own, where your eight-year-old is up sick and flipping channels. Then talk to a pollster. You too will declare you are pessimistic about your country's future; you too will say we are on the wrong track.

Remember your boomer childhood in the towns and suburbs. You had physical security. You were safe. It is a cliché to say it, but it can't be said enough: We didn't lock the doors at night in the old America. We slept with the windows open. The cities were better. A man and a woman falling in love could stroll the parks of a city at 2:00 A.M. Douglas Edwards, the venerable newscaster, once told me about what he called the best time. He sat back in the newsroom one afternoon in the late seventies, in the middle of the creation of the current world, and said, "New York in the fifties—there was nothing like it, it was clean and it was peaceful. You could walk the streets!" And he stopped and laughed at celebrating with such emotion what should be commonplace.

You know what else I bet he thought, though he didn't say

it. It was a more human world in that it was a sexier world, because sex was still a story. Each high school senior class had exactly one girl who got pregnant and one guy who was the father, and it was the town's annual scandal. Either she went somewhere and had the baby and put it up for adoption, or she brought it home as a new baby sister, or the couple got married and the town topic changed. It was a stricter, tougher society, but its bruising sanctions came from ancient wisdom.

We have all had a moment when all of a sudden we looked around and thought: The world is changing, I am seeing it change. This is for me the moment when the new America began: I was at a graduation ceremony at a public high school in New Jersey. It was 1971 or 1972. One by one a stream of black-robed students walked across the stage and received their diplomas. And a pretty girl with red hair, big under her graduation gown, walked up to receive hers. The auditorium stood and applauded. I looked at my sister, who sat beside me. "She's going to have a baby," she explained.

The girl was eight months pregnant and had had the courage to go through with her pregnancy and take her finals and finish school despite society's disapproval.

But society wasn't disapproving. It was applauding. Applause is a right and generous response for a young girl with grit and heart. And yet, in the sound of that applause I heard a wall falling, a thousand-year wall, a wall of sanctions that said: We as a society do not approve of teenaged unwed motherhood because it is not good for the child, not good for the mother, and not good for us.

The old America had a more delicate sense of the difference between the general ("We disapprove") and the particular ("Let's go help her"). We had the moral self-confidence to sustain the paradox, to sustain the distance between "official" disapproval and "unofficial" succor. The old America would not have applauded the girl in the big graduation gown, but some of its individuals would have helped her not only materially but with some measure of emotional support. We don't so much anymore. For all our tolerance and talk we don't show much love to what used to be called girls in trouble. As we've gotten more open-minded we've gotten more closed-hearted.

Message to society: What you applaud, you encourage. Watch out what you celebrate. [This part was written just before the Dan Quayle—Murphy Brown flap, about which one might say he said the right thing in the wrong way and was the wrong man to say it. There is a kind of darkish heavy-handedness that comes over some Republican men when they talk about matters requiring some delicacy. They always sound judgmental, when they mean to show concern.]

Forbes published the piece in September '92. Even now, just a year later, there are things I would quarrel with in it. I don't, on second thought, think any real journey is beginning with the New Age movement. I think it's more a detour, a truck stop on the way to the Rockies. More important, I think some of the generational emphasis, or thinking, was off. I kept sort of referring to America's loss of faith as the boomers were being born, but really, of course, it's a story with a longer time frame. Looking at my family and the families of my friends I can say of almost all of us that our grandparents' generation was, by and large, a pretty faithful and religious one. But their children—the parents of the boomers—had, many of them, already distanced themselves from deep belief and worship, gone beyond it. Some of them thought it was peasanty, immigranty, like their parents. They wanted to be modern. They *were* modern. They drank and smoked and discovered Marilyn Monroe, they listened to Sinatra, worried about the bomb, built fallout shelters. They had their babies in hospitals, and the mothers didn't breastfeed them like someone who couldn't afford milk—they bought bottles and rubber nipples and those big old sterilizers. They were in their own way, even the ones who weren't Norman Mailer, hipsters. They were, even the ones who weren't John Kennedy, Superman at the Supermarket. The Catholics among them were the first Catholics who really made it in America. The affluence they knew, after such effort, distanced them from the spiritual by distancing them from problems that have long led men to "flee from petty tyrants to the throne." The Catholics of my parents' generation had not only a few dollars but a social acceptance and worldly possibilities their parents had not known. They had a president. Who needs God when you've got America? And from what I've seen, a lot of this applies to Jews too, at least Jews of the East, whose people came over in the last hundred years or so. If you're Jewish and a boomer, your parents probably believed in politics, or professionalism. But their parents—poorer, more segregated from society—did not more of them seriously observe their faith?

Anyway, our parents: we inherited our distance from religion in part from them.

—

But wonderful things followed the *Forbes* article.

Religious people from all over started sending me letters and books and I read them all, and I finally understood something that had confused me. The simpleminded ecstasy of people who love Jesus and who have discovered his love for them and who write of it—I had always found this embarrassing and irritating. Years ago I had read or tried to read the autobiography of Saint Thérèse of Lisieux and had thought: Why do people call this great? But now, reading in a new way, I saw that her joy, their joy, is only what Edith Wharton meant when she observed that all love letters are alike whether written by geniuses or dolts—I love you, I adore you, you're so good, so wonderful, thank you. It is the limited, limitless language of love. And Saint Thérèse was great because her autobiography was the purest, most innocent and grateful verbalization of love the Church had ever seen. She was in love with God.

There was the man in the bookshop on Lexington Avenue. I was looking for a book—I was with my son and I think it was for a book for him, because he was at that in-between age, five, in which *Goodnight Moon* was behind him and *Boy's Life of Abe Lincoln* is ahead, and he can't yet read but has a sophisticated interest in, of all things, science, and finding the right books to read to him at night is suddenly difficult. I got into a conversation with the man at the cash register. I don't recall what we were talking about, but I don't think it had anything to do with religion. But he picked up a book from a pile of books near the cash register and said, "You might be interested in this." It was called *Centering Prayer*, by Basil Pennington. So I took it home and there, in the first few pages, was the God of Revelations: "Look, I am standing at the door, knocking. If one of you hears me calling and opens the door, I will come in to share his meal, side by side with him." It struck me hard: I had never thought of him at the door trying to get to me, I thought I was at the door trying to get to him.

That phrase began to follow me. A week later, at Mass, the priest used as the central image in his homily a stained-glass window near the back of the church. In it, he noted, Christ is standing at a door, and waiting for those inside, us, to open it to him. Take a look as you leave, he said, you'll notice there is only one handle on the door, and it faces those inside the room. Only they can open it, Christ cannot. He waits; he is humble.

Then my friend Allie from Connecticut read the *Forbes* piece, took it to a Bible-study meeting, came back and called and said: "I'm starting a new Bible study, a New York chapter for all you heathens, will you come?" Yes, I will.

And at the first meeting we read, "I am standing at the door, knocking . . ."

—

A few months later I met a priest at the taping of a TV show on PBS, and I wrote to him and asked: "Can you help me learn to pray?" He responded with a four-page handwritten letter full of encouragement and sound advice. He said:

You have privileged me by sharing a part of your soul with me. I've been thinking about what to say for a week, off & on, & carrying you in my prayers—which I will continue. If I say, "God help us both," that's a prayer, and not a facetious one. Souls, after all, are serious business. St. Don Bosco took as his motto (from the Latin of Genesis 14:21) "Give me souls, & take away the rest," & that remains our motto. . . . That you're seeking God, seeking Jesus, seeking the spirit is already wonderful & endears you to the Father, the Son, & the Spirit. You're like the woman at the well in next Sunday's gospel, thirsting for you don't know quite what, or like Zaccheus the tax collector (Luke 19:1-10), or so many others.

You're a unique person (we all are), so any advice or suggestion I can send your way must be tentative. Even in the spiritual life we need a lot of trial & error, like your sampling of prayer books. . . . But the place to begin is really with the scriptures, especially the gospels. In them we meet Jesus first-hand (nearly—he is "translated" by Mathew, Mark, Luke & John). A woman who works in our building said recently that this Lent she's getting back to daily Bible reading, a half hour or so, & it makes such a difference in her life. (She's a wife, mother of at least one teenager & a pre-adolescent, & part-time worker with her CPA husband). . . .

Lives of the saints are also inspiring, i.e., they enliven the Spirit within us. Saints are images of Christ, real people with real problems & real relationships who found God & Jesus in all of us. . . . (You wrote) "Maybe books aren't the way." They're one way. But the goal is God in Jesus, thru the Spirit. Whatever we read has to lead us to better prayer & more Christ-like living. Prayer, Peggy, is just conversation with God (addressed as Father, or Son, or Spirit, or all 3) or with Mary or a saint. You've got plenty to talk about: your son, life in New York, your bills, your ex, Bill Clinton, sick friends or relatives, some joy or other. . . . You can speak as freely as you like in prayer: question, thank, ponder, ask forgiveness, be angry, exult. . . .

And the sacraments are really important—Mass every Sunday, reconciliation (confession) about monthly. St. Francis de Sales advised: Only 2 kinds of people need frequent communion—the not-so-good, that they might become better; & the good, that they might stay that way. If you haven't already, look for a church with good liturgy & good preaching—& God will take it from there. . . .

Naturally it hurt me a little to be compared to a tax collector, but it was good advice first to last, and I took it.

I was asked by a friend the other night, "How has this changed you?" And I don't know the answer because I feel I'm on a journey and not there yet, so I don't have a vantage point from which to point and say, Ah, that was the valley, this is the top of the first hill. I can tell you that I often go to Mass during the week, and sometimes afterward stay and say the Rosary with a half-dozen women who are there, in front of the candles in front of the Virgin, every day. They are mostly old, but not all. They have German, Irish and Filipino accents. One of them is the nanny of a friend of my son. We are always surprised and delighted and embarrassed to see each other. I am often self-conscious; I am embarrassed to be here and embarrassed that I am embarrassed. I am afraid someone will see me, for only people in trouble are in church in the afternoon saying the Rosary. Only people who have lost something. But I have found something. I fortify myself, tug back and forth, try to maintain concentration. The good news is that it's like doing any odd thing—the more you do it, the less odd it feels.

—

I mentioned the Bible-study group that my friend Allie started. A dozen of us get together each Tuesday morning for about two hours. One of the nice things about the group is that its members have a very practical way of translating spiritual truths into daily lessons, of turning How To Live into how to live each day. A few weeks ago Allie mused aloud about how people torment themselves with If Onlys. If only I'd developed my talents, if only I'd known it was the wrong school, if only I'd married the other one. We forget, she said, to think about the What Ifs. What if I hadn't fastened the seat belt, what if I had taken that flight, or decided the law degree wasn't worth it.

This, she says, is something everyone has to remember: *The What Ifs redeem the If Onlys.* Don't worry about the past or the future, today's problems are sufficient to today. And we will all gain greater perspective and greater peace if we remember something simple and difficult: We must live in the kingdom of God, and not in the world. The world is around us with all its pleasures, joys and temptations, but there is no peace there. The only peace is in the Kingdom of God, which is not far away on a map but within you. Which is not to suggest, of course, that it is an easy journey.

—

A paradox: The great changes and reforms that have swept the Christian churches the past twenty-five years, including the ecumenical movement, and the modernization of text and prayer that accompanied it, have helped drive many serious Christians from the big mainline churches. A lot of the women at Bible study go now to smaller Protestant churches or to a nearby Baptist church for the preaching. They don't seem to really think of themselves as Episcopalians or Presbyterians anymore. They think of themselves as Christians. They get their spiritual nourishment from unofficial, voluntary groups such as this, the spirit and membership of which is profoundly ecumenical.

This is where the real ecumenicism is happening now in America, in groups such as ours, and in the Bible-study groups that have for some time been springing up all over New York and Washington, all over the country.

———

A friend is back from an ashram in upstate New York where an Indian guru—a woman, late thirties, dignified—instructed a thousand followers and would-be believers in the way of the spirit.

"This is such a strange country," says my friend, who went as a journalist. "There are all these people who look like regular people from New York and they're sitting in front of this swami lady, and they're all looking for something, for belief."

"Who are they?"

"Lawyers, dentists, accountants. Melanie Griffith goes there, a lot of celebrities, a lot of Jews."

"Why don't they try to find God in a temple?"

"Because it's not really emotional enough, it doesn't really involve or encourage the transcendent."

"Tell me about the guru in this way: we all respect spiritual inquiry that is sincere and honest and looking for God, but is she a serious person in search, or a thief manipulating needy people?"

"Well, that's the question. I don't know. She tells her followers among other things that if they follow her path they will have success and prosperity."

"Mmmmmmm. Some Christians have prosperity theology, but most Christians believe that to find Christ is to find peace but there's no promise of prosperity or success. Not in this world, anyway."

"These people seem to want to have it both ways, here and in other lives."

She was told to wear a long skirt. She bought one and put it on her expense account. In one of the seminars they were told that extramarital sex is wrong and not the correct choice, that for the unmarried the proper decision is celibacy. This was greeted with silence.

"What about masturbation?" a woman asked.

"There is some disagreement about that," said the group leader, "but we would ask that you refrain from it here."

"That got silence too." My friend laughed.

"Was it for you, the weekend, a spiritual experience?"

"I tried to be spiritual, but I couldn't really feel it."

"Did a lot of the people there?"

"Oh yes. Some of them were in kind of trances."

"Maybe the good thing about ashrams and all this is it can make clear to you that God is the destination. Then you go home and sit down and figure, This is a good destination but I think I'll take another route. I think I'll go by that church down the block and get a road map. I think I'll go talk to my rabbi."

"Oh, Peggy, maybe. That's— You're talking to a skeptic at the ashram, honey."

I told her one of the most impressive things about her is that she manages to live without religious belief and not die every day of depression.

"But I'm always depressed," she said, with pride. "Haven't you noticed?"

"Oh yes. There is that. But seriously. Life is so— It's many wonderful things but ultimately the facts of life are so difficult and tragic, and there you are burrowing through with yourself and your courage. And it just seems so brave and hearty. I feel like now and then I want to—tip my hat. To your human heartiness."

"Really? To me belief seems like the hard thing. All the reasons not to."

—

Later I thought: There are people who don't believe in God, angels and saints because, first of all, to start with the obvious, they have never seen them. But they have full faith in the existence of black holes, quarks and neutrinos, and they've never seen them, either. My friend might say, "But I've seen the effects of their existence." But you could pick up a flower and see the effects of God's existence. "If I were inclined to see things that way, yes," she would gently reply.

Maybe it does come down to inclination, to a turn of mind. The modern mind is inclined to believe in science. The unmodern mind is inclined to believe in God and his creation, about which we can discover much through science. How do you get the unmodern inclination in the modern age? Through grace, say many Christians. And grace can come through many ways and many things.

When I was seven I was lucky to be taught my religion through the stark and unambiguous Baltimore Catechism. *Who made us? God made us.* We sat in a little room off a church in Massapequa, Long Island, a little room that was like a shack, all made of rough wood. They must have been building something. Actually, if I'm remembering correctly, they were building the new modern church that's there now. They must have been building, and we were in a little annex.

Christian Doctrine class was at night. I went with a girl down the block. There was a nun who taught us. I don't remember anything about her but that she dressed in the old habit, with the tall white part on top pressing into her forehead. She was a figure of respect, and no one ever sassed her. But then we were not at that point a sassy generation. I think she must have had no particular gift for dealing with children, as I don't remember anything warm or interesting she ever said. I seem to recall her carrying a yardstick, but that may be from reading Catholic memoirs.

I would like to say I rebelled from her doctrinaire teaching, but I didn't. I believed everything she said. I thought it was all true. And so, I think, did all the other children. I wish I still had that old dog-eared catechism so I could see what went into our minds, how it all worked. But I'm sure part of it was the power of simplicity, of clear and unadorned assertion. Like saying water's wet.

—

This afternoon I thought of Mary Jane Cuddihy McGuire. Once when I was a teenager, I think, I read Stephen Birmingham's *Real Lace*, a breezy social chronicle of the Irish in America. One of the stories he told was of a big family named Cuddihy that made its fortune in Midwestern meat-packing and then went east and discovered the Hamptons. It was the twenties and I think the island wasn't quite respectable yet, it was Fanny Brice and Nicky Arnstein and the Gatsbys. The Cuddihys had their series of star-crossed generations and things changed, and here at the end of the book Birmingham was interviewing Mary Jane Cuddihy McGuire, who was middle-aged and living in Manhattan. She'd been a girl in the book. The talk turned to faith, and Mary Jane Cuddihy McGuire told Birmingham of the peace and pleasure she receives each day from going to Mass and taking communion. "If I didn't have it I'd just die," she said. "I'd just die."

Her words, when I read them years ago, opened a door. And then I let it shut. But what she said stayed in my mind. When I left Washington and came back to Manhattan in 1989 and was looking for an apartment, a friend introduced me to his friend Jack, and Jack said, "Oh, you must go talk to my sister, she's in real estate." And she was the fabled-in-my-imagination Mary Jane Cuddihy McGuire, now a real estate agent. I met her and just fell in love. She was small and spry and blond and we ran around the East Side smoking cigarettes and looking at sublets I couldn't afford. We traded life stories. She said, "You should meet my friend the monsignor. He'd be a good friend. He's Irish but not dumb Irish, if you know what I mean."

One day we were looking at a rental on Ninetieth and she said, "We're near the monsignor, let's go say hello." So we walked into a little rectory on Eighty-ninth Street and she pushed open the door and said to the secretary, who hopped to "Mary Jane Cuddihy McGuire for the monsignor." And soon the monsignor had us in his office and she was telling him the story of my life. I listened with fascination. He asked me questions. I told him actually something very big was bothering me; for the first time in my life there was someone who was giving me such a hard time, who was being so bad, that I actually had moments when I thought: I wish he would die.

The monsignor looked at the ceiling and made a little steeple with his hands and tapped them together. Then he nodded. "Actually most of us have had moments like that. But they do no one any good, and of course it's not right. So what I think you should do, the next time this fellow does something and you feel that way, try thinking instead: 'Wouldn't it be wonderful if God took John home to his bosom soon.' And we'll work on from there."

I started to laugh and so did the monsignor, and Mary Jane Cuddihy McGuire nudged my arm and shook her head. "That's not all she needs," she told the priest. And he said, "I know." He said, "I think you need the protection of your Church." And we began the process that would include me, again, in its life.

In time Mary Jane Cuddihy McGuire got me a sublet in her huge apartment building in the sixties, and I called her to say "Come say hi to my son." She put me off and then told me she wasn't well, hadn't actually been well in some time, but when she felt better she'd come, and was I still seeing the monsignor? And then, in a few months, she was dead. I was, as she would have put it, her last big deal. I certainly had the winning end of it. But I cannot think it an accident that in the last year of her life this woman who had made such an impression on me when I was young came into mine, and pushed open a door, and kept her foot in, and wouldn't let it close. Grace works that way too, with others who know themselves unangelic as its angelic agents.

—

The central problem for Catholics who have returned to the Church in the past decade or so is the continuing surprise that the Church they left has disappeared. The Church of the fifties and sixties, the Church of certitude and confidence, is gone. In its place is a more open and less stern thing, a less mysterious thing, too. I miss the mystery; you could almost see it in the old days in the dark, shadowed corners and the candles flickering below saints with imploring hands. Now we have big airy suburban churches that look like Dulles Airport, bright, clean and arid, no shadows, few saints, little battery-operated candles in case some grandma needs to light one. (If only priests knew that one of the ways parents get little kids to come to church is by promising them they can light a candle at the end.)

And still Catholics come. What a testimony to the power of faith.

—

We didn't have liberal parishes and conservative parishes, as we do now. In this we are like the Jews with their Reform, Conservative and Orthodox synagogues. But Jews have these because they still debate what Judaism is. Catholics used to know what Catholicism is.

Priests were understood to be celibate, a condition all assumed to be difficult but doable. There were no sex scandals involving priests, or none we knew of. Now we know some occurred and were covered up, the victims, mostly children, abandoned by their Church and forced to go through decades of silent shame. There was a piece on *PrimeTime Live* recently that had the saddest sentence. A young woman talked about how she'd been molested by her priest as a child; she was afraid to tell and it ruined her life. "He took God from me," she said.

Catholics both lapsed and adhering talk about these scandals a lot. Most everyone is still shocked by them. When the stories started surfacing in the news a few years ago, some of us thought they were individual and unusual cases that were being trumpeted by a media ever ready to demonstrate the truth of somebody's observation that anti-Catholicism is the anti-Semitism of the intellectual. It's the last accepted bigotry. But in time, as the testimonies mounted, I realized, no. Media enthusiasm for these stories may or may not reflect unattractive biases in producers and reporters, but if the American Catholic Church is infested with unworthy and corrupt men it's no favor to the Church to hide it. It is a favor to reveal it. (I think I'm being unfair to members of the media to this extent: newspapers like the *Times* have not been sensational in their coverage of the scandals, in part I suspect because reporters and editors at the *Times* know they have a bias against the Church and have tried hard to resist it, or at least not betray it.)

I also think this, narrow-minded person that I am: The great enemy on earth of the evil one is the Church, and what better time to infiltrate it than when it was at its most triumphant, in the past few decades when the Pope's troops were day by day defeating Communism.

—

A small irony. Actually, probably not so small. The reign of the Latin Mass, in which Catholics in every country in the world said the Mass in the same Latin, ended in 1964. Just six years later the 747 came in, the jumbo jet that, with its low ticket prices, freed average Catholics, for the first time, to travel the world over. These accidental tourists would go to Mass in whatever country they were in and not understand a word that was being said because the locals were celebrating Mass in their native tongue.

Soon after began the massive influx of immigrants into half of Europe and much of the Americas; the Latin Mass would have provided a helpful continuity, a helpful religious and social reality, to all the new Catholics in their new countries. All of which is to say that in one of those strange ironies with which history amuses itself, just at the moment when the Latin Mass was beginning to have its clearest practical purpose—in the modern era, when Catholics began to traverse the globe—it was ended.

—

A few years ago I read Thomas Merton's *The Seven Storey Mountain*, the memoir of his journey from artistically ambitious Columbia College student to Trappist monk. I was late in getting to it. People were reading it when I was in college, and for some reason I thought it was about drugs. I can't remember why. Anyway, I used to think that those who, in telling us of their conversions, repeatedly refer to themselves as king of sin, most sinful person ever, were bragging, or neurotically exaggerating their culpability, as if finding their new selves had made them hate their former selves, rather than transcending them. But finally it occurred to me that Merton insists on the ugliness of his moral character because he is honest—he thinks his younger, scheming, dreaming, rutting self was disgusting. And because he means to encourage. He wants you to know bums can become saints; he knows, it happened to him. He also wants to communicate: This world you love so much, these pleasures—they're not only empty, they are nothing compared with the pleasure of God's love. You are hungry and stuck at the hors d'oeuvres tray, you're stuffing yourself and missing the entrée, which is where the really delicious, good-for-you things are.

Anyway, there is much that is wonderful in this great memoir, but something has struck me hard the past few days when I picked it up again. When Merton graduated from Columbia he went to teach and study at a Catholic college in upstate New York. One night he went to hear a speaker who came to the school. She was Baroness de Hueck, "who was working among the Negroes in Harlem."

Merton wrote—it was 1948—

Now a woman, standing all alone on a stage, in front of a big lighted hall, without any directions or costume or special lighting effects, just in the glare of the hall lights, is at a disadvantage. It is not very likely that she will make much of an impression. And this particular woman was dressed in clothes that were nondescript and plain, even poor. She had no artful way of walking around, either. She had no fancy tricks, nothing for the gallery. And yet as soon as I came in the door, the impression she was making on that room full of nuns and clerics and priests and various lay-people pervaded the place with such power that it nearly knocked me backwards down the stairs which I had just ascended.

She had a strong voice, and strong convictions, and strong things to say, and she was saying them in the simplest, most unvarnished, bluntest possible kind of talk, and with such uncompromising directness that it stunned. You could feel right away that most of her audience was hanging on her words, and that some of them were frightened, and that one or two were angry, but that everybody was intent on the things she had to say.

What she was saying boiled down to this:

Catholics are worried about Communism: and they have a

right to be, because the Communist revolution aims, among other things, at wiping out the Church. But few Catholics stop to think that Communism would make very little progress in the world, or none at all, if Catholics really lived up to their obligations, and really did the things Christ came on earth to teach them to do: that is, if they really loved one another, and saw Christ in one another, and lived as saints, and did something to win justice for the poor. . . .

If Catholics, she said, were able to see Harlem as they should see it, with the eyes of faith, as a challenge to their love of Christ, as a test of their Christianity, the Communists would be able to do nothing there.

But, on the contrary, in Harlem the Communists were strong. . . . They were doing some of the things, performing some of the works of mercy that Christians should be expected to do. . . . If some Negro is dying, and is refused admission to a hospital, the Communists show up, and get someone to take care of him, and furthermore see to it that the injustice is publicized all over the city. If a Negro family is evicted because they can't pay the rent, the Communists are there, and find shelter for them. . . . And every time they do these things, more and more people begin to say: "See, the Communists really love the poor! They are really trying to do something for us!"

When I was a teenager and in my twenties I thought the kind of thing Merton wrote and the baroness said was true. Later, in my late twenties and thirties I thought it wasn't. I was by then, in the seventies and eighties, impatient with such thinking. I'd think, Please, it is unhelpful to say the least to encourage the suggestion that the natural and unending imperfection of man, his unwillingness to be saintly, in any way legitimizes the existence of a soul-killing machine like Communism.

And now I think—Oh hell, Merton was right. The baroness was

right. If everyone lived as Christ asked, Communism would have had no converts but the devil.

But man will likely not start living as Christ asked anytime soon. I won't, will you? I didn't think so.

And if we won't, that economic system that promises the greatest, broadest amount of personal freedom and personal prosperity, the one that goes furthest toward guaranteeing a job that can support a family, is of course the one to choose. And that, in our time, is free-market democratic capitalism, the profits of which are not taxed to such an extent that the job-producing engine clogs, sputters or dies. The socialism I thought was the right arrangement when I was seventeen, the welfare-state spending that seemed compassionate and kind when I was twenty seemed, ten years later, not only unhelpful but destructive.

I also thought by my thirties and think: If you believe in the Old and New Testaments, you know man is fallen. And if man is fallen, if he is in fact too often a little snake, it is not wise to put great power in the hands of a band of men, i.e., a snakes' nest, and a band of men making decisions from on high is what rules Socialist and Communist countries. It is wiser to keep as much power as possible in the hands of the individual, in the hands of the woman who writes the rent check or the man who runs the hardware store. This is not a faultless system, but it is like Churchill's comment on democracy: it is the most imperfect system, except for all the others.

But it hasn't solved the problem of poverty.

I think as a nation we've gotten to a point where we've given up on welfare as a means of alleviating human suffering, or as a means of encouraging human improvement. I think we've gotten to the point, as a nation, where we're only trying to buy off our conscience with the welfare program. I think it has degenerated from a program of compassionate assistance to a program that consists of the weary paying of protection money, in the form of welfare checks, to unhappy people in unhappy places in hopes this will make them simply leave us alone.

One result is that welfare recipients are profoundly segregated, not only by neighborhood but much more profoundly by circumstance. It is the segregation of souls. You stay home and take dope and live your wayward life and we'll pay for it—but don't come out and hurt us.

I have never heard a politician in Washington, Democrat or Republican, say he or she thinks the welfare system works. Not one. Most of them know and some will tell you that welfare has not only not eased the pathology of poverty, it has contributed to it, spurred it. Clinton does nothing because it's no. 8 on his list of things to do and he will probably never get below 3 or 4, which is probably a good thing, as he'd be whipped by the pressure groups that run his party into reform that is only change, not improvement. The Democrats do nothing because their constituent groups won't let them, and because some of them actually believe the left-wing things they say. The Republicans have ideas but insufficient congressional power, and at any rate they are afraid of being accused of two things: balancing the budget on the backs of the poor, and looking at welfare because they are racist. Willie Horton may or may not have hurt Mike Dukakis, but he certainly hurt those Republicans whose every effort at reform is scrutinized within a context of Hortonism.

Third- and fourth-generation welfare recipients deserve to be integrated into society, not through some ignorant public-housing scheme like that of HUD's Henry Cisneros, who believes the answer is putting up public housing in middle-class suburbs, but through the great and reliable integrator of American history: work.

They should work in the world. They should be part of the world. They should know the dignity and discipline of taking part and belonging, of slapping the top of the alarm clock and groaning like everyone else and joining the fray. Joining life. They should be detached from their loneliness and attached to the daily life of the nation.

How to do this? I suppose you start with the knowledge that people are people, they are autonomous, they will do what they want. They don't necessarily desire your advice, thank you, and might be inclined to tell those who've come to instruct them on how to live that perhaps it would be a good idea if you would go away like a nice person.

This is their right. But we who pay for their food and their rent also have rights. We have the right to say, We respect your position and will no longer bother you with either our advice or our welfare payments. Have a nice day.

But many recipients would no doubt like a break, a possibility. Before you come up with ways to give them a break—and there are members of both parties who study how to give them a break—you should quickly read two books. One is E. B. White's marvelous and tender tribute *Here is New York*. White, of course, was a liberal in the 1949 sense of being a hopeful person who had respect for all. He had a very modern assumption that nice, smart good-thinking liberals who meant, seriously, to improve the life of the poor could probably, working together and with the power of government, do it.

You could start out reading just one poignant paragraph:

The slums are gradually giving way to the lofty housing projects—high in stature, high in purpose, low in rent. There are a couple of dozen of these new developments scattered around; each is a city in itself (one of them in the Bronx accommodates twelve thousand families), sky acreage hitherto untilled, lifting people far above the street, standardizing their sanitary life, giving them some place to sit other than an orange crate.

Slums giving way? Lifting people? Standardizing their sanitary life? Well, at least that happened, but not as White intended. In this one paragraph you can hear the sound of the liberal dream breaking. It is just sad: a public housing project in the Bronx is, now, the heart of the horror.

You couldn't be smarter or more humane than E. B. White. And still in these big things he was wrong.

I do not mean to suggest that all effort is pointless. I do not mean all schemes are doomed. I do not even mean to suggest that White's words demonstrate the truth of Woody Allen's third law of thermo-dynamics: Sooner or later everything turns to shit.

I do mean the obvious: social engineers, the builders and planners and movers of public housing and public policy, almost always get it wrong. It's not that they are intellectuals, and therefore by defini-tion stupid. It's that in their own way they are dreamers. They are in a dream of ideas. They forget that their abstract notions about justice have a real and concrete impact on the daily lives of individual humans. They live in their heads, the way poets and serial killers do, the way Brendan Behan did and Jeffrey Dahmer does, and are just a tad insensitive to the humans around them. They get ideas; they can actually think people who are sick, abused and abusive will start acting like members of the Westchester Parent-Teacher Association just because you want them to, just because you gave them an apartment on the fourteenth floor. And they are modern, and so can never figure in the existence of those old reliables—evil, weakness and bad behavior.

There is at least one other must-read, Jane Jacobs's classic *The Death and Life of American Cities.* She warned, back in 1963, that the nerdish urban planners who were tearing up the city were doing it with a mindless indifference to the habits, views and insights of the people who live on the block. Any old Italian grandma sitting in front of a small apartment building on a folding chair could have told you that razing a block of apartments to put up a big office building would make a good neighborhood bad. No one with a stake in the neighborhood—no one who knew Johnny was cutting school and his parents weren't watching him, who knew what the normal traffic was in and out of the deli—would be there during the day. No one would be there at night to put on a light and look out the window. You're not making things more shining and modern with your new buildings, she said, you're making them more dangerous and open to neglect.

But it was the sixties; they weren't listening to grandma. They're not listening to grandma today.

May I take a wild leap and tell you my fantasy of the city? It is only a fantasy, but it will perhaps give a sense of what goes through one conservative's imagination when the subject is poverty. It reflects a faith that human beings are often motivated by two things that are opposites but that often work well together: self-interest and altruism.

Also it has this going for it: when liberals give you fantasies you pay for them, but this one is free.

Here it is.

By the mid-1990s in America it had long been obvious that the efforts of government to help the intractable poor had come to nothing. And so America enlisted business, enlisted entrepreneurs and professionals, to try to turn the situation around. Why not? We have so many of each; they are there to be used, and are even often eager.

The federal government in Washington, with the almost unanimous backing of big-city mayors and state governors, adopted the Kempian notions advanced by some Republicans in the 1980s and announced to every business in the country, "Move into the worst part of the inner city and set up your factory, store, or office and we will not charge you a penny of federal state or city tax for fifty years. Not a penny. And we'll help you every way we can. You'll make a lot of money, which your shareholders will enjoy a lot. But there's a price, of course. You have to commit to the community. You have to train and hire local people. You have to live with them. You have to help them make their lives and, much more to the point, their children's lives better."

This is how it works:

If you're a department store you go into the South Bronx, and you'll be so relieved at not paying taxes and having a new low overhead that you'll offer considerably lower prices than at the store you operate in midtown Manhattan, and bargain hunters will flock to you. This will be a fairly typical dialogue:

Woman in front of $800,000 house in Montclair, New Jersey:
    Hi, Jane, where are you going?
Jane, the neighbor next door: To the South Bronx to shop.
Woman: You must be insane.
Neighbor: Armani jackets, $350.
Woman: I'll get my coat.
Neighbor: Don't forget your gun!
Woman: Oh, hon, I'm out of ammo.
Neighbor: That's okay, I've got some!
Woman: Let's go!

You must employ the people who live in the neighborhood. This will require a lot of job training from you, but that's okay because you're making a heck of a lot of money and your shareholders are about to vote you CEO for life. You're going to find a lot of single mothers with kids. A lot of them are young, a lot of them are disturbed and some of them are addicted to dope and alcohol, but you're going to handle that too. You're going to have on-site day care and you're going to employ a lot of doctors and nurses who come in part-time, in the evenings or afternoons, from the big-city hospitals, to help the mothers with drug counseling and the kids with the psychic abuse they've absorbed over the years. The doctors and nurses are going to come because they get a free pass on their federal income tax every year they work with you. They'll get some AFDC mothers out of the house and back into the work force; some of the mothers will start to work part-time in the day-care centers. You're paying for the day-care centers too.

Refurbish old apartment buildings for your employees to live in down the block from the factory—and we want a bunch of your employees to live in the area and not just work in it—and we will not tax the buildings or mess them up with any of our rent laws.

All the churches and synagogues are going to be there helping, which isn't new, as a lot of them are there already. The Catholics in particular will be helpful. They have a lot of decent and energetic left-wing nuns and priests who like to talk about fighting the oppressors of the oppressor class, like the wondrous Sister Prejean of *Dead Men Walking*. The Church will put her in charge of its efforts here. In time she'll write another book in which she talks about how the oppressor-class Big Widget Company is making the slums work.

In time she and other religious will become more deeply convinced that what the poor want from them is what everybody else wants from them, not political agitation but spiritual help.

A young priest will notice that his new flock, oddly enough, seems to respond most deeply to talk about Christ, and His way. This will make the young priest, who is a decent fellow who wants to help, give them Christ. In this way the young priest will himself rediscover God, and forget his earlier belief, which was politics. This will save the young priest's soul. Which is why canny old Cardinal O'Connor sent him there.

The young priest will so fully find God that he will become

generous in his judgments. One day he will come upon a lady in the new Barney's on Willis Avenue who is out of it, confused, on Valium, perhaps, or vodka. Her hair is in disarray, as if she'd fallen asleep in her car, which she did. She will babble. They will sit on the steps near the third-floor ladies' room and she will say, Help me. They will strike up a friendship, they will talk on the phone, and in time he will see that he is needed where she lives, where souls are lost and needy—a moral desert in need of a good priest. He will ask to be reassigned from the South Bronx.

"I want to help the most troubled people in society," he will tell his bishop.

The bishop will nod solemnly, for he will understand. "You mean . . . Greenwich?"

The young priest gulps. "Yes. And Cos Cob."

"All right. You've got guts, son. Good luck."

The welfare working will, if they wish, be able to designate a portion of their pay to go to buying their public-housing apartments. In time, with a paycheck, and a newly bustling street and the day care and the counseling, particularly from a really nice nurse from Forest Hills, Queens, who has become her friend, an AFDC mother with three kids and a coupon book telling her she is 10 percent there on buying the apartment will, having met the neighbors, one of whom is a salesman from Hempstead whose hobby is gardening, decide she wants some flowers on her windowsill. Luckily, a guy who used to run a flower shop on Lexington in the seventies will have opened one down the block. She will go there, taking her oldest son. They will stand in that warm-mist smell. She will talk with a clerk about watering schedules and Miracle-Gro. Her son will watch, see the plants, see the cactuses and tall trees and little flowers in little green plastic holders, and see his mother—who is afraid of clerks, afraid of people in stores, afraid of all authority or what she thinks is authority—actually having a conversation with a guy who purports to know about something. Years later the boy will think, It's funny that that's my first memory, as I was already seven. He will remember his mother saying, "I'll take the pink ones, and these ones too. And the cactus for my son."

Of course that alone won't do it.

The young men and boys who are crime in the cities: we'll have to help them, too. We're going to take some of the soldiers laid off in the downsizing of the armed forces, and we're going to remove some troops from Europe, and we're going to give them a new job: Soldiers of the City. Saviors of the country.

They're going to police the streets, and they're also going to run a CCC-type training camp. It's going to be a few miles from the new factories and stores. Or maybe it will be upstate in rural areas, I'm not sure. Big gyms, big fields, big auditoriums with classrooms, computers donated by IBM and Apple, which have parts-manufacturing plants nearby. They'll also provide trainers who, needless to say, will be well paid and untaxed.

To get into the training camp you have to be young, under twenty or so, and you have to have a record or be from a family that isn't working. There's going to be a tough top sergeant, Sergeant Toughlove. He's straight and trim as Louis Gossett, Jr., in *An Officer and a Gentleman,* and he barks at the kids with a ruthlessness that belies his inner decency. "I break 'em down and I put 'em back together," he says. In time he'll love the boys and love his work. He's going to fall in love with a local AFDC mother of three kids who need a father. He met her at the day-care center. No, he met her at the flower shop when she was buying flowers for the windowsill.

He'll get the boys up and using their energy for good things— studying, reading, cleaning up vacant lots, fixing vacant buildings, planting things. They'll read Robert Frost and Langston Hughes, read *Raisin in the Sun,* and *The Member of the Wedding,* and Shakespeare and William Inge. Sergeant Toughlove will make sure they're up and out there and not missing computer class, where they're going to channel their young male aggression into first learning computers through computer games that are fun and then learning computer skills that are demanding. Oh—religious education is mandatory. They read the Old Testament, they read the New Testament, and rabbis and priests and ministers and nuns and mystics will come and tell them: This is the way, this is your culture, this is the new old America—consider it.

The first graduating class will be addressed in 1998 by the new president, who actually cares about the cities, who sees them not as a problem we have to buy off but a place full of potential. He is a man—or she is a woman—who thinks this isn't a matter of polls but a matter having to do with what is right.

And: all the congressmen and local pols are going to sign a pact in blood promising never to interfere and, ten years in, when the extent of your success and the size of your profits are clear, decide to change the deal, impose taxes or launch an investigation. The Reverend Al will have no right, no ability, to muck it up.

In short, we're going to take a chance and try something new.

Why not? We have nothing to lose. When nothing you've tried works, you have reached the point of total freedom: you can try anything.

—

For no reason that I fully understand I think often these days of a conversation between Winston Churchill and Violet Asquith. It was early on in his career, and he'd just been appointed home secretary. As such he was in charge of England's prison system. One night he was at a dinner party, where he sat with Asquith. They talked about prison, and she said the one thing she couldn't stand would be a life sentence, she'd choose to hang instead. And Churchill protested, in his vehement way, "Never abandon life. There is a way out of everything except death."

Never abandon life. Always choose life. These words are so simple and beautiful, their truth is so obvious, and we are shocked when someone we know, or know of, ignores them.

A year after his death almost everyone I know is still talking about Vincent Foster, and not only because of the recent revelations about the Whitewater scandal, and what may have been its role in his life, and death.

At first, when the story broke, there were reporters all over Little Rock interviewing Foster's friends and relations, and all over the death site on the Potomac looking for something, anything, that would make sense of it. And I knew how those reporters felt. I think I know why they were so frantic to find the reason Foster killed himself. Because if there wasn't a big untold story behind it, then it could happen to them. They have everything to live for too, they're at the top of their game too, they're his age, they have families and kids and a personal relationship with the president. And if Vincent Foster could kill himself, then they could kill themselves. It wasn't only journalistic curiosity, it was fear.

That's why he couldn't die of sadness, it had to be something else. And of course perhaps it was. Perhaps it was Whitewater, perhaps he had knowledge of an intrigue, perhaps he was being blackmailed, perhaps there was a scandal that was about to come out and the only way he could stop it was by killing himself. I have followed this trail in my imagination, mostly because of the violence of the act. Some instinct told me that when he put the gun to his head he was really killing his tormentors, blowing them apart.

—

There was another reason to be preoccupied by the Foster case: no one in the White House commits suicide. This is literally true: there has never been a suicide by a sitting White House staffer. They're too busy to die. They're on top of the world, they're running America, when they drive through the gates each morning they're entering history.

White House staffers are not as a group more mentally healthy than others, they're as screwy as everyone else, but the demons they tend to have are quelled by the life they are living. Jung said all neuroses are an attempt to avoid legitimate suffering, and the White House offers many opportunities for avoidance. Workaholism and its sweet balm of exhaustion, which leaves you too tired to see or face your sadness. Addiction to fear, and its distracting close calls. (Clinton, I think, has this; that's why when he has two months to prepare a big speech he can't complete it until eighteen minutes before broadcast, and then cannot rehearse, as he must, on TelePrompTer. He needs the fear. He needs to defeat it.) Obsessed immersion in your area of responsibility, which bestows a sense of personal meaning, the sense that your life has a point. Is your problem a gnawing lifelong sense of inferiority? Lunching with the president will tend to soothe that condition.

Anyway, they don't kill themselves.

It was all a reminder that emotions can override intellect, anguish defeat will, that all your defenses can blow away like an old picket fence when a hard wind comes.

Perhaps the Foster case will turn out to have been one of those detective stories where the most important clue was in the most obvious place, a place so unhidden that we all missed it—his eyes. In all the many smiling photographs of him—in a cluster with the Clintons, posing with law partners, walking into the concert hall—his smile never reaches his eyes. They are wary and sad-seeming. What his mouth is doing does not connect with what his eyes are doing. He must have been sad, or alone, for a long time.

But I still can't get my brain around it. He was a good man who loved his family and he left them with this horror, this unforgettable terrible thing, and he wasn't drunk and he wasn't drugged and he didn't get a ticket on the way to the little park on the Potomac. For weeks I couldn't stop thinking about the reports that the day he died he ate his lunch in his office, talked on the phone and acted as if it were a regular day and showed no particular sadness, no high melancholy. Maybe he was relieved, because as he walked around the White House that last day he knew, My pain will soon be over, my pain is going to end.

No one who doesn't do it understands the lure. Today I read the words of another Vincent, who, unlike this one, was quite mad, and a genius. Van Gogh had written with strange lucidity, weeks before he took his life, to his brother Theo, "Just as we take the train to get to Tarascon or Rouen, we take death to reach a star. . . . So it seems possible that cholera, gravel, tuberculosis and cancer are the celestial means of locomotion, just as steamboats, buses and railways are the terrestrial means. To die quietly of old age would be to go there on foot."

———

Washington suicide has its own drama not only because it is so public, so publicized. Washington suicide is usually a highly unusual kind of suicide in which one kills not oneself but the most real part of one's self: one's career. The self-destructive don't blow out their brains, they blow up their careers. Gary Hart is one. He is bitter still at what happened to him, but it is the strange bitterness of a man who played Russian roulette, got shot and is angry at the bullets.

There is Dick Darman. A man of great gifts, great accomplishments, who, still in his forties, was just about running the government. He wanted, I always thought, to be the finest public servant of his era; he wanted to be a Wise Man. And then, with the Bush loss of '92 coming, he tried to deflect blame by giving interviews to his best friend, Bob Woodward, who produced a series in which Darman denigrated Bush, whom he allowed to be painted as his philosophical and intellectual inferior. All this four weeks before the election.

Woodward printed the series earlier than Darman expected, earlier than Woodward said he would and with Darman revealed more clearly as the source than Darman anticipated. And when the series came out, when Woodward betrayed the betrayer, Darman was roundly reviled. On the right they claimed new proof that he was what they'd always said he was: a devious operator. In the middle, around Bush, they saw him as utterly and completely disloyal. Boyden Gray, the president's counselor, would later tell the reporter Owen Ullman, "[Darman] spun such an enormous web of deception that it was impossible for anyone in the White House to comprehend the extent of his deceit. When I began to see the full scope of it, I was amazed. I still am." On the left, they laughed or shook their heads: they always knew Bush and everyone around him was cynical.

Darman had committed a kind of suicide, a professional suicide. For treachery on such a scale can be neither hidden nor forgotten, and the day he left government, which was the day of Clinton's inaugural, he must have known that he had retired from political life forever.

What a waste of gifts. There was something moving about his expertise. There was something moving about his struggles. He was the smartest man I ever knew in government. He was the only person I knew, in five years in Washington, who actually seemed to understand how the government, in all its parts and pieces, worked.

There was something seductive about his intelligence. You saw it, saw him, and somehow you'd want to be in the circle of his regard. It's what did Sununu in, and, in a way, Bush. Some gifted people have this. I know a brilliant writer who has it; every time I see him or deal with him I am irritated by my desire for his approval, irritated because I don't even like him, he's not a nice person.

Why do we want the approval of the intelligent, what ratification do we think they can bestow? Especially when their intelligence isn't their power, how we react to it is their power. Which means the only power they have is the power we give them. Most everyone Dick knew gave him that power, and later regretted it.

He wanted to be one of the Wise Men, but not one of those old gentlemen would have betrayed his president, nor turned on his former colleagues, and for such a low thing as spin.

I think part of the lesson is this: if your whole life is calculation, if your mental processes are devoted primarily to plotting to advance yourself or enhance yourself, then sooner or later you'll trip yourself up. Because one can neither consistently calibrate action perfectly nor predict reaction perfectly; spin is not a science. Life is messy, mysterious and confounding. You can't always know outcomes.

Dick did not figure a friend of twenty years would betray him, a strange miscalculation because Dick, in pursuit of a goal, might well have betrayed a friend of twenty years. But he forgot to know that. In this most cerebral of men it was his heart—well, his assumption that affection would maintain, prevail, protect him—that tripped him up. He depended on Woodward's friendship. But Woodward no longer needed him; Woodward knew the architect of the budget deal, and his boss, were finished; Woodward did what you'd expect a reporter with a story to do to a source he no longer needed: he burned him. For the good of history, of course.

Pious connivers all, Flannery O'Connor said of journalists, pious connivers all.

And Ed Rollins. No one will ever know why Ed Rollins told a group of journalists at an on-the-record Sperling breakfast that the Republicans, in the New Jersey gubernatorial race of '93, tried to suppress the black vote by giving money to black ministers. No one will ever know why he did it because Ed doesn't know why he did it. He says he didn't plan to say it. He says he decided to say it because he wanted to make his nemesis, the Democratic strategist James Carville, go crazy. He says he never lies; he says what he said at the Sperling was a fiction.

I talked to Ed about it for *Vanity Fair* a few weeks after what he called the firestorm broke. He was hurting, and he was funny, and he was poignant and frustrating. He told me that no, he doesn't really think he's self-destructive, and no, he doesn't think he's addicted to fear, but yes, there is some truth in the idea that he wanted to leave politics and couldn't because he was such a success at it; and yes, maybe after winning the Jersey campaign, after making a spectacular personal comeback, maybe he was a little disappointed that he was back on top and couldn't leave, couldn't get his freedom back, and so maybe, just maybe . . . he blew his career to pieces at the Sperling to blow himself out of politics.

And maybe that's true. At any rate, he told me that the whole firestorm had sent him back to the Catholic Church, and naturally I found this fascinating but—well, did Ed know I had undergone something similar with regard to refinding belief? Yes, he said, his eyes flickering. And I realized this good guy, this bright and funny man, was probably both telling me a truth and spinning me.

Why not. In Washington life is spin, period. It is a place of big stakes, big power, big parties, big weirdness, a place where friendships often prove fraudulent. In a pile of letters left, possibly for my benefit, in an otherwise meticulous kitchen, I saw one on top that said, "Dear Ed and Sherrie, If I tell you that this too shall pass will you believe me? This is a hideous time, but it will not always be this way. In the meantime when and if you decide to do an interview, I hope you will do it with me."

After two days with Ed I concluded that there were perhaps Three Rules for Young Political Operatives to be sifted from the experience. (1) Never spin your friends; it adds distance. (2) Never network in a psychiatric ward; some of the people you cultivate may prove unreliable. (3) Never stop being nervous; the day of the Sperling Ed Rollins was calm.

But, you know, I think Ed was an accidental suicide. He's going to come back, but as a different person and, after his near-death experience, a better one.

—

It is New Year's Day, 1994, a good day to look back, and forward. Matthew Ridgway died last year, the hero who, the night before D-Day, tossed on his cot and thought of the words God spoke to Joshua: *I will not fail thee nor forget thee.* The other day the man who hid Anne Frank passed away, after a life marked by meaning. More and more we are entering a new era without their generation's sturdy, practical, soulful presence; we will miss the great survivors.

One senses in Americans these days a new dynamic, an odd unease. During World War II people worried about the war and its daily privations. During the Depression people worried about issues of similar personal urgency: where to live, how to pay the rent, what to eat. Where are we now as a country? In a funny place: relatively content, most of us, in the day-to-day, but worried about long-term trends. Today isn't the source of our unease, it is the imagined tomorrow.

In the world, too many countries are percolating with the heat too high; we can't help experiencing this era as not the placid dawn of a peaceful age but the illusory calm before stern storms.

At home certain trends—crime, cultural tension, some cultural Balkanization—will, we fear, continue; some will worsen. In my darker moments I have a bad hunch. The fraying of the bonds that keep us together, the strangeness and anomie of our popular culture, the increase in walled communities, the weakening of the old assumption that the stranger you see on the street is decent, sane and law-abiding, the rising radicalism of the politically correct who run our great universities and who seem to hold little intellectual or emotional attachment to the Constitution, the increased demand of all levels of government for the money of the people, the spotty success with which we are communicating to the young America's reason for being and founding beliefs, the growth of cities where English is becoming the second language . . . these things may well come together at some point in our lifetimes and produce something painful indeed. I can imagine, for instance, in the year 2020 or so, a movement in some states to break away from the union. Which would bring about, of course, a drama of Lincolnian darkness.

But America, the old galleon, has known higher seas. (Another dark thing to say: you will know that things have reached a bad pass when *Newsweek* and *Time*, if they still exist fifteen years from now, do cover stories on a surprising and disturbing trend: aging baby boomers leaving America, taking what savings they have to live the rest of their lives in places like Africa and Ireland. Strange as they are as a generation, boomers love their country. If they're quoted as saying things like "I came back to Dublin for the freedom," you'll know things have taken a turn.)

——

I'll stop being apocalyptic now. There are in fact many hopeful facts and trends. Here is a hopeful thing:

There is still much talk about the culture's war against religion, about the crèche-less public square and the television shows that depict believers only in negative terms, as crazed book burners, venal televangelists, duped naïfs. It troubles some people terribly; it used to trouble me. But it has finally occurred to me that the opposition of the elites is not so bad. Christianity, after all, is at its purest, its most vital, when it knows it is what it has always been: countercultural.

Serious Christian, Orthodox Jews, some others—they are the real counterculture in this society. And there is something good in this, something promising. It is what Christianity began as. So why be disheartened by its low status among the elites, among the people who run networks and publish books, among the intelligentsia. Pagans have been trying to kill Christianity for two thousand years, and each day it dies, and each day it rises. Force it underground and you empower it. You draw rebels, real rebels, the kind society doesn't acknowledge till half a century later, but powerful people nonetheless. The faith will not only endure but flourish, and, as it does in times of adversity, produce real saints.

It is odd that some Christians see themselves as the media do, as bland guys in gray suits with gray buzzcuts. They ought to see themselves as young Marlon Brando on a Harley, for they are the true anti-establishment, the true rebels, and with a cause.

Another hopeful sign: A man I know who is a television programmer told me a year ago that in a recent meeting of executives from various networks—a small meeting, but those in attendance were important in their areas—he decided to pipe up that he was often embarrassed about the grunge they all serve up on TV. He said, "If you are totally comfortable allowing your kids to watch what you put on TV, will you raise your hand?" No one did. "We ought to think about this," he told me he told them. I think he was telling the truth. I found this promising.

Shortly after this I was, by luck, seated next to the president of a network at a lunch. We got talking, and first he complained about rock lyrics, then he talked with real feeling about crime, and then he criticized the culture in general. I was taken aback, and said, "You know, you're starting to sound like me." I meant it as a warning. I had known him slightly years before, when he was an unpassionate political leftist who'd partly inherited his views and partly held them because he wanted to be like everyone else in media.

"Life makes conservatives of us all," he said.

I said, "Oh my. That is—quite a portentous statement."

He actually blushed, and said, "Well, I've just had a child. I'm thinking differently now."

Life makes conservatives of us all.

It is true. Even in the age, or era, or moment of Clinton.

—

I'll tell you something I think about when I get dem ol' history-related blues. I cheer myself up remembering a tired conversation at a party. It was just after the Bush loss, and I'd had a day in which the sadness of the squandered legacy hit me with full force. I was with a man, a businessman who had just come in from Paris on the Concorde. I told him I'd never taken it—what's it like? He said what's always surprising is how small it is, how compact. People, he said, are always surprised by this.

He said that yesterday when he left New York the plane departed three hours late, which caused considerable consternation among the passengers. The jet shot above the Atlantic, and as they neared Orly he noticed a couple sitting up front, their heads together and talking intently, as if they were solving a problem. All of a sudden the man got up, went to the bathroom and returned, marching down the aisle in white tie and tails. They were going to be late for a ball; he'd changed in the bathroom, which is a feat because it's about a foot by a foot and a half. As he went down the aisle to return to his seat the passengers looked up and applauded. He bowed, like a gentleman.

Then his wife got up, went into the bathroom with a bag and emerged in a huge silk ball gown, fully made up, wearing jewels— and she came down the aisle and now there was applause and cheers, and she turned to all the passengers and curtsied deeply before she took her seat.

"It was so—oh." He shrugs like a Frenchman.

"Merry," I say.

"Yes! So merry." He laughed with bright eyes.

It gave me a small epiphany, one I've had before—a déjà vu epiphany about unexpected gaiety and the lift it brings. I found myself absurdly moved. It reminded me of what most of us, really, know: that pessimism and despair are childish, that the only realistic stance toward life is optimism. Because we always survive. Through the most terrible and horrendous moments of human history, through all the purges, long marches, wars, gulags and floods, we survive and go on and increase and make our rude progress. A family begins, a baby is born, a young man gets out of law school and puts up a shingle, a lady in a ball dress is applauded and curtsies back in tribute.

When I got home I thought of words that sometimes roll like a tape through my mind; I found the book in a bookcase and looked for the wise old man of Ecclesiastes. Some find his words depressing, but I do not find them so. It's just another way of saying that in spite of the facts, in spite of who we are, we go on and increase and endure.

Vanity of vanities, saith the Preacher; vanity of vanities, all is vanity. What profit hath man of all his labors wherein he laboreth under the sun? One generation goeth, and one generation cometh; but the earth abideth forever. The sun also ariseth, and the sun goes down, and hasteth to its place where it ariseth. The wind goeth toward the south, and turneth about unto the north; it turneth about continually in its course, and the wind returneth again to its circuits. All the rivers run into the sea, yet the sea is not full; unto the place whither the rivers go, thither they go again. . . . That which hath been is that which shall be; and that which hath been done is that which shall be done; and there is no new thing under the sun. . . . I the Preacher was king over Israel in Jerusalem. And I applied my heart to seek and to search out by wisdom concerning all that is done under heaven . . . I have seen all the works that are done under the sun; and behold, all is vanity and a striving after wind. . . ."

I think this: that we are all inadequate players in an incompetent drama, that defeat is part of the script, you can't escape it, it's not part of life, it's the essence of life—so you might as well just do your best and give your love and know your God and do your work.

And be good to your troupe. Amen.

ABOUT THE TYPE

The text of this book was set in Palatino, designed by the German typographer Hermann Zapf. It was named after the Renaissance calligrapher Giovanbattista Palatino. Zapf designed it between 1948 and 1952, and it was his first typeface to be introduced in America. It is a face of unusual elegance.